THE DIVIDED HEROINE

BY THE SAME AUTHOR

The Forked Flame: A Study of D. H. Lawrence
Dickens and the Art of Analogy
Joseph Conrad: The Way of Dispossession

THE DIVIDED HEROINE

*A Recurrent Pattern in
Six English Novels*

H. M. Daleski

HOLMES & MEIER PUBLISHERS, INC.
New York   London

First published in the United States of America 1984 by
Holmes & Meier Publishers, Inc.
30 Irving Place
New York, N.Y. 10003

Great Britain:
Holmes & Meier Publishers, Ltd.
131 Trafalgar Road
Greenwich, London SE10 9TX

Book design by Stephanie Barton

Library of Congress Cataloging in Publication Data

Daleski, H. M. (Hillel Matthew), 1926–
The divided heroine.

Includes bibliographical references and index.
1. English fiction—History and criticism.
2. Heroines in literature.   3. Women in literature.
4. Split self in literature.   5. Body and soul in
literature.   I. Title.
PR830.H4D34 1983   823'.009'352042   83-12897
ISBN 0-8419-0885-0

Manufactured in the United States of America

To Debbie, Gil, Arit, and Yonat

Between extremities
Man runs his course;
A brand, or flaming breath,
Comes to destroy
All those antinomies
Of day and night . . .

—W. B. Yeats, "Vacillation"

CONTENTS

CHAPTER 7
The End of the Affair
The Eternal Triangle
133

NOTES
151

INDEX
161

ACKNOWLEDGMENTS

A shortened version of Chapter Four has appeared in *Essays in Criticism*, October 1980. I am grateful to the Editors for permission to use this material.

I wish to thank the Hebrew University for a grant towards the cost of typing.

I am grateful to the following for permission to quote from copyright material: to Viking Penguin, Inc., Laurence Pollinger Ltd., and the Estate of Mrs. Frieda Lawrence Ravagli for passages from *The White Peacock*, *Fantasia of the Unconscious*, and *The Collected Letters of D. H. Lawrence;* to the Author's Literary Estate, The Hogarth Press, and Harcourt Brace Jovanovich, Inc., for passages from *Mrs. Dalloway*, by Virginia Woolf, copyright 1925 by Harcourt Brace Jovanovich, Inc.; renewed 1953 by Leonard Woolf; to Harcourt Brace Jovanovich, Inc. for *A Writer's Diary*, by Virginia Woolf, copyright 1953, 1954 by Virginia Woolf; renewed 1981, 1982 by Quentin Bell and Angelica Garnett; and to Mr. Graham Greene, William Heinemann, Ltd., The Bodley Head, Ltd., and Viking Penguin, Inc., for passages from *The End of the Affair*, by Graham Greene, copyright 1951, renewed © 1979 by Graham Greene.

While this book was in preparation, a number of colleagues were good enough to read parts of it and make helpful suggestions for its improvement. I should like to thank the following for their welcome comments: Edward Alexander and Richard J. Dunn of the University of Washington; Dorothea Krook of Tel-Aviv University; and, at the Hebrew University, Baruch Hochman, Shulamith Barzilai, Shlomith Rimmon-Kenan, A. A. Mendilow, and Aviva Furedy.

My chief debt is to Ruth Nevo and my wife, Shirley, both of whom read the book as it was being written, chapter by chapter. I have now had the inestimable privilege of showing drafts of my work to Ruth Nevo for some twenty years, and the great good fortune with this book that her eye—quite against nature—grows sharper as time passes. My wife has not only shown much forbearance and understanding during the process of composition but also commented on the typescript with great acuteness and penetration.

THE DIVIDED HEROINE

CHAPTER 1

The Pattern

Plato's figure of the charioteer and the horses in the *Phaedrus* is so richly suggestive, so accommodating of meaning, that it is perhaps not altogether outrageous to lift it out of its context and apply it in non-Platonic ways. The figure concretizes the opposed pulls to which the charioteer is subject; and if in Plato it serves to represent a tripartite soul, it also lends itself to an image of dual being, with the two horses projecting a division within the charioteer, the manner in which he is pulled by two opposing forces. Such a view, indeed, is consistent with what Socrates says earlier in the same dialogue: "Let us note that in every one of us there are two guiding and ruling principles which lead us whither they will; one is the natural desire of pleasure, the other is an acquired opinion which aspires after the best; and these two are sometimes in harmony and then again at war, and sometimes the one, sometimes the other conquers."[1]

In elaborating the figure of the charioteer and the horses, Plato is primarily concerned to describe how the unruly steed, the one that is "of a dark colour" and said to be "bad," repeatedly "plunges and runs away" when the charioteer sees "the vision of love," taking "the bit in his teeth and [pulling] shamelessly." When this happens, Plato envisages two possibilities: either the dark horse gets his way and forces both the charioteer and the white horse (which is said to be "good") "to approach the beloved," making them "yield and agree to do as he bids them"; or the charioteer succeeds in reining in "the wild steed," covering "his abusive tongue and jaws with blood," forcing "his legs and haunches to the ground," and doing this again and again until he is "tamed and humbled" and follows the charioteer's will (pp. 257–58). But the figure also allows for two further—if non-Socratic—possibilities: the white horse may succeed in pulling both the charioteer and the dark horse in the direction he

3

wishes to take; or both horses may at the same time pull with equal strength in opposite directions.

The figure may thus be said to yield four possibilities of dual being. When the dark horse takes the bit between his teeth and drags the other horse after him, forcing the charioteer to go in the direction he has chosen, we have an image of self-division, of one-sided being in which one half of the self is effectively negated. Were the white horse to pull both the dark horse and the charioteer after him, we would have a similar though reverse image of one-sidedness. When the horses pull together and are under the control of the charioteer, the opposing forces within the self are reconciled and we have an image of harmonious or integrated being. If the two horses were to pull in opposite directions at the same time, we would have an image of disintegration, for the charioteer would then be subject to two conflicting and equally powerful pulls and torn in two.

It is with anatomies of self-division and disintegration that I am concerned in this book—as they present themselves in a number of English novels in an analogous figure. The figure is a love triangle. In the novels to be studied the protagonist is a woman, though the figure may appear in novels in which the protagonist is a man, and *Jude the Obscure*, for instance, provides as striking an example of the pattern as *Tess of the d'Urbervilles*—as does Melville's *Pierre* in the American novel. The self-division of the protagonist is externalized in her strong attraction to two lovers who are presented as thoroughgoing opposites and embody opposed tendencies within herself. When she is drawn to one of the lovers, therefore, one of the steeds within her is given its head, as it were, and negates the other. When she moves from one lover to the other, the process is reversed. Both the reversal and the movement from one lover to the other are essential to the pattern. The most distinctive feature of the pattern, however, is that she is eventually caught between the two men, either bound to one and longing for the other, or unable to choose finally between them, and is consequently torn in two. Her disintegration is projected either in the breakdown of madness or the loss of the will to live; and it is usually consummated in her actual death, which sometimes has suicidal overtones. The fate of the protagonist, whatever her circumstances, is thus first and foremost a result of her inability to reconcile the opposed forces within herself.

This is the pattern which I believe may be discerned in the works selected for discussion: in Emily Brontë's *Wuthering Heights* (which also provides a unique example, with its two generations, of a subsequent and contrary pattern of integration), George Eliot's *The Mill on the Floss*, Thomas Hardy's *Tess of the d'Urbervilles*, D. H. Lawrence's *The White*

Peacock, Virginia Woolf's *Mrs. Dalloway* (where the breakdown is projected in a double of the protagonist), and Graham Greene's *The End of the Affair* (in which the triangle of the protagonist, her husband, and her lover is given a theological transfiguration). But since love has always been a central theme in the novel—Leslie Fiedler has remarked that it is "as necessary and as expected as battle in Homer or revenge in the Renaissance drama"[2]—and since a theme is most forcefully dramatized in terms of conflict, novels abound in love triangles. At the outset, therefore, I should like to emphasize the ways in which the pattern to be studied differs from that represented by some other kinds of triangle.

First, the protagonist is genuinely torn between her two lovers. Accordingly, the sort of triangle that is established in Dickens's *Our Mutual Friend* by Lizzie Hexam's relations with Eugene Wrayburn and Bradley Headstone does not conform to the pattern. Both the men are in love with her; and though Eugene is the one who marries her in the end, Bradley proposes marriage to her and is sufficiently in earnest to try to murder Eugene. But Lizzie is never for one moment interested in or drawn to Bradley; and though he pesters her, he is never able to pull her towards him and away from Eugene. What at first sight seems to be a similar sort of triangle is to be found in Jane Austen's *Mansfield Park*. Fanny Price is also involved with two men, Edmund Bertram and Henry Crawford, and—like Lizzie Hexam—she appears to be quite indifferent to one of them. Henry, however, the one she disdains, eventually succeeds in winning her regard in spite of herself. Before the *dénouement*, it seems as if her resistance to Henry's suit may conceivably be worn down even though we know she loves Edmund, the more especially since *he* is otherwise engaged. The triangle in *Mansfield Park*, therefore, involves the heroine more strongly in rival claims than that in *Our Mutual Friend*, but it differs from the stated pattern in another important respect. Edmund and Henry are very different in temperament and character, and may even be viewed as opposites, but the opposition projected by them is not the reflection of an inner conflict in Fanny. Self-division is not one of Fanny's problems, and Crawford does not embody even a potentiality of her being. A second feature of the selected pattern, therefore, is that the contending forces are not only clearly embodied in the rival men but also evident within the protagonist.

The triangle in Charlotte Brontë's *Jane Eyre* strikingly presents these initial features of the pattern. Jane is passionately in love with Edward Rochester, yet she almost marries St. John Rivers. Rochester and St. John, moreover, as Masao Miyoshi has stated, are boldly presented as opposites, and body forth opposed tendencies in Jane:

Where Rochester is Gothic, St. John is "classic"; where he is fire, St. John is "ice"; and where Rochester is all passion, St. John is reason itself. But just as there is that substantial likeness between Rochester and Jane, between St. John and Jane too there is a tie: "She [Rosamond Oliver] said I was like Mr. Rivers."[3]

In *Jane Eyre* we accordingly have the emotional involvement of the heroine with two very different men; the reflection of her own central conflict between abandon and control in the opposition between them and in her relations with them; and the distinctive movement from one man to the other, with Jane being called on at the crisis of her relationship with each to inhibit a fundamental part of her nature. But though *Jane Eyre* is thus much like the works discussed in this book, it is nevertheless different from them in one essential respect. Jane is indeed caught between Rochester and St. John, but she is finally able (if with supernatural aid) to make a decisive choice between them and, leaving St. John, to return to Rochester and marry him. In the selected pattern the protagonist is, crucially, unable to resolve her conflict.

Such a conflict may also be resolved by an equally decisive if different kind of choice on the part of the protagonist—the decision to withdraw from both entanglements. This is what we are shown in Lawrence's *Sons and Lovers*, where Paul Morel in the end decides to reject both Miriam Leivers and Clara Dawes, refusing to accept the "halfness" or "partness" which a permanent relationship with either woman would entail for him, and determining to seek a wholeness of being apart from both of them. Paul in effect follows the course recommended, in a different context, by Alan Sillitoe, behind whose pronouncement hovers a nightmarish reminiscence of Plato's figure: "While gleaning for the truth, despair calls from one side and hope beckons at the other, and they try and draw you apart. When such horse-mares struggle for your inner vision you manage to walk, or take a spade and dig the soil over."[4] Though the pattern in *Sons and Lovers* is much like that in the selected texts (allowing, of course, for the protagonist's difference of sex), Paul's resolution of his conflict radically differentiates this work from the others.

The novels to be studied should also be distinguished from novels in which the heroine is led to breakdown and death, even suicide, as a result of her relations with more than one man, but in which the tragic development is not the product of a distinctive disintegrative pull exerted by two men. In Scott's *The Bride of Lammermoor*, for instance, Lucy Ashton is in love with the Master of Ravenswood but agrees to marry the Laird of Bucklaw; on the night of the wedding, however, she goes insane, kills her husband, and thereupon falls into convulsions and dies. Lucy's end, therefore, is much like that of the protagonists in the selected texts, but her story differs from the given pattern because though she is in effect caught between the two men, she is not drawn to both of them: she is never interested in Bucklaw, and is tricked into marrying him by her parents. Similarly, in Hardy's *A Pair of Blue Eyes* Elfride Swancourt is in love with Henry Knight but marries Lord Luxellian and dies as the result of a miscarriage. But Luxellian is the third man in her life, her emotions having been invested first in Stephen Smith and then irrevocably in Knight, and her death is expressive not of emotional conflict but of the loss of the will to live which follows her abandonment by Knight. The stories of two famous continental heroines both end in suicide, but they too follow a different pattern. Both Emma Bovary and Anna Karenina become involved in adulterous relationships, but they are not torn between their husbands and their lovers: once they give themselves to their lovers their commitment to them is absolute, and their suicides are not the result of conflicting drives but of despair at having failed to win a like commitment from the lovers.[5]

Finally, the novels to be discussed should be distinguished not only from works (such as those referred to) which might at first seem to resemble them but also from the main line of the English novel. Conflict is the life-blood of the novel, the means by which both its plots and its characterization are dynamically set in motion, and the prevailing thrust of novels within the main tradition is towards the successful resolution of conflict. The resolution of conflict, indeed, usually serves as a natural point of termination not only for the plot but for the characterization too since it coincides with the postulated achievement of selfhood in the protagonist. From *Tom Jones* onwards, it is the protagonist's working through to such an achieved self that perhaps constitutes *the* distinctive feature of the main tradition. The novels to be studied, therefore, may be thought of as spinning off the main tradition onto a track which runs parallel to it. Though they follow the lines of traditional love stories, they move not to a liberating resolution of conflict but to a state of deadlock; and they lead not to a consummation of self in the protagonist but to a disintegration of being. Starting with *Wuthering Heights* in 1847, they present a striking and recurrent mode of failure, forming over the years a series of counter-statements, and dramatizing what in *The Mill on the Floss* is referred to as that "divided action of our nature" which "makes half the tragedy of the human lot."

II

If the pattern to be studied posits the duality of the protagonist, it is St. Paul who stamped a particular mode of dual being on the Christian consciousness, insisting on the opposition between flesh and spirit. In this he went beyond anything Jesus envisaged. As Matthew Arnold notes in his sympathetic study of Paul in *St. Paul and Protestantism*, "for Jesus, the uncertain conflict between the law in our members, and the law of the spirit did not appear to exist. Those eternal vicissitudes of victory and defeat, which drove Paul to despair, in Jesus were absent."[6] Paul, however, was quite uncompromising in his insistence on the recalcitrance of the flesh:

> For the good that I would I do not; but the evil which I would not, that I do.
> Now if I do that I would not, it is no more I that do it, but sin that dwelleth in me.
> I find then a law, that, when I would do good, evil is present with me.
> For I delight in the law of God after the inward man.
> But I see another law in my members, warring against the law of my mind, and bringing me into captivity to the law of sin which is in my members. (Romans 7:19–23)

And again:

> This I say then, Walk in the Spirit, and ye shall not fulfil the lust of the flesh.
> For the flesh lusteth against the Spirit, and the Spirit against the flesh: and these are contrary the one to the other: so that ye cannot do the things that ye would.
> But if ye be led of the Spirit, ye are not under the law. . . .
> And they that are Christ's have crucified the flesh with the affections and lusts.
> If we live in the Spirit, let us also walk in the Spirit. (Galatians 5:16– 18, 24–25)

What Paul will not conceive of is the possibility of reconciling the flesh and the spirit. For him "these are contrary the one to the other"; and the consequence of this is that he who would "walk in the Spirit" must die to the flesh, as Christ did, must indeed "crucify" the flesh. And such an extinction of the unruly members brings the kind of serenity which is true life: "For they that are after the flesh do mind the things of the flesh; but they that are after the Spirit the things of the Spirit. For to be carnally minded is death; but to be spiritually minded is life and peace" (Romans 8:5–6).

What Paul insists on as a virtue is a prescription for self-division, a willed negation of one half of being. The insistence, moreover, invites a contrary negation in those in whom the flesh obdurately refuses to be subdued, the denial of the spirit. It is such a propensity to extinguish one half of self—and then in reaction to assert it in repudiation of the other— that characterizes the protagonists in the novels to be studied. That their self-division, though directly expressed in varied terms, should posit an underlying, fundamental opposition between the flesh and the spirit would seem to be attributable to the vitality of the Pauline dichotomy— and to the forcefulness with which it was mediated for the nineteenth century by John Wesley. Noel Annan has said that "Evangelical morality was the single most widespread influence in Victorian England";[7] and George Ford has stated that though "it would be difficult to name a Victorian writer of any consequence who remained an Evangelical in the true sense of the term, it would be equally difficult to name one who was not affected by what Evangelicalism had stood for."[8] For Wesley the need to oppose the spirit to the flesh was at the heart of Pauline doctrine and of a Christian way of life. In his sermon "On Sin in Believers," for instance, he inflexibly insists on this:

> [St. Paul] is speaking to believers, and describing the state of believers in general, when he says, "The flesh lusteth against the Spirit, and the Spirit against the flesh: these are contrary the one to the other," Gal. v:17. Nothing can be more express. The Apostle here directly affirms that the flesh, evil nature, opposes the Spirit, even in believers; that even in the regenerate, there are two principles, "contrary the one to the other." . . .
>
> Indeed this grand point, that there are two contrary principles in believers, nature and grace, the flesh and the Spirit, runs through all the epistles of St. Paul, yea, through all the Holy Scriptures: almost all the directions and exhortations therein, are founded on this supposition: pointing at wrong tempers in those, who were notwithstanding, acknowledged by the inspired writers to be believers. And they are continually exhorted to fight and conquer these, by the power of the faith which was in them.[9]

The hundred odd years between the publication of *Wuthering Heights* and *The End of the Affair* may have been a period in which the power of Pauline Christianity was thoroughly undermined, but the force of its opposition between flesh and spirit persisted nonetheless—and is evident even in the work of those who might well have been persuaded of their own liberation from it. That it is clearly apparent in *Wuthering Heights* is perhaps not surprising since Emily Brontë was subject to the influence of both her Evangelical father, an Anglican clergyman, and her Methodist aunt, who brought her up after her mother died. The novel is shot through with "contrary principles"; and though it may subsume, it does not escape, the Pauline opposition.[10] More unexpectedly this opposition also dominates the work of free thinkers such as George Eliot and Thomas Hardy. Though it is true that George Eliot, as she herself stated, was "strongly under the influence of Evangelical belief" in her late teens,[11] she decisively broke with Christianity in her twenties, lived her life as an agnostic, and was even regarded as "the outstanding exponent, in the public mind, of the doctrine of free love."[12] Yet in her major work, *Mid-*

dlemarch, the scene at the beginning of the novel in which Dorothea Brooke first disdains and then succumbs to the lure of her mother's jewels strikingly points to the way in which the life of the heroine is to be cast between the contrary pulls of flesh and spirit; and in *The Mill on the Floss* Maggie Tulliver's basic conflict is the same though it is more immediately presented as one between animal and intellectual being. Moreover, though one of George Eliot's remarks about her art inverts the Pauline injunction, it strongly suggests its hold on her imagination: she declared she had repeatedly gone through "the severe effort of trying to make certain ideas thoroughly incarnate, as if they had revealed themselves to [her] first in the flesh and not in the spirit."[13] Thomas Hardy, in turn, may have declared at the age of fifty that he had "been looking for God [for] fifty years," but he added: "I think that if he had existed I should have discovered him"; and he liked to think of himself as a "harmless agnostic."[14] In novel after novel, however, Hardy seems to be obsessively preoccupied with the opposition between flesh and spirit. This is most clearly pronounced in *Tess of the d'Urbervilles* and *Jude the Obscure*, Hardy indeed declaring in the Preface to the First Edition of *Jude* that his aim had been "to tell, without a mincing of words, of a deadly war waged between flesh and spirit."

Nor is the heritage of Paul less in evidence among the twentieth-century novelists to be studied. They all may be thought of as laboring under the yoke of the Pauline dichotomy, for the more they pull away from it—transposing its terms—the more closely do they seem to be held by it. For D. H. Lawrence the Pauline denigration of the flesh constitutes the very basis of his attack on Christianity; and in his first novel, *The White Peacock*, he tries to transvalue the division of flesh and spirit by transforming it into one of blood-consciousness and mental consciousness and reversing the terms of disparagement—a prelude to his ultimate attempt, in the late work "The Man Who Died," to transform and transvalue the Christian myth itself. Virginia Woolf was brought up in the freethinking home of her father, Leslie Stephen, but is on record to confirm the lasting power of St. Paul: "Even today [i.e., 1938] it is probable that a woman has to fight a psychological battle of some severity with the ghost of St. Paul, before she can have intercourse with a man other than her husband."[15] What her work suggests, particularly *Mrs. Dalloway*, is that such a battle has to be fought before a woman can have intercourse at all; and that the heroine's fear of giving herself in the flesh underlies the central opposition in this novel between a desire for connection and an inclination for withdrawal. In Graham Greene, the professing Catholic, the Pauline view is accepted but significantly modified; and in *The End of the Affair*, though the heroine is torn between the flesh and the spirit, it is asserted that the way to the spirit lies through the flesh, that the carnal is a stepping-stone to the divine.

The imprint of Pauline doctrine may thus be discerned in all the works to be studied, but its effects are more immediately devastating in the nineteenth-century novels. Hardy may be regarded as the great divide in this respect. In his work the conflict between flesh and spirit is not only at its most intense but exacts an unmitigated tragic toll. Thereafter, with the decline in strength of Evangelical influence, the modern novelists seem better able than their predecessors to imagine effective resistance to the kind of disintegrative conflict epitomized by a Tess Durbeyfield or a Jude Fawley. The heroine of Lawrence's first novel, it is true, is thoroughly undermined by her conflict, but she avoids overt tragedy; and after his first two apprentice novels, Lawrence's lifework constitutes a strong counter-statement, an assertion of the need for—and the possibilities of—integrated being. Likewise, Virginia Woolf's Clarissa Dalloway is a victim of fears of the flesh, but she is not destroyed by them—and (as distinct from her double) she is able, in the end, to "assemble" herself for life. Finally, it is only in sublunary terms (though I shall argue that these must be given their full weight) that Graham Greene's heroine is undone; in the perspective the novelist wishes to enforce, her conflict is intended to be seen as leading to her sanctification.

III

Eric Trudgill has stated it was "Evangelical propaganda of the 1790s and after" that "fostered the acceptance of a new veneration for the good woman and a new abhorrence of the fallen . . ."[16] The strong feelings aroused by these opposed views of woman were related to two other polarized images in nineteenth-century England, what Alexander Welsh has called "the basic antithesis of home and the streets."[17] The Victorian home was the abode of virtue. Walter E. Houghton has described it as "not only a peaceful" but "a sacred place," for as the power of Christianity diminished, "the living church more and more became the 'temple of the hearth.'"[18] The streets, on the other hand, were the sphere of vice; and Dickens, for example, in seeking to differentiate *Oliver Twist* from the more romantic genre of the Newgate novel, was at pains to declare in the Preface which he wrote for the third edition of his novel that he had located his thieves not on "moonlit heaths" or in "the snuggest of . . . caverns" but, especially, in "the cold, wet, shelterless midnight streets of London." In *Oliver Twist*, moreover, as I argued in another connection, the streets are associated with the darkness of a hell on earth.[19] It is not surprising, therefore, that the opposed images of woman should have crystallized as the Angel in the House and the Fallen Woman of the Streets.

Dickens may be said to have stamped these images on the Victorian consciousness in his presentation, at the outset of his career, of the two contrasted young women of *Oliver Twist*, Rose Maylie, the heroine, and Nancy, the prostitute. Rose is introduced to the reader in the following terms:

> The younger lady was in the lovely bloom and spring-time of womanhood; at that age, when, if ever angels be for God's good purposes enthroned in mortal forms, they may be, without impiety, supposed to abide in such as hers.
> She was not past seventeen. Cast in so slight and exquisite a mould; so mild and gentle; so pure and beautiful; that earth seemed not her element, nor its rough creatures her fit companions. The very intelligence that shone in her deep blue eye, and was stamped upon her noble head, seemed scarcely of her age or of the world; and yet the changing expression of sweetness and good humour; the thousand lights that played about the face, and left no shadow there; above all, the smile; the cheerful, happy smile; were made for Home; for fireside peace and happiness.[20]

The passage is striking in the way it contrives to evoke a burgeoning womanhood—and to spiritualize it out of existence. Rose, we are told, is "in the lovely bloom and spring-time of womanhood," but we are to understand there is nothing earthy about her flowering, for "earth" does not seem to be "her element." Indeed, the mould in which she is cast is "so slight" that she is hardly there in the flesh, and it is no surprise that lights which play about her face should leave "no shadow." Her shadowless incorporeality is to be seen as a measure of her unstained radiance, for she is "so pure" that she is like an angel. And the angel, of course, is "enthroned" not only in Rose's "mortal form" but in a domestic kingdom— "Home," complete with capital. Nearly twenty years before Coventry Patmore put a name to it, Dickens had thus epitomized an Angel in the House, though as yet an unmarried one. Patmore's poem may celebrate a fruitful married love, the "sweetness" of "the ten-years' wife," but he is no less adept than Dickens at transforming flesh into spirit; and his lover's view of his beloved during courtship clearly indicates the nature of her future symbolic role:

> I loved her in the name of God,
>   And for the ray she was of Him;
> I ought to admire much more, not less;
>   Her beauty was a godly grace;
> The mystery of loveliness,
>   Which made an altar of her face,
> Was not of the flesh, though that was fair,

> But a most pure and living light
> Without a name, by which the rare
> And virtuous spirit flamed to sight.[21]

The flame of this virtuous spirit would seem to consume the flesh it illuminates.

Not only the woman was transformed by such views of her, but the quality of the love that was directed to such an object, desire presumably being channeled to ethereal regions, as was the flesh. Lust was for the streets—and for the likes of Nancy, who states that her "eyes and senses [opened] on London streets," that "the alley and the gutter" were her "cradle," and that she has "no certain roof but the coffin-lid" (pp. 271, 275). This is the way Nancy, along with Bet, is first presented:

> They wore a good deal of hair: not very neatly turned up behind; and were rather untidy about the shoes and stockings. They were not exactly pretty, perhaps; but they had a great deal of colour in their faces; and looked quite stout and hearty. Being remarkably free and agreeable in their manners, Oliver thought them very nice girls indeed. As there is no doubt they were. (p. 55)

Though we are not told very much about the "nice girls," the narrator's glance sweeping from head to foot, they are sufficiently placed for us. That seemingly curious reference to their untidy shoes and stockings makes us realize that, unlike Rose, they have their feet on the ground. The "stout and hearty" girls are of the earth earthy and exist unmitigatedly in the flesh, the "great deal of colour in their faces" being the outward sign of their errant blood, as the "good deal of hair" that they wear not very neatly would seem to be the immediate locus of their unruly sexuality. The contrast between Nancy and Rose is of course further developed in moral terms:

> The girl's life had been squandered in the streets, and among the most noisome of the stews and dens of London, but there was something of the woman's original nature left in her still . . .
> The miserable companion of thieves and ruffians, the fallen outcast of low haunts, the associate of the scourings of the jails and hulks, living within the shadow of the gallows itself,—even this degraded being felt too proud to betray a feeble gleam of the womanly feeling which she thought a weakness, but which alone connected her with that humanity, of which her wasting life had obliterated so many, many traces when a very child. (p. 270)

Where Rose is the Angel in the House, Nancy is a "fallen outcast" of the streets, whose forlorn aspiration is "not to die in the same hell in which [she has] lived" (p. 275). Where Rose is notable not only for her purity but also for her intelligence and nobility, Nancy bears all the marks of "degraded being," of the waste of shame in which she has squandered her life. If Rose and Nancy are thus portrayed as decided opposites, it is instructive to note that in one revealing respect their presentation is similar: just as the woman is hardly there in the angel, so is she virtually eliminated in the prostitute, for if there is "something of the woman's original nature left in [Nancy] still," it has been largely "obliterated" by her "wasting life."

What is notable, of course, is that these images of Madonnas and Magdalens, as Eric Trudgill calls them, of angels of the spirit and fallen women of the flesh, these images which leave the woman out—are conceived by the male imagination. Nor is Dickens their only begetter. Thackeray, for instance, may be regarded as working in the same tradition that produced a Rose and a Nancy, though with a greater subtlety and complexity of characterization, in his portrayal in *Vanity Fair* of the seemingly angelic, sexless Amelia Sedley as opposed to the demonic, sexy Becky Sharp. But according to Freud "what, in the conscious, is found split into a pair of opposites often occurs in the unconscious as a unity"; and in Freudian terms the whole behind these two images in the male consciousness would appear to be the mother, viewed on the one hand as an angelic embodiment of absolute purity, and on the other—in resentful acceptance of the fact of her sexuality—as not far removed from a whore.[22] One of the interests of this study of female protagonists who are fundamentally divided between the spirit and the flesh is accordingly to see how the novelists concerned reassemble the polarized images and put woman together again. It would seem to be more than a coincidence of literary history that the challenge to the Dickensian conception of woman came most strongly from women novelists—though in making it they in turn proceeded to polarize the men to whom the heroines are attracted. Once the Brontës had shown the way with a Catherine Earnshaw and a Jane Eyre, and George Eliot had consolidated it with a Maggie Tulliver and a Dorothea Brooke, Hardy was liberated for his Tess Durbeyfield. But the split remains, even though it is now internalized in their protagonists, and in Cathy and Maggie and Tess it proves to be productive of the sort of irresolvable dilemma that makes for tragedy. That the attempt of the nineteenth-century novelists to give full expression to the nature of their heroines should result in the depiction of tragic disintegration rather than wholeness of being is perhaps a measure of the strength and persistence of the prevalent view of woman. For the achievement of wholeness, we have to wait for D. H. Lawrence's Ursula Brangwen. And the Angel cast a long shadow—even for writers in the twentieth century: Virginia Woolf has roundly declared that "killing the Angel in the House was part of the occupation of a woman writer."[23]

IV

In *The Divided Self: A Perspective on the Literature of the Victorians*, Masao Miyoshi distinguishes "three broad categories" of the phenomenon announced by his title: the "formal," which relates to "the breakdown of formal unity" in the work of a given writer; the "thematic or ideological," which relates to instances in a given work either of "self-duplication" (manifested in a doppelgänger or in "the Romantic ideal") or of "self-division" (of a kind exemplified by "the Gothic villain, the Byronic hero, and the Jekyll-Hyde split personality"); and the "biographical," which relates to "the dual personality as a fact of the author's life" (pp. x–xi). Miyoshi concentrates on the second category, the thematic or ideological, and is particularly concerned with its manifestation in Victorian literature, maintaining that Victorian writers experienced and expressed "the self-division endemic to their times" (p. ix). He also believes, and cites Walter Jackson Bate and Leslie Fiedler in support of his view, that it was "the collapse of Neoclassicism" that "brought about the first expression of the divided self" (p. xix), though earlier instances of self-division would seem to be clearly evident in Shakespeare, not to mention Chaucer's Cryseyde. At all events, Miyoshi begins his wide-ranging survey with a discussion of Gothicism and Romanticism, arguing that these traditions "together created the prototypes of man divided that . . . reappear throughout Victorian literature: the Gothic villain, the Byronic hero, and the Shelleyan solipsist" (p. xiv). He holds, furthermore, that the Gothic novel was "the first modern prose form disposed to fairly intensive concern with the various phenomena of the divided self" (p. 38); and considers especially the "violent oscillation of evil deed and penitent mood that makes the Gothic villain a modern archetype for alienated man divided against himself" (p. 5).

Miyoshi's conception of the divided self is thus much wider and more elastic than the specific variety of it that I am concerned with in this book, the suppression or negation of one part of the self. It is significant, however, that the figure of the love triangle as I have described it should make its appearance in fiction in the nineteenth century. Since the figure is a means of delineating a particular kind of self-division, J. Hillis Miller's observation that in "eighteenth-century England the stability of the social order, sustained by divine Providence," was a "guarantee of the stability of selfhood"[24] is suggestive. The removal of that sustaining presence, therefore—or, in Miller's terms, the disappearance of God—may be thought of as fracturing the self; and in this light the novels to be studied may be seen as one reflection of the progressive undermining of Christianity that began in the nineteenth century. It is true, of course, that both Emily Brontë and Graham Greene are Christians, but then, at least in the works to be discussed, their views can hardly be said to rest firmly on orthodox beliefs.

Whatever the reason for the emergence of this particular form of the love triangle in the nineteenth century, I know of no similar instance in the eighteenth-century English novel; and among Gothic novels the only one I am aware of in which an analogous pattern is discernible is *The Monk* (1796) by M. G. Lewis. Allowing for a male protagonist, most of the outward features of the pattern are to be found in *The Monk*, even though it lacks its inner dynamic. It therefore merits consideration, but—*pace* John Berryman, who calls it "one of the authentic prodigies of English fiction"[25]—it seems to me to be so much the product of a sick imagination as to place it in an altogether different class from the novels to be studied.

Ambrosio, the abbot of a Capuchin monastery in Madrid, is surnamed "The Man of Holiness" and is presented as a matchless example of virtue. Having been found "while yet an infant at the abbey-door," he has spent his whole life in the monastery, and "every hour" of the thirty years he has lived "has been passed in study, total seclusion from the world, and mortification of the flesh." Ambrosio appears to be a man serenely at peace with himself, an epitome of wholeness of being; but his apparent wholeness is of course founded on a lifelong denial of one part of the self, to a degree that he is "reported to be so strict an observer of chastity, that he knows not in what consists the difference of man and woman" (pp. 43–45).

What follows, not unexpectedly, is his conquest by the flesh. Ambrosio is seduced by Matilda, who has smuggled herself into the monastery in the guise of the novice Rosario and in the end turns out to be an agent of the devil. When Ambrosio discovers Rosario is a woman and in love with him, he reflects that "to vanquish temptation [is] an infinitely greater merit than to avoid it" (p. 103) and allows the novice to remain in the monastery; but ultimately he yields to her and, "drunk with desire," clasps her "rapturously in his arms," forgetting "his vows, his sanctity, and his fame" (p. 109). Though the monk is soon "glutted with the fullness of pleasure" and within a week is "wearied of his paramour," their illicit relationship continues since he is still "led to her arms, not by love, but the cravings of brutal appetite" (pp. 236–37).

Subdued to his lust, Ambrosio experiences the kind of reversal that is provoked by one-sided being, and is now as immoderately given to the flesh as he was previously divorced from it. At the same time he maintains his position as abbot, and so becomes a sort of otherworldly Dr. Jekyll, with "the different sentiments with which education and nature had inspired him . . . combating in his bosom" (p. 239). It is at this point that he comes in contact with Antonia, who approaches him to beg him to remember her sick mother in his prayers, and to recommend a confessor for her.

When the second woman comes into his life, it seems as if Ambrosio's story will follow a pattern much like that which will be studied in this book. Antonia is the opposite of Matilda. Where Matilda is devilish, she is "formed in the mould of angels" (p. 266); where Matilda's eyes sparkle with a "wanton expression," with a "wild luxurious fire," hers enchant with their "timid innocence." Accordingly the emotions she first arouses in Ambrosio are "totally different from those inspired by Matilda." For her he feels not "the provocation of lust" but "a mingled sentiment of tenderness, admiration, and respect"; and whereas he realizes that Matilda has "glutted" him with enjoyment, "even to loathing," he is enthralled by Antonia's "inexpressible charm of modesty" (p. 243).

As Ambrosio becomes enraptured with Antonia, it seems as though it is the deposed spirit in him that is about to revive. But in fact his development at this point should be sharply differentiated from that, at an analogous stage, of the protagonists in the selected texts. His movement from one woman to the other is not the occasion for a reversal of being, for the liberation or reassertion of a negated part of the self, but for an intensification of the same one-sidedness, for an even more decisive lapse into the flesh. It might perhaps be argued that Ambrosio's inordinate desire for the angelic Antonia can be taken, symbolically, to represent a wish to repossess an innocence he has lost; but on the literal level there is no doubt about the implacable lust which drives him to pursue the woman. It is as a very Hyde that Ambrosio closes in on "his prey" (p. 261). In the course of stalking her, he first kills her mother; then contrives (with Matilda's aid) to have her conveyed to one of the burial vaults of the adjoining convent after she has been administered a magic drug and is believed—like Romeo's Juliet—to be dead; and finally comes to claim possession of his "sleeping beauty" as she lies "by the side of three putrid half-corrupted bodies" (p. 363). Of his "fondness" for her, by this time, "none but the grosser particles" remain, and he longs "for the possession of her person" (p. 365). When she awakes, the "objects of mortality" which she sees around her are "ill calculated to inspire her with those emotions by which the friar [is] agitated," and so he proceeds to rape her (pp. 367–68). When people approach and she calls out, he murders her. For good measure, it later emerges that her mother is his mother and she his sister.

It is also notable that Ambrosio's affections are not divided between the two women. His new interest in Antonia makes an incipient revulsion from Matilda complete, leading him at once to tear her "once-admired" picture from the wall, spurn it with his foot, and call her "the prostitute"

(p. 244). Thereafter, while he waits for "the opportunity of satisfying his unwarrantable lust" for Antonia, "every day [increases] his coldness for Matilda" (p. 256). Ambrosio therefore experiences no inner conflict over the transfer of his passion from one woman to the other, and his rejection of Matilda, once he has determined on it, is absolute. Nor is he in any way ever drawn back to her. Accordingly he is not in the end torn in two, either by opposed pulls exerted by the women or by an opposition within the self between flesh and spirit. He unreservedly pursues Antonia, and gives himself wholly to the flesh. Though he may be regarded as recklessly setting out on a course which leads, in effect, to self-destruction, his is a story of the progressive corruption of self rather than of its inner rending. Accused of rape, murder, and sorcery—and actually guilty as well of incest, matricide, and sororicide—he is tried by the Inquisition and sentenced to die in an auto da fé; but—in a final gesture of ultimate corruption—he avoids the stake by making his soul over to Lucifer. Having claimed him, the devil makes his death a symbolic reenactment of his life, dropping him from "a dreadful height": "Headlong fell the monk through the airy waste" to be mangled on the rocks beneath and, after six days of suffering, to be washed away on the seventh by a river in flood (pp. 419–20).

V

It may be noted that the love triangle as it has been described here links up indirectly with the figure of the double or the second self as this appears in literary works. In his survey of the critical literature on the subject, C. F. Keppler concludes that the "common theory" underlying various approaches to it amounts to this: "that the figure of the second self is created by its author, either consciously or unconsciously, to express in fictional form the division within his own psyche, whether caused by purely personal problems or by the wider problems of his culture or by both." It is generally held that the second self embodies the "darker side" of the author, and is "a figure of menace and loathing, who arouses shame, fear, and often murderous hatred in his counterpart, the first self, with whom the author tends to identify himself." But one of Keppler's own contributions to the study of the second self is to insist that it need not necessarily be evil, and that, in a number of examples which he discusses, it functions as what he calls the "Saviour."[26]

In the love triangles to be considered here, the opposed lovers in any instance should clearly not be regarded as doubles or second selves of the heroine. I take it that a primary function of the double in a literary work is to give dramatic expression to what is no more than a potentiality of being in the protagonist. This function is strikingly exemplified in one of the finest stories of doubles in the language: in Joseph Conrad's "The Secret Sharer," the chief mate, Leggatt, who kills a member of his crew in an emergency, actually gives way to the kind of impulse to which, it is implied, the captain-narrator (to whom Leggatt plays double) might well have succumbed though he is not in fact tested in this way. In the selected texts, therefore, the lovers should not be considered doubles of the protagonist, for they embody aspects of self which she herself actively seeks to realize in action, to live out, as it were.

At the same time, the prevailing view of the likely impulsion behind the creation of doubles or second selves that Keppler summarizes links up with Hillis Miller's notion of the undermining of the self in the nineteenth century and suggests that in the novels under consideration the self-division of the protagonists reflects a similar psychological condition in the novelists.[27] If this is so, then the pattern of the love triangle may be seen as offering the novelist an alternative means of handling inner conflict, one that allows him directly to portray the divided self of the protagonist and also to project the opposed elements within it in his presentation of the lovers, instead of merely implying self-division by embodying a contrary element in a double. In the light of the fundamental Pauline dichotomy that underlies the pattern, moreover, it may also be seen as reflecting unresolved religious conflict in the novelists concerned, and—in most of the cases—the vestiges of a war that Christianity waged with them rather than they with Christianity. I should like to make it clear, however, that it is no part of my purpose, in the analysis of these novels, to consider further the biographical dimensions of the conflicts which are at their center and may perhaps be related to the lives of the novelists. My interest is exclusively in the literary fashioning of the pattern.

The love triangle also links up with what Robert Rogers calls "decomposition." He says that "this concept is not well known outside of psychoanalytic writings and not even used consistently in them," and that it "remains a minor concept in psychoanalytic theory"; but he suggests that it may serve to describe the phenomenon of "dual and multiple fragmentation" of character in literature, and he uses the term as synonymous with "doubling," "splitting," and "fragmentation."[28] Rogers states that "when an author wishes to depict mental conflict within a single mind a most natural way for him to dramatize it is to represent that mind by two or more characters" (p. 29); and that "decomposition tends to occur wherever an artist feels moved, however unconsciously, to depict Manichaean extremes of good and evil within a single personality . . ." (p. 46). Rogers quotes Ernest Jones's description (in his study of *Hamlet*) of decomposition in "myth formation": "In this way one person, of complex character, gets replaced by several, each of whom possesses a different aspect of the character that in a simpler form of the myth was combined in one being" (p. 12). Rogers also refers to Freud's view that Macbeth and Lady Macbeth "together . . . exhaust the possibilities of reaction to the crime, like two disunited parts of the mind of a single individuality, and perhaps they are the divided images of a single prototype" (p. 48). The principle of decomposition is thus most suggestive, but the way in which Rogers applies it as a critical tool, in his discussion of a work such as *Billy Budd*, for instance, is open to objection. He says that Billy and Claggart "may be regarded as a composite character, each representing different aspects of the psychological son" (p. 153); and that "present in the work itself is the composite mind of Billy-Claggart whose parts (one that of the rebellious, heterosexually-oriented son and the other that of the loyal, homosexually-oriented son) may be said to be enacted on an oedipal stage before the eyes of the father, Vere, who combines both the tender and the punishing aspects of the psychological father . . ." And he adds: "We may also speak, with reservation, of the minds of Billy and Claggart as though they were independent without forgetting that they form a composite one" (p. 157). The "reservation" with which we are enjoined to speak should surely relate not to the palpably independent and fully realized presences of Billy and Claggart but to their "composite mind," which is certainly not manifestly "present in the work itself" and would seem to exist rather in the psychoanalytic construct of the critic. In the works to be discussed, however, a composite mind *is* present, and a process of "decomposition" is evident inasmuch as the conflict within the protagonist is projected in the opposition embodied in her two lovers.

VI

Though it would seem to be a far cry from Paul of Tarsus to the "Strange Case of Dr. Jekyll and Mr. Hyde," Dr. Jekyll is strongly aware of "man's dual nature," and—in a phrase that directly recalls Paul—is filled with the "consciousness of the perennial war among his members."[29] The story of Dr. Jekyll, moreover, presents a literal instance of decomposition. But the particular interest of the tale for this study is that its chosen mode of science fiction serves to highlight some of the implications of a denial of one half of the self, and therefore of the greater perplexities of being faced by the protagonists in the selected texts.

Dr. Jekyll is a wealthy, industrious, and respected man, but he soon becomes aware that his public image—the "more than commonly grave countenance" that he "wears" in public—is at odds with "a certain impatient gaiety of disposition." He indulges this disposition but conceals his "pleasures," and by the time he reaches the "years of reflection," finds himself "committed to a profound duplicity of life" (p. 428). Jekyll is so shamed by his pleasures and his aspirations continue to be so "exacting" that the "provinces of good and ill which divide and compound man's dual nature" are "severed" in him, with "even a deeper trench than in the majority of men" (p. 429). The image of the trench vividly suggests the consequence of a denial of one constituent of the self, the gap in being that this creates, and the severance of parts that previously were joined. What is imaged, indeed, is the way the stage is set for an inner falling apart.

The severance is followed, in the science fiction, by actual separation. Jekyll accepts that he is "radically both" of the "two natures" that contend in his consciousness, but he becomes more and more obsessed by the thought of the possible "separation of these elements" (p. 430). He experiments with drugs, and eventually compounds one which will enable him to give a physical "form and countenance" to the "lower elements" of his soul, thus releasing Edward Hyde from Henry Jekyll when the doctor drinks the chemical mixture he has prepared (pp. 431–33). It is notable that Hyde is said to be "projected" (p. 435) from Jekyll, as though he were thrown out of him. Hyde, of course, is Jekyll's opposite, and the opposition between them is asserted both physically and morally: Hyde is "pale and dwarfish," and gives "an impression of deformity" (p. 365), whereas Jekyll is "a large, well-made, smooth-faced man of fifty," with "every mark of capacity and kindness" (p. 370); Hyde has evil "written broadly and plainly" on his face, while good "[shines] upon the countenance" of Jekyll (p. 434). A different kind of potion enables Hyde to change back into Jekyll.

Dr. Jekyll is thus a composite figure, being made up of Jekyll and Hyde; but Mr. Hyde is a man who has crucified the Jekyll in him, as it were, dying to him, and coming to life unadulterated. This would seem to be what is meant when Hyde is said to be "pure evil" (p. 434)—and proceeds to indulge his evil propensities to the full. Dr. Jekyll, therefore, is not exactly the "alternating personality" that C. F. Keppler calls him because it is a Jekyll-and-Hyde self which alternates with Hyde; whereas Keppler says that "the 'split personality' is almost always to some extent an 'alternating personality,' in which now one and now another of the combatant elements in the psyche appears on top"; and that "genuine alternation means the total temporary eclipse of the displaced personality half . . ."[30]

In its radical dramatization Stevenson's tale helps illuminate the more subtle process that, in the texts to be studied, is figured in the relations of the protagonists with their lovers. When in these novels the heroine is drawn to one man, clearly attracted to him by the reflection in him of one part of her own composite nature, and when in her relations with him she does the utmost to deny and negate the antithetical part of her self, she may be said to be like the doctor who is Jekyll-and-Hyde but presents himself to the world as Dr. Jekyll. When the reversal takes place and she is in turn attracted to a man who is the opposite of the first, trying then to negate the other part of her self, she is like a creature Stevenson did not imagine—a man who goes abroad as Mr. Hyde but is really Hyde-and-Jekyll. Outside the realm of science fiction there are no Hydes.[31]

The story of Dr. Jekyll and Mr. Hyde takes a sudden turn when Jekyll begins to change into Hyde involuntarily, that is without his taking the potion: "Yes, I had gone to bed Henry Jekyll, I had awakened Edward Hyde" (p. 439). Jekyll concludes that, whereas his initial difficulty had been "to throw off the body of Jekyll," the involuntary transformation indicates that he is becoming "slowly incorporated" with his "second and worse" self (p. 441). He realizes that he must now choose between the two selves though the choice is not easy: "To cast in my lot with Jekyll, was to die to those appetites which I had long secretly indulged and had of late begun to pamper. To cast it in with Hyde, was to die to a thousand interests and aspirations, and to become, at a blow and for ever, despised and friendless" (p. 442). He chooses to be Jekyll, but after a time succumbs, swallows "the transforming draught," and in the person of Hyde commits a murder, thereby becoming a wanted man and forfeiting his freedom to be Hyde. Subsequently Jekyll loses more and more control of his metamorphoses, until it is only "by a great effort as of gymnastics, and only under the immediate stimulation of the drug," that he is able "to wear the countenance of Jekyll" (p. 451). Then his supply of the drug which transforms Hyde back into Jekyll begins to run out, and the draught he makes with a new provision of salt proves to be "without efficiency" (p. 453). When he involuntarily turns into Hyde for the last irrevocable time, he takes his life.

The symbolism of the latter part of Jekyll's story also has some bearing on the pattern I wish to study. Jekyll's repeated involuntary transformation into Hyde betokens, in effect, the paralysis of that part of Dr. Jekyll which is not Hyde. Having created Hyde, having psychologically liberated him, that is, Dr. Jekyll becomes progressively subject to an attrition of self. When he thinks of the way in which Hyde comes to "[prevail] against him," he significantly envisages him as "[deposing] him out of life" (p. 452). That deposition results in the loss of Jekyll's will to live, as well as in his refusal to live as Hyde, and so ultimately in suicide for both. The process enacted in the novels under discussion is more complex, but it is clarified by the exemplary case of Dr. Jekyll. When the protagonists in these novels break down it is because they are torn apart by the contending forces within them; but the disintegration portrayed is so complete because it may be thought of as taking place in a weakened self, the self having been exposed to something like the attrition experienced by Dr. Jekyll as first one half of the self and then the other tries to play Mr. Hyde.

A comic instance of a Jekyll and Hyde type of transformation—one without benefit of potion—is provided by Mr. Wemmick in *Great Expectations*. Working as a clerk to Mr. Jaggers, the lawyer, Wemmick in Little Britain is "a dry man, rather short in stature, with a square wooden face," whose expression seems "to have been imperfectly chipped out with a dull-edged chisel," and whose mouth is "such a post-office of a mouth" that he has "a mechanical appearance of smiling" and, when he eats a biscuit, throws pieces into it "as if he were posting them."[32] His guiding principle is "Get hold of portable property" (p. 190); and when Pip wants to shake hands with him on parting, he looks at Pip's outstretched hand as if he thinks he "[wants] something" (p. 163). At his home at Walworth, however, "a little wooden cottage" which he has made into a castle, complete with cannon and drawbridge over "a chasm about four feet wide and two deep" (p. 195), he gives himself to domestic bliss, solicitously caring for his old father, the Aged P., with "his hard face really softened" when he contemplates him (p. 196), and circumspectly courting the ineffable Miss Skiffins. When he sets out for Little Britain from Walworth, "by degrees" Wemmick gets "dryer and harder" as he goes along, and "his mouth [tightens] into a post-office again" (p. 198).

The opposed parts of Wemmick are thus given a local habitation if not a name, but—like Dr. Jekyll—he makes strenuous efforts to keep them separate. "The office is one thing," he tells Pip, "and private life is another. When I go into the office, I leave the Castle behind me, and when I come into the Castle, I leave the office behind me" (p. 197). When Pip wishes secretly to aid Herbert Pocket by conferring a certain amount of portable property on him, he makes the mistake of consulting Wemmick in Little Britain as to the best means of doing so, and meets with emphatic opposition to the plan; but later at Walworth Wemmick proves far more amenable, and in fact arranges the matter for Pip. In refusing to help Pip at the office, Wemmick states his position plainly: "Mr. Pip," he says, "Walworth is one place, and this office is another. Much as the Aged is one person, and Mr. Jaggers is another. They must not be confounded together. My Walworth sentiments must be taken at Walworth; none but my official sentiments can be taken in this office" (p. 277).

In the comic mode Wemmick therefore finds the perfect formula for disposing his opposed selves; and he suffers no more in the end than an "unmasking" by Pip in the presence of an incredulous Mr. Jaggers. In the selected novels, however, the protagonists are not able to move back and forth with ease between a Walworth and a Little Britain; theirs is a one-way journey—until they suddenly change direction. Nor can they contrive to sidestep conflict, as Wemmick does, by rendering unto Caesar the things which are Caesar's and unto God the things that are God's. When Walworth suddenly intrudes into Little Britain in their case, it results in more than momentary embarrassment. Their fate is to discover they cannot be in both places at the same time.

CHAPTER 2

Wuthering Heights
The Whirl of Contraries

The unconsummated passion of Cathy and Heathcliff may dominate the action of *Wuthering Heights*, but it is the repeated fact of marriage that is the motive force of the plot, and the repeated movement between the two houses, Wuthering Heights and Thrushcross Grange, that is the organizing principle of its structure. Thus in the first generation, Cathy, a child of the Heights, marries Edgar, a child of the Grange, and goes to live with him at the Grange. Their marriage is balanced by that of Isabella and Heathcliff, in which a child of the Grange marries a child of the Heights and goes to live with him at the Heights. This balance is then duplicated in the marriages of the second generation, that between Cathy II and Linton, in which a child of the Grange marries a child of the Heights and goes to live at the Heights; and that between Hareton and Cathy, in which a child of the Heights marries a child of the Grange and goes to live at the Grange.

Given the importance of place in the pattern of the marriages, David Cecil's account of the Heights and the Grange as foci of "storm" and "calm," respectively, remains as suggestive as ever, a good springboard, though we need to ground the distinction more firmly in the text than he does, and then take it further, moving out in a different direction.

Wuthering Heights, with its narrow, deep-set windows and large, defensively jutting corners, is a house that has been built for storm; and what it has chiefly been designed to withstand is "the power of the north wind," which is at once evident to Lockwood in "the excessive slant of a few, stunted firs at the end of the house" (p. 4.).[1] The north wind is an important concretization of the principle of storm, suggesting the kind of powerful, natural, elemental force that finds its analogue in the surging, tempestuous spirit of the characters who are brought up at the Heights. The thrust of this force in them is so insistent that it is imaged as destructive of containment, bursting out of puny limits: "Catherine," says Heathcliff, "has a heart as deep as I have; the sea could be as readily contained in that horse-trough, as her whole affection be monopolized by [Edgar]" (p. 182). Alternatively, were this force to be unnaturally contained, a woman such as Cathy could only languish: Heathcliff claims that Edgar "might as well plant an oak in a flower-pot, and expect it to thrive, as imagine he can restore [Cathy] to vigour in the soil of his shallow cares!" (p. 187). Natural force and stormy energy in Cathy and Heathcliff are also associated with the wild and untamed, and the uncivilized. As children "they both [promise] fair to grow up as rude as savages" (p. 56), and under Hindley's rule Heathcliff becomes "daily more notable for savage sullenness and ferocity" (p. 81). On Lockwood's first meeting with him, Heathcliff speaks "so savagely" to Cathy II that it makes his new tenant start (p. 15).

The savage wildness that is a primary attribute of the principle of storm is epitomized in the dogs at the Heights which attack Lockwood in "an absolute tempest of worrying and yelping," make "wolfishly" for his legs, and seem to him like "a brood of tigers" (pp. 8–9); when he tries to leave the house on a subsequent visit, "two hairy monsters" fly at his throat and knock him down (p. 21). It is characteristic of Emily Brontë's imagination that it is "in the arch of the dresser" that Cathy and Heathcliff as children seek a refuge from Hindley and Frances (p. 25), for it is from "an arch under the dresser," that some twenty-five years later the "huge, liver-coloured bitch pointer" emerges to attack Lockwood (p. 6). It is also characteristic that, when Heathcliff runs away from the Heights, Cathy, who waits outside for him, should be said to be heedless of "the growling thunder" (p. 104); that the adult Heathcliff, when angered, should "[thunder] . . . with savage vehemence" (p. 34); and that Isabella, telling Hindley how Heathcliff trampled on him and kicked him, should add: "And his mouth watered to tear you with his teeth; because he's only half a man—not so much" (p. 222). Catherine indeed had earlier tried to make Isabella realize this, to understand that Heathcliff is "an unreclaimed creature, without refinement—without cultivation; an arid wilderness of furze and whinstone . . . a fierce, pitiless, wolfish man" (p. 126).

Sheltered in a valley and confined within its park, Thrushcross Grange is not exposed, like the Heights, to the north wind; and those, like Edgar Linton, who grow up in it seem, as Nelly Dean says of him, to "[want] spirit in general"—but this lack of spirit goes together with the amiability and grace and intellectual power which Lockwood discerns in the portrait of Edgar that Nelly shows him (p. 82). It goes too with "cold blood"—Cathy accuses Edgar of having veins which are "full of ice-water" (p. 144), whereas she is aware of how her own blood can "rush into a hell of tumult at a few words" (p. 153); and it also goes with softness. The softness is apparent in Edgar's "soft-featured face" (p. 82), and in the appurtenances of the Grange drawing room, in which the Linton children seem to have their being (as Cathy and Heathcliff have theirs on the moors): ". . . ah! it was beautiful—" Heathcliff says of this room to Nelly, "a splendid place carpeted with crimson, and crimson-covered chairs and tables, and a pure white ceiling bordered by gold, a shower of glass-drops hanging in silver chains from the centre, and shimmering with little soft tapers" (p. 58). The Grange, that is, posits an elegant, padded refinement as against the rough, free wildness of the Heights; and an appropriate emblem of its "calm" is the "little dog" which Cathy and Heathcliff watch Isabella and Edgar fighting over: tame and domesticated, this lap dog bears the same relation to Isabella and Edgar as the dogs that are like tigers bear to Cathy and Heathcliff. The children of the Heights cannot help scorning the quarreling Lintons and "[laugh] outright at the petted things" (p. 59). The Grange may be only four miles from the Heights, but the two are worlds apart and indeed Nelly says that the contrast between Heathcliff and Edgar resembles "what you see in exchanging a bleak, hilly, coal country for a beautiful fertile valley" (p. 87).

The principle of storm, then, is set firmly against that of calm, but not, it seems to me, in a vision of "cosmic harmony," as Cecil maintains; nor would the novel appear to be concerned with the disruption of "the working of the natural order" through the discordant presence of Heathcliff, who is viewed as "an extraneous element" though "a child of the storm."[2] Emily Brontë is engaged, if anything, by possibilities of personal rather than cosmic harmony, by the possibilities of reconciling storm and calm—that is, as the imagery suggests, of reconciling animal-like wildness and refined cultivation—in personal relations. The strength with which the children of storm and the children of calm are drawn to their opposites is indicative of their desire for a more comprehensive form of life, for the development of the opposing principle within the self as well as for contact with it in a marriage. The motif of marriage, indeed, would seem to point particularly to the possibility of a metaphorical marriage of opposites within the self; and what is at issue is the instinctive attempt of the individual to reconcile and integrate the two principles, not only within a marriage but within a new wholeness of being. Though the opposed principles are projected predominantly in terms of wildness and cultivation, their association with the passionate and the reasonable suggests that the opposition is a transmutation of the more fundamental dichotomy of flesh and spirit.[3]

If *Wuthering Heights* is concerned with such a marriage of opposites, then it is striking that the actual marriages which point to this theme are extremely short-lived. In the two generations that are the focus of interest, there is only one marriage which may be presumed to last, that of Cathy and Hareton at the end of the novel. Cathy I dies after a year of marriage to Edgar; Isabella leaves Heathcliff after about three months; Linton dies within about a month of his marriage to Cathy II; and (we might add for good measure, though the relationship is not part of the main design) Frances dies within less than two years of her marriage to Hindley. What this points to is division or fragmentation rather than integration, and indeed there are other notable instances of such separations: Heathcliff is separated from Cathy, and then (when he returns) succeeds in dividing her from her husband; Isabella, in marrying Heathcliff, is separated from her brother, who thereafter thinks of the two of them as being "eternally divided" (p. 178); Edgar does not permit Cathy II to visit Linton at the Heights, leaving the boy to hope he will not "remain long so utterly divided" from his cousin (p. 314); and when Cathy is finally lured to the Heights, she is forcibly separated from her dying father.

The idea of division leaves its imaginative stamp on *Wuthering Heights* in other ways too. The narrative is divided between two narrators; and though much has been said about the narrative functions of Nelly Dean and Lockwood and the technical brilliance of Emily Brontë's employment of them as narrators, the fact remains that this division is impressed on us throughout: if Nelly tells most of the story, we are returned to Lockwood at regular intervals and made aware of him as a narrating presence. A natural consequence of this method of narration is a divided or dislocated—rather than a chronologically straightforward—time scheme: Lockwood begins the tale towards the end of its time span; Nelly goes back to the beginning of the *fabula* and then by degrees brings the story forward to the point at which Lockwood started; Lockwood takes it further, only to have Nelly once again fill in a gap for him before he concludes it. The narrative, moreover, despite the overwhelming impression Cathy and Heathcliff make on us, is in fact almost equally divided between the two generations even if this is not generally reflected in the amount of attention paid to the second generation in most critical discussions; and though it is true that Heathcliff straddles the novel, there is a decided division of interest as we switch from Cathy I to Cathy II as foci in the first and second halves, respectively.

The motif of division is thus thrown up in a number of ways, and it has its bearing on the figure which may be said to underlie the pattern of marriage previously referred to, namely, that of the love triangle. In each generation the relationships established by the two Catherines with the men they love take the same form. Cathy I is strongly drawn to Heathcliff and Edgar, two men who embody the opposing principles of storm and calm; and what we witness is the way in which she swings away from Heathcliff to Edgar, and then back to Heathcliff again. Similarly, Cathy II is drawn to both Hareton and Linton, the opposed embodiments of storm and calm in the second generation; and what we watch is how she turns in revulsion from Hareton to Linton, only to turn back to Hareton in the end. The pattern thus provides a repeated image of a self divided between the conflicting principles. But the novelist also uses the pattern to balance a story of disintegration with one of integration, for if Cathy I is torn apart by her conflicts, Cathy II is finally able to reconcile the principles of storm and calm.

II

The story of Cathy and Heathcliff and Edgar may be said to begin when the children of the Heights peep in on and then mock the children of the Grange through its drawing room window, only to have a bulldog set loose on them. Cathy is bitten and held by the dog, and then taken into the house by a servant. Heathcliff follows, and reports to Nelly how Mr. and Mrs. Linton declare him to be a "castaway" and clearly wicked:

> "'A wicked boy, at all events,' remarked the old lady, 'and quite unfit for a decent house! Did you notice his language, Linton? I'm shocked that my children should have heard it.'
>
> "I recommenced cursing—don't be angry, Nelly—and so Robert was ordered to take me off—I refused to go without Cathy—he dragged me into the garden, pushed the lantern into my hand . . . and bidding me march, directly, secured the door again.
>
> "The curtains were still looped up at one corner, and I resumed my station as spy, because, if Catherine had wished to return, I intended shattering their great glass panes to a million fragments, unless they let her out.
>
> "She sat on the sofa quietly. Mrs. Linton took off the grey cloak of the dairy maid which we had borrowed for our excursion, shaking her head, and expostulating with her, I suppose; she was a young lady and they made a distinction between her treatment and mine. Then the woman servant brought a basin of warm water, and washed her feet; and Mr. Linton mixed a tumbler of negus, and Isabella emptied a plateful of cakes into her lap, and Edgar stood gaping at a distance. Afterwards, they dried and combed her beautiful hair, and gave her a pair of enormous slippers, and wheeled her to the fire, and I left her, as merry as she could be, dividing her food between the little dog and Skulker, whose nose she pinched as she ate; and kindling a spark of spirit in the vacant blue eyes of the Lintons—a dim reflection from her own enchanting face—I saw they were full of stupid admiration; she is so immeasurably superior to them—to everybody on earth, is she not, Nelly?" (pp. 62–63)

This episode offers us a wonderfully concentrated prefigurement of later developments in the relationships of the protagonists. Heathcliff throughout remains quite unshakable in his devotion to Cathy, having to be separated from her by force; and his violent readiness to smash the Lintons' great windows into "a million fragments" is premonitory of the way in which he proceeds, when Cathy is finally taken from him, to shatter and fragment the Linton family, gaining entry to their property then by making it his own. Cathy, however, is separated from Heathcliff by a force more subtle than that employed by Robert—by the startling power of the new image of herself that is reflected in the eyes of the Lintons, the image of herself as "a young lady," in contradistinction to that of Heathcliff as a castaway, as someone "quite unfit for a decent house" (just as he will later appear to her to be quite unfit for a decent marriage). When she quietly allows Mrs. Linton to remove the dairymaid's cloak, which (as Cathy subsequently writes in the account that Lockwood reads) the children have "appropriated" so that they can together "have a scamper on the moors, under its shelter" (p. 26), she submits to being divested of more than a garment. Evidently she is strongly drawn to the Lintons and their elegant home, and is glad to take herself at their valuation, for Heathcliff leaves her "as merry as she could be." The Grange bulldog may initially hold her in a grip from which she cannot escape, but she ends by feeding it. She also fills the Lintons, as it were: she "[kindles] a spark of spirit" in their "vacant blue eyes," sustaining them with her abundant fire, to which thereafter Edgar, in particular, is irresistibly impelled.

Cathy stays for five weeks at Thrushcross Grange, and when she returns to Wuthering Heights she appears to be not so much "reformed," as Frances has hoped, as transformed. Her "manners" are said to be "much improved," and Nelly is confronted by "a very dignified person" instead of the "wild, hatless little savage" she expects to jump into the house. Hindley registers the extent of the change for us when he barely recognizes her: "Why, Cathy," he says, "you are quite a beauty! I should scarcely have known you—you look like a lady now . . ." (p. 65). The period spent at the Grange, that is, and Cathy's own revised attitude to the cultivation of the Lintons have served to counter her wildness and foster her own latent civility of nature. It is not so much a new Cathy who comes back to the Heights as a new part of her that is revealed, the "lady" having been superimposed on the "savage." Cathy is both savage and lady, if alternately; and though now the savage may only have been repressed, not expunged, that does not mean that her new manner is false. That it is generally seen as an affectation which belies "her genuine disposition" (p. 89), is due to Nelly Dean:

Catherine had kept up her acquaintance with the Lintons since her five weeks' residence among them; and as she had no temptation to show her rough side in their company, and had the sense to be ashamed of being rude where she experienced such invariable courtesy, she imposed unwittingly on the old lady and gentleman, by her ingenious cordiality; gained the admiration of Isabella, and the heart and soul of her brother—acquisitions that flattered her from the first, for she was full of ambition—and led her to adopt a double character without exactly intending to deceive anyone.

In the place where she had heard Heathcliff termed a "vulgar young ruffian," and "worse than a brute," she took care not to act like him; but at home she had small inclination to practise politeness that would only be laughed at, and restrain an unruly nature when it would bring her neither credit nor praise. (pp. 82–83)

What is apparent here is Nelly's acuteness as an observer—and her extraordinary bias against Cathy. What she perceives is Cathy's "double character," the composite self in which a "rough side" persists and underlies a civil; but her animus towards Cathy is such that she quite misconstrues what she sees. She contrives to turn Cathy into an ambitious hypocrite whose very cordiality is "ingenious" and who artfully (though of course unintentionally) "adopts" her double character in her dealings with the Lintons, and so "imposes" on them (though of course "unwittingly"). Nelly fails to understand that "an unruly nature" may be genuinely "restrained"—and not merely solicitous of credit and praise—when brought into real relationship with a more tractable disposition; and that Cathy, when removed from the tension of relationship with the Lintons that develops her socially and braces her into "politeness," may easily sag back into incivility at the Heights since it is propitious to it and offers no qualification to her wildness.

Nelly's attitude to Cathy is so suspect as to make her an unreliable narrator where she is concerned though there is no reason to doubt her word in other respects. It is difficult to account for her attitude, and the novelist certainly does nothing to help us; but it may possibly be traced back to her somewhat ambiguous relationship to Hindley and Cathy as children. Of an age with Hindley, Nelly is the playmate of brother and sister and yet at the same time a general factotum at the Heights (p. 43); she makes a point of telling Lockwood that Mr. Earnshaw turns to her as well as to Hindley and Cathy when he announces his expedition to Liverpool—"for I sat eating my porridge with them" (p. 43); and she refers to Hindley as her "foster brother" (p. 229). There is perhaps some basis for inferring resentment on her part of Cathy's status, especially after her stay at the Grange. But whatever the grounds of her animosity, she openly admits it exists: "I own I did not like [Cathy], after her infancy was past," she says to Lockwood; "and I vexed her frequently by trying to bring down her arrogance; she never took an aversion to me, though" (p. 82); ". . . she was so proud," she remarks of Cathy on her return from the Grange, "it became really impossible to pity her distresses, till she should be chastened into more humility" (p. 83); "I've said I did not love her, and rather relished mortifying her vanity, now and then," she confesses on another occasion (p. 88); and she always expects the worst of her, as she unconsciously reveals when she admits that it is to her "agreeable disappointment" that Cathy behaves "infinitely better" than she has "dared to expect" on moving to the Grange as Edgar's wife (p. 113).

That Nelly is right about the persistence of the "rough side" beneath Cathy's newly cultivated exterior is brought out when Edgar begins to visit her at the Heights. Acting on Hindley's instructions, Nelly always "[makes] a third party" during these visits; and on one occasion she refuses to leave the room when Cathy wants her to. Cathy thereupon surreptitiously pinches her, "with a prolonged wrench, very spitefully on the arm," and is infuriated when Nelly screams out her resentment:

> "I didn't touch you, you lying creature!" cried she, her fingers tingling to repeat the act, and her ears red with rage. She never had power to conceal her passion, it always set her whole complexion in a blaze. (pp. 87–88)

It is Nelly's exposure of her before Edgar that fires Cathy, as though a bolt of lightning has pierced through her civility, consuming it, and penetrated to a deeper and more passionate level of being, setting it ablaze. This is quite beyond Cathy's volition: like a Dr. Jekyll involuntarily turned into a Mr. Hyde, one part of her is for the time being negated. Quite unable to control herself, Cathy is now "irresistibly impelled" to slap Nelly on the cheek with "a stinging blow that [fills] both eyes with water" when she shows the purple evidence of the pinching; to shake little Hareton "till the poor child [waxes] livid" when he begins to cry in sympathy with Nelly; and finally to strike Edgar over the ear "in a way that [can] not be mistaken for jest" when he tries to free Hareton (p. 88). Edgar's response to the slap is interesting. Initially declaring he will not come to the Heights again, he leaves the house, but glances into the room where Cathy is, as Nelly reports:

> The soft thing looked askance through the window—he possessed the power to depart, as much as a cat possesses the power to leave a mouse half killed, or a bird half eaten—
>
> Ah, I thought, there will be no saving him—He's doomed, and flies to his fate!
>
> And, so it was; he turned abruptly, hastened into the house again, shut the door behind him; and, when I went in a while after . . . , I saw the quarrel had merely effected a closer intimacy—had broken the outworks of

youthful timidity, and enabled them to forsake the disguise of friendship, and confess themselves lovers. (pp. 89–90)

The cat simile is puzzling at first, for one would expect Cathy to be regarded as the devourer rather than Edgar, but what the simile implies is the compulsive pull of unfinished business. Edgar is roused by Cathy's fury, not only masochistically, as the simile indicates; and, implicated with her in violence, he is now impelled to see things through to the end. The episode, indeed, corresponds to the scene in *Women in Love* where Gudrun Brangwen slaps Gerald Crich on the face and he almost at once declares his love for her—though Edgar of course is not racked by the same kind of destructive demons that possess Gerald. We realize, however, that Edgar, like Cathy, has two sides to his nature. The same applies to Heathcliff. It is true that his childhood attempt to match the change in Cathy after her stay at the Grange fails utterly, so that by the age of sixteen he gives "an impression of inward and outward repulsiveness," acquires an "ignoble look," and exaggerates "his naturally reserved disposition" into an "almost idiotic excess of unsociable moroseness" (p. 84). But when he returns to the Heights after his mysterious absence of three years, Nelly is amazed "to behold [his] transformation," even though in his case the outer self (in comparison with that of Cathy and Edgar) gives more direct intimation of the depths within: "[his countenance] looked intelligent, and retained no marks of former degradation. A half-civilized ferocity lurked yet in the depressed brows and eyes full of black fire, but it was subdued; and his manner was even dignified, quite divested of roughness though too stern for grace" (p. 118).

It is on the day she slaps him that Edgar asks Cathy to marry him, and that she accepts him (p. 96); but on the same day she passionately declares to Nelly that she knows—"in [her] soul, and in [her] heart"—that she is "wrong" to do so (p. 98):

> "I've no more business to marry Edgar Linton," [she says], "than I have to be in heaven; and if the wicked man in there [i.e., Hindley] had not brought Heathcliff so low, I shouldn't have thought of it. It would degrade me to marry Heathcliff, now; so he shall never know how I love him; and that, not because he's handsome, Nelly, but because he's more myself than I am. Whatever our souls are made of, his and mine are the same, and Linton's is as different as a moonbeam from lightning, or frost from fire. . . .
> "... surely you and everybody have a notion that there is, or should be, an existence of yours beyond you. What were the use of my creation if I were entirely contained here? My great miseries in this world have been Heathcliff's miseries, and I watched and felt each from the beginning; my great thought in living is himself. If all else perished, and *he* remained, I should still continue to be; and, if all else remained, and he were annihilated, the Universe would turn to a mighty stranger. I should not seem a

part of it. My love for Linton is like the foliage in the woods. Time will change it, I'm well aware, as winter changes the trees—my love for Heathcliff resembles the eternal rocks beneath—a source of little visible delight, but necessary. Nelly, I *am* Heathcliff—he's always, always in my mind—not as a pleasure, any more than I am always a pleasure to myself—but, as my own being—so, don't talk of our separation again . . ." (pp. 100–102)

These are famous and stirring lines, and Cathy's love for Heathcliff is clearly more profound—issuing from an altogether deeper part of herself—than her feeling for Edgar. Our sense of the profundity of her connection with Heathcliff is increased by the transcendental overtones that sound in her declaration of love. Her passion for him, indeed, seems so authoritatively right that our immediate response is to marvel at how wrong she is in marrying Edgar in spite of it, and to lament how willfully she seems to betray not only Heathcliff but herself in doing so. But at the same time her statements have some disquieting implications. If she boasts that time will change her love for Edgar though not for Heathcliff, we remain aware that it is not only foliage in the woods that is changed by time but anything that is alive—and that a love which is like the eternal rocks and does not change would not seem to be amenable to consummation in this world. Indeed her claim that she *is* Heathcliff underlines the point, for one can only be another person by ceasing to be oneself.[4] Her assertion, moreover, that she has "an existence" beyond her *in* Heathcliff would seem to be a prescription for sexual disaster if we allow D. H. Lawrence to serve as our guide here. An acceptance of the otherness of one's partner, Lawrence insisted, is a *sine qua non* of true sexual relationship; and he envisaged sexual union not as a merging of the partners but as a heightening of their distinctness, as a condition of "two in one." Cathy, however, can conceive of her relationship with Heathcliff only as an indivisible, organic oneness, as the trunk of a tree is a seamless whole: whoever should try to separate her and Heathcliff, she tells Nelly, will "meet the fate of Milo" (p. 101). And if her soul is made of the same stuff as Heathcliff's, whereas Edgar's is utterly different, as she perceives, it is the connection with moonbeam and frost, not lightning and fire, that she needs.

The way Cathy announces her intention to accept Edgar's proposal, however, makes it seem like a wayward attempt to have her cake and eat it, to marry Edgar and have Heathcliff remain "as much to [her] as he has been all his lifetime." Her stated belief, moreover, that she will be able to "aid Heathcliff to rise, and place him out of [her] brother's power" if she marries Edgar, seems frivolous and points to her own desire for place and fortune, her own fear of being a "beggar" if she marries Heathcliff

(p. 101). But her overt relationship with Edgar is more than a question of his social attractiveness. If we fail to appreciate that she also loves him, it is because Nelly is there to mislead us. When Nelly asks her whether she loves Edgar, her response is immediate, spontaneous, unqualified: "Who can help it? Of course I do," she says. But Nelly thereupon puts her through a "catechism" as to why she loves him, and not surprisingly elicits only mockingly conventional answers. Nelly, however, proceeds to sum up the situation for Cathy—and for us—in a way which subtly disparages her feeling: ". . . you love Mr. Edgar," she says, "because he is handsome, and young, and cheerful, and rich, and loves you" (pp. 96–97).

It is clear that Cathy's feeling for Heathcliff and Edgar is different in kind, and springs from different levels of her being; indeed it is because each engages only half of her, as it were, that she seems to think she can safely have both. But it is also clear that she loves both of them, and it is this fact that eventually destroys her. Pulled between the two men, she is divided between the opposed principles they represent, between the two sides of her own nature. In the storm that arises on the night of Heathcliff's disappearance (when Cathy communicates her dilemma to Nelly), a large tree at the Heights is "split" in two, and this can be taken to be "nature's adumbration" not only of a "calamitous severance of selves," as Edgar F. Shannon has said,[5] but of a crucial split in Cathy herself. Though Cathy suffers bitterly as a result of it, Heathcliff's departure actually serves as a palliative, enabling her to suspend the immediate conflict and marry Edgar.

The essential feature of Cathy's marriage to Edgar prior to Heathcliff's return—though this tends to get lost to view in the subsequent tempest—is that it works, and seems to be getting better and better. Even Nelly says, "I believe I may assert that they were really in possession of deep and growing happiness" (p. 114); while Isabella declares that "Catherine and Edgar are as fond of each other as any two people can be!" (p. 182), and later remarks on how happy they all were—and especially "how happy Catherine was"—before Heathcliff returned (p. 223). But this of course is not the whole story, and, as we may expect, Cathy has to pay a price for her happiness. In her marriage she has to do without Heathcliff and strongly to contain, if not negate, one side of herself: she tells Nelly later that she has "endured very, very bitter misery" though she has never "expressed the agony [she] frequently felt." When Heathcliff suddenly returns, she declares she is "reconciled . . . to God and humanity!" (p. 123). What she cannot do is reconcile the two men; and Nelly perceives that the calm of Cathy's married life prior to Heathcliff's return should be attributed to the fact that "for the space of half a year, the gunpowder lay as harmless as sand, because no fire came near to explode it" (p. 114). Nelly's image is exact: when Heathcliff comes back, a dormant part of Cathy is ignited, blazing into sudden life.[6]

Cathy persists in believing that she can tranquilly enjoy both men, and she places the blame for the storm that erupts on Heathcliff, who complicates matters by showing an apparent interest in Isabella: ". . . Edgar is restored from the ill-temper he gave way to at your coming," she tells Heathcliff; "I begin to be secure and tranquil; and you, restless to know us at peace, appear resolved on exciting a quarrel . . ." (p. 138). The quarrel is not long in coming. Edgar, informed by Nelly of Heathcliff's "behaviour" with Isabella, confronts him, though he starts quietly, not wishing "to entertain him with any high flights of passion":

> "I have been so far forbearing with you, sir," he said, quietly; "not that I was ignorant of your miserable, degraded character, but I felt you were only partly responsible for that; and Catherine wishing to keep up your acquaintance, I acquiesced—foolishly. Your presence is a moral poison that would contaminate the most virtuous—for that cause, and to prevent worse consequences, I shall deny you, hereafter, admission into this house, and give notice, now, that I require your instant departure. Three minutes' delay will render it involuntary and ignominious."
>
> Heathcliff measured the height and breadth of the speaker with an eye full of derision.
>
> "Cathy, this lamb of yours threatens like a bull!" he said. "It is in danger of splitting its skull against my knuckles. By God, Mr. Linton, I'm mortally sorry that you are not worth knocking down!"
>
> My master glanced towards the passage, and signed me to fetch the men—he had no intention of hazarding a personal encounter.
>
> I obeyed the hint; but Mrs. Linton, suspecting something, followed, and when I attempted to call them, she pulled me back, slammed the door to, and locked it.
>
> "Fair means!" she said, in answer to her husband's look of angry surprise. "If you have not the courage to attack him, make an apology, or allow yourself to be beaten. It will correct you of feigning more valour than you possess. No, I'll swallow the key before you shall get it! I'm delightfully rewarded for my kindness to each! After constant indulgence of one's weak nature, and the other's bad one, I earn, for thanks, two samples of blind ingratitude, stupid to absurdity! Edgar, I was defending you, and yours; and I wish Heathcliff may flog you sick, for daring to think an evil thought of me!" (pp. 140–41)

It is a fine scene, and vividly dramatizes the opposition on which the novel is based. As Edgar begins to speak with controlled restraint, his very syntax an index of the ordered, logical movement of his mind and its firmness a mark of the position he has adopted, it is clear that he takes his stand, essentially, as a social being, a "civilized" man, who never doubts his power to force Heathcliff to abide by the rule of law, and believes unquestioningly in the inviolability of his rights under it. It is preeminently in terms of a right of property—it is his house (not to mention his wife and his sister)—that he "requires" Heathcliff's departure. Heathcliff's immediate response is to measure the physical power that his antagonist commands, opposing the firmness of knuckles (fit to split Edgar's skull) to that of speech. The only rule he recognizes is that of force, the rule that the strong may do and have what they want; and the right he implicitly claims is that of an elemental affinity with Cathy that binds them together, of a natural bond more imperious than marriage.

For Cathy, caught between Edgar and Heathcliff as they confront each other, strikingly placed in that position by the novelist, this is a moment of choice—and she responds with a fiery instinctiveness. As she springs into action, she slams the door not only on the men Edgar would summon but on any possibility of compromise, forcing the "personal encounter" her husband wishes to avoid. And it is clear she conceives of that encounter only in terms of violence, of attacking and beating and flogging. Her spontaneous response, that is, constitutes a denial of all that is represented by the Grange and her marriage, as "her husband's look of angry surprise" indicates—and an identification with Heathcliff and the system of values she has known at the Heights. When Edgar subsequently tries "to wrest the key from Catherine's grasp" and she flings it into "the hottest part of the fire," her repudiation of her husband is complete. For good measure, she declares Edgar's "type is not a lamb, it's a sucking leveret," lending herself to Heathcliff's contemptuous dismissal of him as a "milk-blooded coward" and a "slavering, shivering thing." It is not the wolf or tiger that actually attacks, however, for it is Edgar who is provoked into striking Heathcliff, but the blow with which the scene ends settles nothing (pp. 141–42). When Edgar later explicitly formulates the only alternatives Cathy seems to have left them all—"Will you give up Heathcliff hereafter, or will you give up me? It is impossible for you to be *my* friend and *his* at the same time; and I absolutely *require* to know which you choose"—she proves to be incapable of acting on a choice she has already made in effect, and "requires" in turn to be "let alone" (p. 144).

Cathy thereupon begins to "[dash] her head against the arm of the sofa, and [grind] her teeth, so that you might fancy she would crash them to splinters" (pp. 144–45), this being the rage of a divided self turning upon itself in a frenzy of frustration; for, wanting Heathcliff, she is not ready in fact to give up Edgar and her life at the Grange.[7] Her refusal of food for three days at this point is only a different form of violence against the self. Cathy proceeds to make herself ill, and the delirium that marks the onset of her illness directly figures the pressure of her need for some escape from her condition: in her delirium she flees to childhood, to a time when she was united with Heathcliff (pp. 149–50). When she "revives," she still unavailingly longs to "be herself," to be what she was before Edgar came into her life: ". . . I wish I were a girl again, half savage and hardy, and free . . . and laughing at injuries, not maddening under them! Why am I so changed? why does my blood rush into a hell of tumult at a few words? I'm sure I should be myself were I once among the heather on those hills" (pp. 152–53).

Torn in two by her conflict, it is by breakdown that Cathy is menaced, as she herself seems to divine. Immediately after the confrontation between Edgar and Heathcliff she tells Nelly that she is "nearly distracted," and asks her to remind Edgar that her "passionate temper [verges], when kindled, on frenzy" (p. 143). When she rushes away from Edgar—and his ultimatum—she feels certain "of having a fit, or going raging mad" if he persists in "teasing" her (p. 152). The doctor informs Nelly that "the threatening danger" is "not so much death, as permanent alienation of intellect" (p. 160); and in the end Cathy succumbs to a severe illness that is "denominated a brain fever" (p. 163). Though she recovers from this illness and it is in childbirth that she dies, she never seems to recover the will to live.[8] In the poignant scene in which Heathcliff steals into her room just before her death and passionately embraces her, she bitterly says that he and Edgar have together "broken [her] heart" (pp. 194–95); but Heathcliff does not allow her that view of the rending: "I have not broken your heart—" he says, "*you* have broken it—and in breaking it, you have broken mine. . . . I forgive what you have done to me. I love *my* murderer—but *yours*! How can I?" (p. 198).

III

Ever since Richard Chase's persuasive account of *Wuthering Heights*, it has become customary to consider the second half of the novel as somewhat of an anticlimax, to view Hareton and Cathy II as "but pale replicas of their elders," and to regard the marriage with which the book ends as representing a tame "domestication" of the energies that drive the characters of the first generation.[9] Though it is undoubtedly true that the characters of the second generation do not have the force of the first, to follow Chase's reading is to ignore the fact that Hareton and Linton Heathcliff are presented as being even more extreme embodiments of the principles of storm and calm than Heathcliff and Edgar. And it is not to do justice to the marriage of Cathy and Hareton, which—in a manner that is far from contemptible—represents a reconciliation of the opposed principles.

From an early age Hareton, who is in effect raised by Heathcliff, gives every indication of outdoing his teacher in ferocity. When, at the age of five, he is approached by Nelly, who has been his nurse but has not seen him for ten months, his response to her greeting—"God bless thee, darling!"—is to retreat "out of arm's length," pick up "a large flint," and throw it at her head; and he follows this up with "a string of curses" which distort "his baby features into a shocking expression of malignity" (p. 134). And before he is six he figures in a brutal epiphany when Isabella, in her flight from the Heights, knocks him over while he is engaged in "hanging a litter of puppies from a chair-back in the doorway" (p. 224). Nor is his disposition tempered by time: when Lockwood first encounters him as a young man at the Heights, Hareton looks at him "from the corner of his eyes, for all the world as if there were some mortal feud unavenged between [them]." The wildness which Hareton has pre-served intact into adulthood is not mediated, as is the case with Heathcliff, by a veneer of civility, and Lockwood notes how, in contradistinction to Heathcliff, both Hareton's dress and speech are "rude," his hair rough, and his whiskers "[encroach] bearishly over his cheeks" (p. 14). The wolfish man, we see, has reared Hareton like an animal; and indeed when Hareton resists an apparent inclination to assault Lockwood, he "[smothers] the storm in a brutal curse," thereafter "growls" rather than talks, and is mentally designated a "bear" by the visitor (pp. 16–17). Heathcliff later boasts that Hareton will "never be able to emerge from his bathos of coarseness, and ignorance": "I've got him faster than his scoun-drel of a father secured me," he says, "and lower; for he takes a pride in his brutishness. I've taught him to scorn everything extra-animal as silly and weak—" (p. 267). Lockwood also notes, however, that Hareton's manner is "free, almost haughty" (p. 14), and it is clear that a high spirit blows undiminished in him too. As Joseph says, "He's getten t'raight sperrit in him" (p. 305).

But Hareton is perhaps most vividly placed for us by Nelly. He is eighteen when he first meets Catherine Linton, his young cousin from the Grange. Nelly remarks then that, if Heathcliff appears "to have bent his malevolence on making [Hareton] a brute," having deprived him of the chance of learning how to read and write and ensuring that he has never been "led a single step towards virtue, or guarded by a single precept against vice," he is nevertheless "a well-made, athletic youth, good looking in features, and stout and healthy." Nelly sums up her impression of Hareton in an elaborate image:

> I thought I could detect in his physiognomy a mind owning better qualities than his father ever possessed. Good things lost amid a wilderness of weeds, to be sure, whose rankness far over-topped their neglected growth; yet, notwithstanding, evidence of a wealthy soil that might yield luxuriant crops under other and favourable circumstances. (pp. 240–41)

This image is at the heart of the action of the last section of the novel. What Nelly discerns, going beyond his outer neglect, is that Hareton has a good mind as well as a stout frame, that he is capable of rich growth— and that it is merely cultivation that his rank unweeded garden requires in order to sustain a more ordered luxuriance. At eighteen, that is, Hareton is in much the same position as his aunt was before she left the Heights a little savage and first entered the Grange.

Linton is Heathcliff's son, but as his father promptly asserts on first seeing him, he seems to be his "mother's child, entirely": "Where is *my* share in thee, puling chicken?" Heathcliff disgustedly asks (p. 254). The domestic fowl poised for fright, Linton has few redeeming features; and though Edgar hopes that "the company of a child of his own age will instil new spirit into him soon" (p. 247), he proves to be notably lacking in any spirit at all. Zillah maintains that she "never knew such a faint-hearted creature" (p. 258). Just as Hareton is a wilder Heathcliff (though as an adult he is not placed in situations that elicit a dramatic expression of his brutality), so Linton is a tamer Edgar, an Edgar run to seed, to sickliness and effeminacy. Nelly is quick to draw the distinction for us: "A pale, delicate, effeminate boy, who might have been taken for my master's younger brother, so strong was the resemblance, but there was a sickly peevishness in his aspect that Edgar Linton never had" (p. 245). Linton's peevishness, however, has a vicious side to it, for, as Joseph points out, "we've allas summut uh orther side in us," and Linton does have some of his father in him. It is his response to Hareton's eviction of him from the room with the settle that elicits Joseph's comment, for Linton then shrieks out: "If you don't let me in I'll kill you! If you don't let me in I'll kill you! Devil! devil! I'll kill you, I'll kill you!" (p. 306); and, as Heathcliff says, "Linton can play the little tyrant well. He'll undertake to torture any number of cats if their teeth be drawn, and their claws pared" (p. 333).

Linton's predominant characteristic is epitomized in Cathy's account of his "perfect idea of heaven's happiness":

> "He said the pleasantest manner of spending a hot July day was lying from morning till evening on a bank of heath in the middle of the moors, with the bees humming dreamily about among the bloom, and the larks singing high up over head, and the blue sky and bright sun shining steadily and cloudlessly." (p. 301)

Linton's wanting "all to lie in an ecstasy of peace" (p. 302) is a celebration of stasis; and to Cathy it seems that his heaven is "only half alive"—that it projects a state of paralysis, we might say. In Linton the principle of calm seems to have been denatured, to have become, rather, a principle of becalming.

Cathy's ideal of happiness, as imaged on the same occasion, is sharply differentiated from that of Linton:

". . . mine was rocking in a rustling green tree, with a west wind blowing, and bright, white clouds flitting rapidly above; and not only larks, but throstles, and blackbirds, and linnets, and cuckoos pouring out music on every side, and the moors seen at a distance, broken into cool dusky dells; but close by, great swells of long grass undulating in waves to the breeze; and woods and sounding water, and the whole world awake and wild with joy. He wanted all to lie in an ecstasy of peace; I wanted all to sparkle, and dance in a glorious jubilee." (pp. 301–302)

What Cathy celebrates, in opposition to Linton, is motion; but though she talks of the whole world being awake and "wild with joy," the kind of motion she actually pictures—the rocking in a rustling tree, the clouds flitting, grass undulating in a gentle breeze—is also strikingly distinguished from the tumult associated with the children of storm in the first generation. Where her mother at the end of her life is obsessed with the wish to be out on the stormy moors and it is the roar of the north wind that fills her ears, Cathy's imagination is held by a peaceful summer scene, with the music of birds sounding everywhere and a mild "west wind blowing." In Cathy, it is suggested, the wild, chaotic, destructive energy that drives her mother and Heathcliff is much attenuated, is, indeed, reduced to a disciplined order and control—as it is in the "dance" of jubilee in which her ideal world moves.

Cathy is perhaps too contained, allows too little for the subdued part of her nature, as Nelly unintentionally implies in her description of her as a girl of twelve:

She was the most winning thing that ever brought sunshine into a desolate house—a real beauty in face—with the Earnshaws' handsome dark eyes, but the Lintons' fair skin, and small features, and yellow curling hair. Her spirit was high, though not rough, and qualified by a heart sensitive and lively to excess in its affections. That capacity for intense attachments reminded me of her mother; still she did not resemble her; for she could be soft and mild as a dove, and she had a gentle voice, and pensive expression: her anger was never furious; her love never fierce; it was deep and tender. (p. 232)

With Cathy's mother in mind, Nelly is struck by the superiority of her charge; we cannot help noticing that in Cathy, though she is half Earnshaw and half Linton, the Earnshaw heritage is so submerged as to be barely apparent: though she has the Earnshaws' eyes, these are quite offset by the Lintons' skin and features and hair; if her spirit is "high" in the Earnshaw manner, it is so "qualified" by her Linton sensitivity and affectionateness that it is effectively curbed. As Nelly insists, Cathy is a Linton both in appearance and by temperament, a dove, not a tiger. She is so much a child of the Grange, indeed, that until the age of thirteen she has never been "beyond the range of [its] park by herself," and "Wuthering Heights and Mr. Heathcliff [do] not exist for her." But she longs to go out on to the moors and to Penistone Crags and "the topmost Heights," and will not be put off by Nelly's telling her that she should be content with Thrushcross park, which is "the finest place in the world": " 'But I know the park, and I don't know those,' she [murmurs] to herself" (pp. 233–34). Her life becomes the making of that journey to the Heights—a movement, that is, in a direction opposite from that taken by her mother.

Both Hareton and Linton are Cathy's cousins, and the second half of the novel turns on the question of her proper relation to them. Cathy is sixteen when she first sees them together, and she then turns away from Hareton, siding with Linton against him. Nelly reports how Hareton is led to confess he cannot read the inscription over the main door to the Heights, and how Linton thereupon taunts him with his ignorance:

> "If thou wern't more a lass than a lad, I'd fell thee this minute, I would; pitiful lath of a crater!" retorted the angry boor, retreating, while his face burnt with mingled rage and mortification; for he was conscious of being insulted, and embarrassed how to resent it.
>
> Mr. Heathcliff, having overheard the conversation as well as I, smiled when he saw him go, but immediately afterwards cast a look of singular aversion on the flippant pair, who remained chattering in the door-way: the boy finding animation enough while discussing Hareton's faults and deficiencies, and relating anecdotes of his goings on; and the girl relishing his pert and spiteful sayings, without considering the ill-nature they evinced: but I began to dislike, more than to compassionate, Linton, and to excuse his father, in some measure, for holding him cheap.
>
> We stayed till afternoon: I could not tear Miss Cathy away, before . . .
> (pp. 269–70)

This is the beginning of Cathy's connection with Linton, a connection that quickly becomes so strong it is difficult to "tear [her] away," and that is broken, ultimately, only with his death. It is a connection that is based, first of all, on the "retreat" of the boorish Hareton, but also on the scorn of him that she shares with Linton. Cathy is clearly drawn by Linton's bright maliciousness—it is notable that it is this which "animates" the usually spiritless boy—and, with Hareton having left the field, she is altogether subdued to what Linton works in, for it is with "relish" that she makes one of a "flippant pair."

Cathy's feeling speedily develops into love in the secret correspondence with Linton that follows, but there is more to the relationship than that, as we see when next she meets him:

". . . I think I should not be peevish with you," [said Linton]; "you'd not provoke me, and you'd always be ready to help me, wouldn't you?"

"Yes," said Catherine, stroking his long soft hair, "if I could only get papa's consent, I'd spend half my time with you—Pretty Linton! I wish you were my brother."

"And then you would like me as well as your father?" observed he more cheerfully. "But papa says you would love me better than him, and all the world, if you were my wife—so I'd rather you were that!"

"No! I should never love anybody better than papa," she returned gravely. "And people hate their wives, sometimes, but not their sisters and brothers; and if you were the latter, you would live with us, and papa would be as fond of you as he is of me." (pp. 289–90)

On Linton's side, it is apparent, his mother being dead and his father hating him, there is a frantic hunger for love; and in part Cathy's love for him is a reciprocation of his love for her: when Nelly earlier accuses her of having "led the way in writing . . . absurdities," she answers: "I didn't once think of loving him till—" (p. 276). Her love is also a compassionate response to his need of her: ". . . he'll be under the sod before summer, unless you restore him!" Heathcliff tells her just before her visit on the present occasion (p. 283). But, as she strokes Linton's "long soft hair," it becomes clear that his being "more a lass than a lad," as Hareton puts it, is attractive to her, and that she is drawn to his soft effeminacy as well as to his sharp tongue. And, calling him "pretty Linton," she is drawn, too, to the lap dog in him, as she virtually spells out to Nelly on the way home: "He's a pretty little darling when he's good. I'd make such a pet of him, if he were mine" (p. 295). But above all Cathy is drawn to him as his mother's child, as a Linton like herself; and she is held by the insidious pull of like to like, succumbing to the incestuous feeling that rises to the surface when she expresses the wish that he might be her brother. Cathy's relationship to Linton, that is, is parallel to—though also the obverse of—Cathy I's relationship to Heathcliff. In both cases, like is drawn to like and would be made one with it. But that is to negate the balance of opposites which the novel declares marriage to be, to force nature, as it were. It is suggestive in this respect that, whereas Cathy I and Heathcliff do not marry, the marriage of Cathy and Linton is literally forced, even though Cathy insists to Heathcliff that she loves Linton: ". . . I love him—and why should you wish to force me to do what I'll willingly do of myself?" (p. 332). Their marriage, however, is short-lived, and when Heathcliff demands to know how Cathy feels on Linton's death, she answers: "He's safe, and I'm free" (p. 355).

When Cathy first meets Hareton and is told he is her cousin, she is "upset at the bare notion of relationship with such a clown" (p. 240); yet it is her eventual acceptance of a necessary relation to him that brings her real freedom after Linton dies. Her immediate response to his death is to isolate herself in her room for a fortnight, but then she comes downstairs; and Zillah notes how Hareton tries "to make himself agreeable" (p. 358), at once giving her the books that are too high for her to get at:

> "She continued reading, or seeking for something to read. His attention became, by degrees, quite centred in the study of her thick, silky curls—her face he couldn't see, and she couldn't see him. And, perhaps, not quite awake to what he did, but attracted like a child to a candle, at last he proceeded from staring to touching; he put out his hand and stroked one curl, as gently as if it were a bird. He might have stuck a knife into her neck, she started round in such a taking.
>
> "'Get away, this moment! How dare you touch me? Why are you stopping there?' she cried, in a tone of disgust. 'I can't endure you! I'll go upstairs again, if you come near me.'
>
> "Mr. Hareton recoiled, looking as foolish as he could do . . ." (p. 359)

In this scene, as Hareton artlessly acts on his impulses, we see what draws him to Cathy. As he strokes her hair, "not quite awake" to what he is doing (or to the risk) but "attracted like a child to a candle," he would seem to be impelled not only by a desire to touch her golden curls. What he appears to long for also is contact with her delicate flame of being and access to the light she so effortlessly commands in her books—the books which are closed to him, who is indeed no more than a child in their presence. It is the elusive spirit that he gropes for as his rough hand strokes a curl "as gently as if it were a bird." The violence of Cathy's response to his caress, her starting round as if he has "stuck a knife into her neck," suggests that he has touched her more deeply than her immediate recoil in physical aversion from him indicates. She clings now, however, to her "disgust," to the outraged wound to her sense of herself as being quite beyond the reach of the boor she holds him to be. But, as Lockwood notes later, Hareton has "sensitive though uncultivated feelings," and he strives to reduce the distance between them, ceasing to be "content with daily labour and rough animal enjoyments." He tries to win her approval by secretly teaching himself to read—even though he is provoked into throwing the books he is studying into the fire when she continues to mock him, and the gap between them remains as large as ever (p. 366).

In the end it is Cathy who is kindled by Hareton and allows herself to move towards him. She is forbidden by Heathcliff to go outside the garden, and, as spring comes on, it frets her "to be confined to its narrow bounds"; she is also left alone a great deal, and complains to Nelly "of loneliness." When she suddenly begins to take an interest in Hareton, becoming "incapable of letting him alone" where earlier she has shunned him, she may be seen as seeking to counter her sense of loneliness and restriction, for she still is not allowed beyond the garden, by pushing beyond the confines of her own being in a new relationship (p. 375). It is relationship, at all events, that she now asserts and claims: "I've found out, Hareton," she says, "that I want—that I'm glad—that I should like you to be my cousin, now, if you had not grown so cross to me, and so rough"; and when Hareton refuses to respond, she persists: "Come, you shall take notice of me, Hareton—you are my cousin, and you shall own me" (pp. 378–79).

Hareton remains obdurate at this point, but Nelly urges him to relent, remarking that "it would make [him] another man, to have her for a companion" (p. 380); and when Cathy thereupon proceeds to work at creating a relationship, it is as if he is indeed transformed before Nelly's eyes. Cathy first kisses him gently on the cheek; then makes the further overture of proposing to teach him to read the "handsome book" which she proffers him through Nelly; and, when he finally if grudgingly accepts the present, sits down beside him: "He trembled, and his face glowed—all his rudeness and all his surly harshness had deserted him—he could not summon courage, at first, to utter a syllable, in reply to her questioning look, and her murmured petition" (pp. 381–82). As Nelly has earlier led us to expect, Hareton responds well to cultivation; and though there are "temporary interruptions," for he is "not to be civilized with a wish," since they both want the same thing—"one loving and desiring to esteem, and the other loving and desiring to be esteemed"—they contrive "in the end, to reach it" (p. 384). As their relationship develops, it is evident that it is for them a mutual enrichment, for if it serves to illuminate Hareton's whole being, Cathy—after "[feeling] and [seeing] only death" when Linton dies (p. 355)—is fired by it into abundant new life:

> His honest, warm, and intelligent nature shook off rapidly the clouds of ignorance and degradation in which it had been bred; and Catherine's sincere commendations acted as a spur to his industry. His brightening mind brightened his features, and added spirit and nobility to their aspect—I could hardly fancy it the same individual I had beheld on the day I discovered my little lady at Wuthering Heights, after her expedition to the Crags. . . . The red fire-light glowed on their two bonny heads, and revealed their faces, animated with the eager interest of children; for, though he was twenty-three, and she eighteen, each had so much of novelty to feel and learn, that neither experienced nor evinced the sentiments of sober disenchanted maturity. (pp. 391–92)

It is Heathcliff's witnessing of this scene which leads him to realize that, though he has the "representatives" of his "old enemies" completely in his power, he has lost the will to harm them: "I have lost the faculty of enjoying their destruction," he tells Nelly, "and I am too idle to destroy for nothing" (p. 393). Heathcliff's revenge on his enemies has all along been what he calls "a moral teething," which has led him, as he puts it, to "grind with greater energy, in proportion to the increase of pain" in his victims (p. 186)—though the metaphor he chooses to describe the process reveals surely enough that it is his own pain that drives him. Now after eighteen years it is no longer his own pain alone that engrosses him. Coming on Cathy and Hareton bent over the fire together, Heathcliff suddenly sees the young man as "a personification" of his own youth: "Hareton's aspect," he says to Nelly, "was the ghost of my immortal love, of my wild endeavours to hold my right, my degradation, my pride, my happiness, and my anguish—" (pp. 393–94); and though he will not admit it, this identification plays its part in diverting him from pursuing his revenge. He is primarily diverted, however, by the vision he has had of Cathy I's "passionless features" when Edgar dies and he opens her coffin to find her preserved in her grave after eighteen years (p. 349). During all that time, he confesses, he has been "the sport of . . . intolerable torture" in the belief that she was "on the earth" with him, and seeing her in her grave has "pacified" him a little (p. 351). It also completely obsesses him with the thought of joining her.

After Heathcliff dies, Cathy and Hareton plan to marry and take up life at the Grange, leaving the Heights to Joseph and a lad—and, as Lockwood observes, to "such ghosts as choose to inhabit it," for the country folk swear that Heathcliff and Cathy haunt the area (pp. 412–13). As the younger Cathy and Hareton ready themselves for their new life, it is not only Hareton who has been transformed. Pulled between storm and calm, like her mother, Cathy is not torn in two by the conflict but succeeds in bringing the two sides of her nature into a viable realignment.

CHAPTER 3

The Mill on the Floss
The Dividing of the Seasons

At the end of Book Second of *The Mill on the Floss*, after Maggie Tulliver has brought her brother Tom the news of their father's ruin and illness and brother and sister set out for home together, they are said to begin a "new life of sorrow":

> They had gone forth together into their new life of sorrow, and they would never more see the sunshine undimmed by remembered cares. They had entered the thorny wilderness, and the golden gates of their childhood had for ever closed behind them. (p. 171)[1]

The evocation of their childhood in prelapsarian terms is puzzling since at this stage of the narrative Tom is sixteen and Maggie thirteen, and no suggestion of a loss of innocence would seem to be intended. The passage appears rather to define their paradisal childhood as a time of carefree existence; but though it is true they have hitherto not had to face anything like the magnitude of the trouble that now awaits them, their childhood has certainly not been portrayed as a state of careless bliss. Indeed, the first two books dwell, if anything, on the tribulations of childhood; and objection has often been taken to the view of it enforced by the passage quoted above or in the notorious lines that describe the drowning of Tom and Maggie and refer to their "living through again in one supreme moment the days when they had clasped their little hands in love, and roamed the daisied fields together" (p. 456). A short way of dealing with the disparity is to follow Michael Steig, who says that "the generalizations about Maggie's and Tom's childhood together as an Edenic existence" are "one of the novel's most glaring inconsistencies."[2]

But George Eliot is a meticulous artist, and it is more rewarding to

47

seek an alternative explanation of the evocation of Eden, as John Hagan does: "The essential fact is that, during this period of [Maggie's] life, her father and brother reciprocate her love. This is why at the end of Book II, when [her] childhood is coming to an end, George Eliot can refer to it as having been an Eden . . ."[3] The fact that Maggie's father and brother cease to reciprocate her love, I too shall want to argue, is crucial to her development; but to accept Hagan's reading of the statement at the end of Book Second is arbitrarily to limit its application to Maggie alone, whereas it plainly relates to Tom as well, and there is no question of Tom's thereafter being denied her love—or of its being of overwhelming importance to him. We should rather pay attention, I believe, to a reference to Eden that appears at the beginning of the same chapter in which the quoted statement is made. The chapter is entitled "The Golden Gates Are Passed," and begins by describing how Maggie, as "a young lady" of thirteen, does not dream of keeping her promise to kiss Philip Wakem when she meets him since the promise was given some years previously while she was still a child, and "such a greeting" is now "out of the question":

> The promise was void, like so many other sweet, illusory promises of our childhood; void as promises made in Eden before the seasons were divided, and when the starry blossoms grew side by side with the ripening peach— impossible to be fulfilled when the golden gates had been passed. (pp. 165– 66)

George Eliot, this passage suggests, associates Eden not only with an idea of timelessness but of wholeness, for in the Garden the seasons are not divided, and with an immediate fullness of form rather than a process of growth, for there the blossom coexists with the fruit.[4] Childhood, in other words, is to be seen, however paradoxically, as a time of fullness of being; and what the passing of the golden gates signifies is a fall into self-division. This, at any rate, is what is dramatized in the stories of Tom and Maggie. The period up to the ruin of their father is a time in which opposed forces within the self, which negate each other in the adult personality, are given full expression and allowed to coexist.

II

The opposition that is generally held to be at the heart of the novel is that between Dodsons and Tullivers. Jerome Thale, for instance, says that "the fact that the two ways [of life represented by Dodsons and Tullivers] are antagonistic and yet complementary is dramatized in the account of Tom and Maggie's growing up, and is the very center of their problem"; and he maintains that Maggie is "essentially a Tulliver" and Tom "a

Dodson."⁵ What being a Dodson means is "revering" whatever is "customary and respectable," whatever is "becoming" and belongs to the "eternal fitness of things," whatever is associated with "traditional duty or propriety" (pp. 239–40). The difference between Dodsons and Tullivers, however, would seem to be more a matter of temperament than fundamental distinction, for it is asserted that "the same sort of traditional belief" runs in the veins of the Tullivers even if it is carried "in richer blood, having elements of generous imprudence, warm affection, and hot-tempered rashness" (p. 240). Moreover, though Mrs. Tulliver's Dodson sisters are agreed that the Tulliver blood does "not mix well with the Dodson blood" (p. 54), from the vantage point of the narrator the "emmet-like Dodsons and Tullivers" have much in common, epitomizing alike "the most prosaic form of human life: proud respectability in a gig of unfashionable build: worldliness without side-dishes" (p. 238).

Maggie is certainly not prosaic, and we soon realize that the opposition between Dodsons and Tullivers will not take us very far in our attempt to understand her though it no doubt serves to focus attention on the dual nature as well as the mixed blood of the Tulliver children. From the outset the presentation of Maggie suggests a marked duality of being. Before she makes her first appearance, Mr. Tulliver declares she is "twice as 'cute as Tom," perhaps even "too 'cute for a woman," and he goes on to say that the nine-year-old child "can read almost as well as the parson" (p. 12). Maggie's bright bookishness is again stressed in the conversation between Mr. Tulliver and Mr. Riley: she is "allays at her book," says her father, and understands what she reads "better nor half the folks as are growed up"; and he again insists "a woman's no business wi' being so clever" (p. 16). Mrs. Moss, Maggie's aunt, offers us a similar view of her (p. 72). But when Maggie, the "small mistake of nature" who has darkly failed to resemble her mother, makes her first appearance, it is as a young animal that she figures: she is said to have a habit of "incessantly tossing her head to keep the dark heavy locks out of her gleaming black eyes—an action which [gives] her very much the air of a small Shetland pony" (p. 13). Maggie's head is her most striking feature, but it is not only her intellectual power—her brains—that it may be taken to posit, for with her abundance of hair—the "mane" (p. 13) which she is given to tossing—it at the same time betokens her animal being.

In the narrative as a whole, Maggie's hair seems to have much the same emblematic significance as that which I earlier suggested attaches in *Oliver Twist* to Nancy's hair: it similarly indicates her strong sexuality; and indeed Maggie, too, is eventually regarded as a fallen woman, "to be shrunk from" by every good lady of St. Ogg's who has "to take care of her own reputation—and of Society" (p. 442). In the childhood scenes, as in the Shetland pony passage or when she runs, "shaking the water from her black locks . . . , like a Skye terrier escaped from his bath" (p. 25), her hair projects more generally an unruly animality. Her hair, her mother complains, "won't curl" (p. 12); it is naturally resistant to nurture, that is, or aided to be so by a defiant dipping in water, as when she plays the Skye terrier. And her unruly animality is a quality which the discerning eye of Mr. Wakem detects in the adult woman too: "She's not the sort of woman your mother was, though, Phil," he says. "I saw her at church—she's handsomer than this—deuced fine eyes and fine figure, I saw; but rather dangerous and unmanageable, eh?" (p. 374).

The significance of the animal imagery is extended in a passage of authorial commentary in which it is directly stated that Maggie and Tom are "still very much like young animals":

> We learn to restrain ourselves as we get older. We keep apart when we have quarrelled, express ourselves in well-bred phrases, and in this way preserve a dignified alienation, showing much firmness on one side, and swallowing much grief on the other. We no longer approximate in our behaviour to the mere impulsiveness of the lower animals, but conduct ourselves in every respect like members of a highly civilised society. (p. 35)

The animal is associated here with impulsiveness or a quality of abandon; and this wild immediacy is opposed to the restraint or self-command that is viewed (for all the irony) as a mark of civilization. The passage thus strikingly mediates not only between some of the polarities of *Wuthering Heights*, where, as we have seen, an animal-like wildness is opposed to the cultivation of civilized existence, but also those of *Tess of the d'Urbervilles*, where, I shall argue, the opposition between abandon and control is central. And the three novels are further linked by a common concern with the fundamental antinomy between flesh and spirit.

In *The Mill on the Floss* it is the connection between restraint and civilization that is expressly insisted on, both in the final thrust of the plot, and in direct statements such as that quoted above or the following: "a high state of civilisation" is said to introduce complexity into the emotions, for "in the enlightened child of civilisation the abandonment characteristic of grief is checked and varied in the subtlest manner" (p. 51). The connection is also dramatized in miniature, as it were, when Maggie, having often been told she is "like a gypsy, and 'half wild'" (p. 94), on one occasion actually runs away to the gypsies when she summons up "the daring that comes from overmastering impulse," and sets out to seek with them a "refuge from all the blighting obloquy that [has] pursued her in civilised life" (p. 96). Self-command is also associated with the mature and the adult as well as the civilized: in the family discussion about Mr.

Tulliver's ruin, Tom displays "a remarkable manifestation of self-command and practical judgment in a lad of fifteen," speaks with a "sudden manliness of tone," and is throughout determined to "behave like a man" (pp. 188–90). Maggie, on the other hand, during the same discussion allows herself a "mad outbreak," confronting the family with "her eyes flashing like the eyes of a young lioness" (p. 190); and she is later said to be "strangely old for her years in everything except in her entire want of that prudence and self-command which were the qualities that made Tom manly in the midst of his intellectual boyishness" (pp. 241–42).

The point to register about Maggie is that, up until about the age of thirteen when the golden gates close behind her, animality coexists in her quite comfortably with intellectuality, neither in any way negating or frustrating the free expression of the other. The quickness and sharpness of her intellect, for example, is at once apparent in the way she runs rings round Mr. Riley at the age of nine:

> "Well," said Mr. Riley, in an admonitory patronising tone, as he patted Maggie on the head, "I advise you to put by the 'History of the Devil,' and read some prettier book. Have you no prettier books?"
>
> "O yes," said Maggie . . . "I've got 'Aesop's Fables,' and a book about Kangaroos and things, and the 'Pilgrim's Progress.'" . . .
>
> "Ah, a beautiful book," said Mr. Riley; "you can't read a better."
>
> "Well, but there's a great deal about the devil in that," said Maggie triumphantly . . . (p. 17)

The coexistence is nicely dramatized when Maggie impulsively leaves civilization for the gypsies, for she immediately begins "to instruct" them in necessary elements of knowledge (p. 98). It is true that Maggie, in her pursuit of the joys of intellect, has to contend with her inferior status as a girl, Mr. Stelling, for instance, declaring that if members of her sex are "quick," they are also "shallow" and so not really up to the sort of education he provides for boys (p. 134); but her appetite for things of the mind (just like her appetite for love) remains insatiable and accounts for how she appears to Philip Wakem just before she is first allowed to go to boarding-school: "What was it, he wondered, that made Maggie's dark eyes remind him of the stories about princesses being turned into animals? . . . . . . I think it was that her eyes were full of unsatisfied intelligence, and unsatisfied, beseeching affection" (p. 158). When misfortune strikes, it is a quality of intellect as much as feeling that lifts the girl of thirteen to sudden profundity in the face of the loss of her books, including her beloved *Pilgrim's Progress:* "I thought we should never part with that while we lived," she says, "—everything is going away from us—the end of our lives will have nothing in it like the beginning!" (p. 212). Indeed, when she enters The Valley of Humiliation, Maggie accepts as "part of the hardship of her life" that there is "laid upon her the burthen of larger wants" than others seem to feel; and, a very Dorothea Brooke in the making, she endures a "wide hopeless yearning for that something, whatever it [is], that [is] greatest and best on this earth" (p. 252).

Nor does the free play of intellect serve in Maggie to curb the rush of impulse, as two of the most dramatic of the childhood episodes indicate. In the first episode attention is drawn once again to Maggie's hair, which is made the object of a critical survey by her aunts. "I think the gell has too much hair," says Mrs. Pullet. "I'd have it thinned and cut shorter, sister, if I was you: it isn't good for her health. It's that as makes her skin so brown, I shouldn't wonder" (p. 56). It is clearly Maggie's luxuriance of physical being that offends Mrs. Pullet, her overflowing vitality that poses a threat to notions of cautious well-being. And even her loving father, who declares that she is "healthy enough," cannot refrain from adding that "it 'ud be as well if Bessy 'ud have the child's hair cut, so as it 'ud lie smooth" (p. 56), thus conceding the need to temper unruliness. When Mrs. Tulliver thereupon tells her to go and get her hair brushed "for shame," Maggie, taking Tom with her, goes upstairs, cuts her hair "straight across the middle of her forehead," and asks Tom to "cut it behind" for her, not heeding his admonition that she will "catch it":

> "Never mind—make haste!" said Maggie, giving a little stamp with her foot. Her cheeks were quite flushed.
> The black locks were so thick—nothing could be more tempting to a lad who had already tasted the forbidden pleasure of cutting the pony's mane. . . . One delicious grinding snip, and then another and another, and the hinder-locks fell heavily on the floor, and Maggie stood cropped in a jagged, uneven manner, but with a sense of clearness and freedom, as if she had emerged from a wood into the open plain. (pp. 57–58)

When Maggie stamps her foot and the blood rushes to her cheeks, it is the young animal in her that demands satisfaction of its needs, as the analogical reference to the pony immediately emphasizes. Paradoxically, though it is her hair which is the basis of the animal imagery associated with her, its cropping does not indicate any curtailment of this aspect of her nature; on the contrary, the animal in her may be said to be given its impulsive head in this scene. It is this, I take it, which accounts—over and above her sense of "deliverance" from previous constraint, from "her teasing hair and teasing remarks about it" (p. 58)—for her exhilaration, for the feeling of "clearness and freedom": Maggie here experiences the release of spontaneously doing what she wants and so of unclogged, uninhibited being. Not that it lasts long. When Tom laughs at her cropped appearance and she allows herself to reflect about what she has done, she is quick to grasp that now she will "have to hear and think more about her hair than ever; for Maggie rushed to her deeds with passionate impulse, and then saw not only their consequences, but what would have happened if they had not been done, with all the detail and exaggerated circumstance of an active imagination" (p. 58).

In the second episode, ponies and terriers are supplanted and Maggie's hair figures more menacingly as that of the Gorgon: when Tom coldly ignores her and devotes all his attention to their cousin, Lucy Deane, Maggie is said (in a brilliant phrase) to look "like a small Medusa with her snakes cropped," the snakes pointing to "the small demons" that now "take possession" of her soul (p. 88). Though she is filled with anger and jealousy, Lucy is a mere mouse to her snake—Maggie has previously believed she "could never be cross with pretty little Lucy, any more than she could be cruel to a little white mouse"—and at first she succeeds in restraining herself, even if she now begins to think she "should like to make Lucy cry, by slapping or pinching her" (p. 89). A little later, however, when Tom not only shows Lucy a water-snake but tells Maggie to "get away"—"there's no room for you on the grass here," he says to her. "Nobody asked *you* to come—she "abandons herself to her impulse" (to use a phrase which Hardy employs in relation to Tess Durbeyfield) and pushes "poor little pink-and-white Lucy into the cow-trodden mud," an area, we may assume, which has previously been designated a "dirty place" for good reason. On this occasion the joy of release is not evoked, but Maggie remains quite "impenitent" and the pale cast of thought does not shadow the "small Medusa face" with which she looks after Tom and Lucy as they retire from the scene (pp. 90–91). Indeed, at this point Maggie embraces wildness altogether—and goes off to the gypsies.

When Tom leaves with Lucy he informs Maggie that he intends to tell their mother what she has done, for he feels "justice clearly [demands] that Maggie should be visited with the utmost punishment" (p. 91). An unremitting and merciless sense of justice becomes Tom's most striking characteristic, as distinctive in him as his sister's sharp-wittedness is in her. Until the golden gates close behind him, however, this quality does not dominate his personality to the exclusion of all else; and, we remember, he is also said (like Maggie) to be at the same time very much like a young animal. The presentation of Tom is not as dramatic as that of Maggie, but there is sufficient indication—as in the scene with the jam puffs or the fight with Bob Jakin—that his developing nature as readily accommodates the existence of opposed tendencies. From the time that he is forced to leave Mr. Stelling's as a result of his father's failure, however, his sense of what is right and just makes him quite monomaniacal in his determination to ensure that his father's creditors will all be paid back in full. Tom now fiercely suppresses his "very strong appetite for pleasure" (p. 270), giving himself exclusively to the making of money, and this has a profound effect on Maggie.

The key to Maggie is her need of love, the need both to love and be loved; and in her childhood this is satisfied by her relationships with her father and Tom, even though the connection with her brother is on occasion tempestuous. At the outset of the narrative, it is said that "the need of being loved" is "the strongest need in poor Maggie's nature" (p. 34); and indeed not only in hers: "It is a wonderful subduer, this need of love—this hunger of the heart—as peremptory as that other hunger by which Nature forces us to submit to the yoke, and change the face of the world" (p. 35). Because love, that is, is a vital principle, because the satisfaction of the "hunger of the heart" is as vital to life as that of the hunger of the flesh, we are subdued by this need and compelled to find some way of relieving it, just as we have been forced continually to find new ways of producing food. If the passage implies that the evolution of civilization may be ascribed to our need to feed ourselves, so then the history of any individual may be viewed in terms of his or her attempts to provide for love. This is certainly the perspective in which Maggie's story would appear to be placed.

When her father is ruined, the centrality of Maggie's need for love is brought home to her: "And if life had no love in it, what else was there for Maggie? Nothing but poverty and the companionship of her mother's narrow griefs—perhaps of her father's heart-cutting childish dependence" (p. 208). But as Tom devotes himself singlemindedly to the pursuit of cash, he becomes less and less aware of her; and even her father's love now becomes "mingled with bitterness, like everything else":

> When Maggie laid down her work at night, it was her habit to get a low stool and sit by her father's knee, leaning her cheek against it. How she wished he would stroke her head, or give some sign that he was soothed by the sense that he had a daughter who loved him! But now she got no answer to her little caresses, either from her father or from Tom—the two idols of her life. Tom was weary and abstracted in the short intervals when he was at home, and her father was bitterly preoccupied . . . (p. 245)

What the repeated tableau vividly if simply depicts is the way in which the flow of Maggie's love is now obstructed, blocked by the hard imperviousness of both her father and her brother, who in their abstraction cease to register her. Denied even a modicum of sustenance, she attempts to make do with nothing—and turns to Thomas à Kempis. But that is when she ceases to be at one with herself.

III

In retrospect George Eliot was dissatisfied with the structure of *The Mill on the Floss:* "My love of the childhood scenes," she said, "made me linger over them; so that I could not develop as fully as I wished the concluding book in which the tragedy occurs, and which I had looked forward to with attentive premeditation from the beginning."[6] It is perhaps true that disproportionate space is given to the childhood scenes—we are almost halfway through the novel before the golden gates close on Tom and Maggie, and well past the midpoint by the time Maggie reaches the age of seventeen, and her real conflicts begin. But the elaboration of the childhood section is not merely nostalgic on the novelist's part; it has the clear function of presenting the wholeness of being that Maggie enjoys in childhood as a tangible criterion against which her later self-division may be measured and judged.

When Maggie comes across the Thomas à Kempis among the books which Bob Jakin brings her as a present, she finds a guide who enables her to face up to her changed circumstances and helps her "through years of loneliness" (p. 256). The voice that speaks out of "the little, old, clumsy book" exhorts her to adopt a stern code of renunciation:

> "If thou desire to mount unto this height, thou must set out courageously, and lay the axe to the root, that thou mayst pluck up and destroy that hidden inordinate inclination to thyself, and unto all private and earthly good. . . . In heaven ought to be thy dwelling, and all earthly things are to be looked on as they forward thy journey thither. (pp. 253–54).

In the injunction to cut roots, to sever connection with a self that clings to earth and earthly goods so as to be free to mount on high, there sounds the Pauline insistence that one die to the flesh in order to live in the spirit. That this should be regarded as the primary direction of Maggie's effort at renunciation as she follows her teacher during the difficult years between thirteen and seventeen (though this is a period that the novelist does not chronicle in detail) is implied by a significant gesture when she first embraces the new creed:

> Maggie drew a long breath and pushed her heavy hair back, as if to see a sudden vision more clearly. Here, then, was a secret of life that would enable her to renounce all other secrets—here was a sublime height to be reached without the help of outward things—here was insight, and strength, and conquest, to be won by means entirely within her own soul, where a supreme Teacher was waiting to be heard. (p. 254)

It is her animal being which she now sets out to push aside, even though she often strives after "too high a flight" and comes down "with her poor little half-fledged wings dabbled in the mud" (p. 256).

But it is not the animal in her alone that Maggie now denies, the
flesh alone that she "rises above":

> The old books, Virgil, Euclid, and Aldrich—that wrinkled fruit of the
> tree of knowledge—had been all laid by; for Maggie had turned her back on
> the vain ambition to share the thoughts of the wise. In her first ardour she
> flung away the books with a sort of triumph that she had risen above the
> need of them; and if they had been her own, she would have burned them
> . . . She read so eagerly and constantly in her three books, the Bible,
> Thomas-à-Kempis, and the "Christian Year" . . . that they filled her mind
> with a continual stream of rhythmic memories . . . (p. 257)

Maggie's mind may be full, but we are to understand that it is essentially
unused, in effect discarded along with the books she would burn. The
strength that she derives from Kempis, therefore, is not unlike the
strength that Tom displays during these years—the strength of negation,
based on what she can later see is no more than a "negative peace" (p. 336).
During these years, that is to say, Maggie tries to exist as a sort of shadow
self, striving to suppress both the animal and intellectual components of
her being. But willy-nilly, axe and root and Thomas à Kempis notwith-
standing, she enters the period of "blossoming youth," and though her
form is outwardly irradiated by the glow of spirit, it is inwardly rocked by
eruptions of the flesh:

> Hanging diligently over her sewing, Maggie was a sight any one might
> have been pleased to look at. That new inward life of hers, notwithstanding
> some volcanic upheavings of imprisoned passions, yet shone out in her face
> with a tender soft light that mingled itself as added loveliness with the
> gradually enriched colour and outline of her blossoming youth. (p. 257)

When Maggie, at the age of seventeen, renews her childhood friendship with Philip Wakem and begins to meet him at the Red Deeps, her
appearance is expressive of a robust femininity: her "broad-chested figure"
is said to have "the mould of early womanhood," her "eyes are liquid," her
"brown cheek is firm and rounded," and her "full lips are red." Indeed it is
the firm establishment of her physical being that is stressed, for her "kinship with the grand Scotch firs" which grow in the Deeps would seem to
be more than a matter of her "dark colouring and jet crown surmounting
her tall figure." At the same time, however, a discordant note is struck by
her expression:

> Yet one has a sense of uneasiness in looking at her—a sense of opposing
> elements, of which a fierce collision is imminent: surely there is a hushed
> expression, such as one often sees in older faces under borderless caps, out
> of keeping with the resistant youth, which one expects to flash out in a
> sudden, passionate glance, that will dissipate all the quietude, like a damp
> fire leaping out again when all seemed safe. (p. 261)

The spirit which here threatens collision with the opposed element of flesh speaks in her "hushed expression" and "quietude," which would silence her "resistant youth" and extinguish its fires. But it is also intimated that these fires can never wholly be dampened, and that they are liable to leap out again in a flash. Accordingly, the way would seem to be prepared for Maggie to burst into passion when she is now thrown together with Philip, but in fact in relation to him her negation of the earthy, animal side of her nature becomes even more insistent.

Philip's appeal is to her intellect; and as Joan Bennett has pointed out, she is drawn to him in much the same way as Dorothea is initially attracted to Casaubon in *Middlemarch*.[7] Philip's humpback, his physical deficiency, is also indicative of a deficiency of physical force on his part, of the animality which is so pronounced a feature of Maggie's being. As a boy his hair "[waves] and [curls] at the ends like a girl's," and Tom finds him "a pale, puny fellow" (p. 143); as a young man of twenty-two he is said to be "by nature half feminine in sensitiveness" (p. 289). His physical disability, however, is compensated for by his intellectual capacity. As a pupil at Mr. Stelling's, he is notably "advanced" and "apt" in his studies (p. 151); and when Maggie first sees him after an interval of five years, she is filled with a sense of how much he must have developed: "I know you are so clever," she tells him, "and you must have seen and learnt so much to fill your mind: I was not quite sure you would care about me now" (p. 266). Philip is in many ways a kindred spirit to Maggie, is himself a Maggie, as it were, with all animality thoroughly tamed, if not quite left out. Not only does he care, as she used to do, for art and things of the mind—"I care for painting and music," he tells her; "I care for classic literature, and mediaeval literature, and modern literature" (though he adds: "I flutter all ways, and fly in none") (p. 286)—he also strives, as she used to do, to rise "above the dead level of provincial existence" (p. 286), and confesses that he hungers, just as she used to, for things that he feels "to be beautiful and good" (p. 264).

Philip's humpback has a double bearing on his relationship with Maggie. As far as he is concerned, it leads him to snatch with the greater intensity and desperation at the chance of making "an element in her life" since he feels he is "excepted" from what is "a matter of course with others." As far as she is concerned, it means that "the thought of his being her lover never [enters] her mind" (p. 289), and that in effect she sees him as a disembodied intellect. It is the prospect of a meeting of minds that draws her to him, even though at first she feels she must resist the temptation:

> I said that Maggie went home that evening from the Red Deeps with a mental conflict already begun. You have seen clearly enough, in her inter-

view with Philip, what that conflict was. Here suddenly was an opening in
the rocky wall which shut in the narrow valley of humiliation, where all her
prospect was the remote unfathomed sky; and some of the memory-
haunting earthly delights were no longer out of her reach. She might have
books, converse, affection—she might hear tidings of the world from which
her mind had not yet lost its sense of exile; and it would be a kindness to
Philip too, who was pitiable—clearly not happy; and perhaps here was an
opportunity indicated for making her mind more worthy of its highest
service—perhaps the noblest, completest devoutness could hardly exist
without some width of knowledge: *must* she always live in this resigned
imprisonment? (p. 284)

Maggie's attempt to follow the Teacher and make her dwelling in heaven,
we see, has left her by the age of seventeen with the exclusive prospect of a
"remote unfathomed sky"—and with an oppressive sense of narrow enclosure, of being "shut in" by a "rocky wall." The image is echoed when
Philip later tells her she is "shutting herself up in a narrow self-delusive
fanaticism" (p. 286). The motif of enclosure is important in the presentation of Maggie's development: we remember her exhilaration as a child
when her hair is cropped and she feels as if she has "emerged from a wood
into the open plain": she is now filled with something like the same longing for release when she registers that her chosen path of renunciation has
led her to the dead end of that rocky wall, to a "resigned imprisonment."
What the relationship with Philip—the "opening" in the wall—
accordingly offers is both liberation and enlargement, a chance to move
beyond the barred confines of her asceticism and venture out into the wide
world once again.[8] It is only in the expanses of the mind, however, that
she is now tempted to wander, for if it is "the world" she has renounced
and is in exile from, it is more specifically a "width of knowledge" she is
seeking. "Earthly delights," for Maggie, are "books, converse, affection."
But to make her way through the opening in the wall means also to expose
herself, to open herself to "the seductive guidance of illimitable wants";
and dreading the loss of her "simple rule of renunciation" as much as the
concealment which meetings with Philip will necessarily entail, she tells
him they must give each other up (pp. 284–85).[9]

Faced by her prohibition, Philip makes a final appeal to her:

"Maggie," he said, in a tone of remonstrance, "don't persist in this
wilful, senseless privation. It makes me wretched to see you benumbing and
cramping your nature in this way. You were so full of life when you were a
child: I thought you would be a brilliant woman—all wit and bright imagination. And it flashes out in your face still, until you draw that veil of dull
quiescence over it."

"Why do you speak so bitterly to me, Philip?" said Maggie.

"Because I foresee it will not end well: you can never carry on this self-
torture."

"I shall have strength given me," said Maggie, tremulously.

"No, you will not, Maggie: no one has strength given to do what is unnatural. It is mere cowardice to seek safety in negations. No character becomes strong in that way. You will be thrown into the world some day, and then every rational satisfaction of your nature that you deny now, will assault you like a savage appetite." (pp. 287–88)

This exchange between Maggie and Philip is dense with implication. Not only does it have a strong proleptic quality; in a manner that he is quite unaware of, Philip diagnoses the likely consequences of Maggie's entering into a relationship with him while warning her about the results of her holding back from it. When he remarks on how "full of life" she was as a child in comparison with her present ascetic condition, it is her fullness of being that is evoked, the childhood self which readily contained and expressed "opposed elements." But this appeal to her is all in the name of one side of her being only: it is an appeal to her not to "starve into dullness" all "the highest powers of [her] nature" (p. 286), and these are then implicitly defined as the brilliant flash of wit and imagination. The language Philip employs, however, is suggestive of the thrust of powers of her being that he is tacitly ignoring: when he declares that unsatisfied parts of her nature will some day assault her "like a savage appetite," it is the animal in her which exists beyond the pale of civilization that is conjured up for us, not a starved intellect. It is not merely that Philip unwittingly foretells the form her later involvement with Stephen Guest will take; he also unwittingly indicates the inevitable result for her of a prolonged association with him, that "benumbing and cramping" of her nature which he maintains will be like a "long suicide" (p. 288) and which we once again tend to refer to physical rather than intellectual being.

In the end Maggie continues to see Philip. In the course of insisting they must give each other up, she reveals her imperative need for love, and it would seem to be this that finally impels her to relent: "What a dear, good brother you would have been, Philip," she says. "I think you would have made as much fuss about me, and been as pleased for me to love you, as would have satisfied even me" (p. 287). Having relented, Maggie clings during the year that they meet secretly to the kind of relationship implied by her artless comparison, and continues to cling to it even when Philip finally declares his love for her (p. 294). But the intellectual stimulation she has received from Philip, it is evident, has left its imprint on her: there is now a sparkle to her conversation—"I've never any pity for conceited people," she declares, "because I think they carry their comfort about with them" (p. 292)—and though Philip has by no means taken the full measure of her self, the change in her lends support to his claim that their meetings have led to her "reviving into [her] real self" (p. 293).

After confessing his love for her, Philip asks her directly whether she loves him. Maggie, who until this moment has never even thought of his "being [her] lover," turns "rather pale," and is decidedly evasive: "I think I could hardly love any one better: there is nothing but what I love you for," she tells him (pp. 292–93). Before they part that day, however, she not only tacitly allows him to believe that she is ready to return his love but seems to convince herself of this too. At this point she begins that willed negation of one half of her being which thereafter characterizes her relationship with him, for if she registers that the relationship will demand a "sacrifice" of her, it is one that she is willing to make in a renewed sense of the riches of renunciation:

> "Then my life will be filled with hope, Maggie—and I shall be happier than other men, in spite of all? We *do* belong to each other—for always—whether we are apart or together?"
> "Yes, Philip: I should like never to part: I should like to make your life very happy."
> "I am waiting for something else—I wonder whether it will come."
> Maggie smiled, with glistening tears, and then stooped her tall head to kiss the pale face that was full of pleading, timid love—like a woman's.
> She had a moment of real happiness then—a moment of belief that, if there were sacrifice in this love, it was all the richer and more satisfying. (pp. 294–95)

The sacrifice, however, necessitates a forcing of her deepest being, as is thereafter suggested on more than one occasion. This first becomes apparent when Tom learns about her secret meetings with Philip and compels her to agree not to see him again without his knowledge: "And yet, how was it that she was now and then conscious of a certain dim background of relief in the forced separation from Philip? Surely it was only because the sense of a deliverance from concealment was welcome at any cost" (p. 305). The narrator's comment points here in its very emphases to the hidden nature of Maggie's relief, the sense of reprieve she experiences in a now permitted relaxation of her will. More forcibly, some two years later, when she tells Lucy about her relationship with Philip, and Lucy says she will try "to contrive some plot" that will enable her cousin to marry Philip when she marries Stephen Guest, Maggie is startled into an involuntary betrayal of her physical shrinking from Philip:

> "Wouldn't that be a pretty ending to all my poor, poor Maggie's troubles?"
> Maggie tried to smile, but shivered, as if she felt a sudden chill.
> "Ah, dear, you are cold," said Lucy. "You must go to bed; and so must I . . . ." (p. 338)

Maggie persists, however, in affirming her wish to marry Philip—

though, when Mr. Wakem is prepared to sanction the marriage, she falls back, somewhat desperately, on Tom's continued opposition to it:

> "Maggie, is it that you don't love Philip well enough to marry him?—tell me—trust me."
>
> Maggie held Lucy's hands tightly in silence a little while. Her own hands were quite cold. But when she spoke, her voice was quite clear and distinct.
>
> "Yes, Lucy, I would choose to marry him. I think it would be the best and highest lot for me—to make his life happy. He loved me first. No one else could be quite what he is to me. But I can't divide myself from my brother for life. I must go away, and wait. Pray, don't speak to me again about it." (p. 384)

Once again, we note, Maggie is evasive about the nature of her love for Philip, and once again the thought of marriage to him seems to chill her. When she does bring herself, after a considerable pause, to state her position, it is significant that she justifies it by saying this would be "the best and highest" for her, as if she admits to herself that it is a lower, inferior self that has impelled her towards Stephen. It is one of the ironies of the novel that Philip's love for her is indeed "high," noble and generous in its selflessness, as is perhaps most strikingly evident in his final moving letter to her on her return to St. Ogg's after her involvement with Stephen. But this is not to gainsay that his is a love which cannot wholly satisfy her; and once again, when he castigates her in general terms, he unwittingly fixes the price she would be called on to pay in continued relation to him: "You want to find out a mode of renunciation that will be an escape from pain," he says to her. "I tell you again, there is no such escape possible except by perverting or mutilating one's nature" (p. 361).

IV

When Tom discovers that Maggie has been meeting Philip secretly and criticizes her bitterly for conduct that is "likely to disgrace" them all, he tells her that she is given to "ridiculous flights first into one extreme and then into another" (p. 304). That there is some truth in the accusation is shown in her subsequent relationship with Stephen Guest. The opening presentation of Stephen is decidedly ironic: an apparently worthless fop, he is first shown idly teasing Lucy's lap dog with a scissors, from which he has to be rescued when they slip over his knuckles ("it seems"), a "Hercules" reduced to holding out "his entrapped fingers hopelessly"; and we are told that his "diamond ring, attar of roses, and air of nonchalant leisure, at twelve o'clock in the day, are the graceful and odoriferous result of the largest oil-mill and the most extensive wharf in St. Ogg's" (p. 316). Stephen has accordingly been made the object of considerable and continuing critical abuse, a note sounded early and strong by Leslie Stephen:

> . . . Mr. Guest is a typical provincial coxcomb . . . No attempt is made to suggest that he is anything but a self-satisfied commonplace young gentleman . . .
>   . . . we might even have forgiven [Maggie] if, after being a little overpowered by the dandified Stephen, she had shown some power of perceiving what a very poor animal he was.[10]

Whatever one may say about Stephen, the whole point about him is that he is not a poor animal. On the very next page we are also told that he is "a rather striking young man of five-and-twenty, with a square forehead, short dark-brown hair standing erect, with a slight wave at the end, like a thick crop of corn" (p. 317). By the time Stephen is introduced, Maggie's hair has assumed such symbolic weight that we would do well to heed this description. What Stephen, like her, would seem abundantly to possess is bodily potency and a rich physical vitality—in a word, what Philip lacks. And his physical force—and attractiveness—is rendered convincingly enough for us to understand and accept how Maggie, moving from one extreme to another, is drawn to him. In both Maggie and Stephen it is animal appetite that imperiously demands to be satisfied: he looks into her eyes "as a thirsty man looks towards the track of the distant brook" (p. 356), and his own eyes are said to "devour" her (p. 385); when he passionately declares his love for her, his words seem to her "like nectar held close to thirsty lips" (p. 411).[11]

As Maggie's lips hover over the nectar, she reflects that there must be "a life for mortals here below which [is] not hard and chill—in which affection [will] no longer be self-sacrifice" (p. 411). Her feeling for Philip may be assumed to be a major constituent of her sense of what her life has become, and it should be contrasted with the "glowing gladness at heart" which she feels when Stephen approaches her at the dance at Park House: "This one, this last night, she might expand unrestrainedly in the warmth of the present, without those chill eating thoughts of the past and the future" (p. 386). The contrast points up the opposition between the two men; and indeed they—together with Maggie, who is caught between them—embody the cluster of polarities operative in the novel. Animal being is associated with warmth and with passion; with abandon—it is to an "overpowering passion" (p. 449) that Stephen finally gives way; with a living for the moment, brute existence in the present; and with extension of self, a sense of expansion. Intellectual being by contrast is associated with chill and with reflection—the way in which Maggie is subject to "eating thoughts," it may be remarked, is strikingly similar to that in which Angel Clare is "eaten out with thinking" in *Tess of the d'Urbervilles;* with restraint—Philip is a man who "seldom [loses] his self-control" (p. 358); with a "civilized" concern for the past and the future; and with diminution of self, with self-sacrifice. If each of the two men epitomizes one set of qualities, Maggie, whose childhood self was capacious enough to contain the major opposition projected by them, is tempted in relation first to one man and then to the other to negate one half of her self. It is in these terms that Philip makes his final pronouncement about her relationship with Stephen: "I believe," he writes to her, "that the strong attraction which drew you together proceeded only from one side of your characters, and belonged to that partial, divided action of our nature which makes half the tragedy of the human lot" (p. 439). But then the same applies to her relationship with him.

The developing attraction between Maggie and Stephen flares into the open at the dance at Park House. Walking with Stephen in the conservatory, Maggie lifts her arm to pick a "large half-opened rose that [has] attracted her":

> A mad impulse seized on Stephen; he darted towards the arm, and showered kisses on it, clasping the wrist.
> But the next moment Maggie snatched it from him, and glared at him like a wounded war-goddess, quivering with rage and humiliation.
> "How dare you?"—she spoke in a deeply-shaken, half-smothered voice. "What right have I given you to insult me?"
> She darted from him into the adjoining room, and threw herself on the sofa, panting and trembling. (p. 387)

It is in its nonrational, animal abandon that Stephen's impulse is "mad," and when it seizes on him, taking possession of him as Maggie was possessed as a child by her snaky demons when she pushed Lucy into the mud, it consumes civility. Maggie's response is indicative of a complex mixture of emotion, the half-opened rose presiding over her dilemma. With one part of her she really is resentful and humiliated, it being a "wound to her self-respect" (p. 388) that he has inflicted; but the wound also implies that he has drawn blood. The extremity of the war-goddess's rage thus suggests it is not only a wild, savage Maggie he has touched into life, a Maggie who pants as well as trembles, but also a customarily contained Maggie who is desperately trying to repress the eruption of a presence that is threatening to her.

The "savage enemy who [has] feigned death" is said to "leap to life" again a few days later when Stephen seeks Maggie out at her aunt Moss's (p. 390). He apologizes for having taken "an unwarrantable liberty" in the conservatory by way of declaring his passionate love for her (p. 391); and then there follows an exchange between them which is at the moral core of the novel. She begs him to "think of Lucy," and adds that she has "other ties" apart from her:

> "You are engaged to Philip Wakem?" said Stephen, hastily. "Is it so?"
> "I consider myself engaged to him—I don't mean to marry any one else."
> Stephen was silent again until they had turned out of the sun into a side lane, all grassy and sheltered. Then he burst out impetuously—
> "It is unnatural—it is horrible. Maggie, if you loved me as I love you, we should throw everything else to the winds for the sake of belonging to each other. We should break all these mistaken ties that were made in blindness, and determine to marry each other."
> "I would rather die than fall into that temptation," said Maggie, with deep, slow distinctness—all the gathered spiritual force of painful years coming to her aid in this extremity. She drew her arm from his as she spoke.
> "Tell me, then, that you don't care for me," he said, almost violently. "Tell me that you love some one else better."
> It darted through Maggie's mind that here was a mode of releasing herself from outward struggle—to tell Stephen that her whole heart was Philip's. But her lips would not utter that, and she was silent. (p. 393)

In the exchange Stephen (rather like Heathcliff in relation to Cathy) takes his stand on nature and love, on what he later refers to as "natural law" (p. 417). For him this is paramount, taking precedence over everything else, which should be cast "to the winds" in free abandon. Maggie opposes him on the grounds of inculcated principle, of a belief in what she calls "faithfulness" (p. 394), the necessity for accepting the restraint which "ties" to others impose. It is difficult to say whose case is stronger morally, for it would seem to be no better morally to be true to others than to oneself—or vice versa. Practically, however, Stephen's position appears to be more convincing. If for Maggie it is preeminently a question of ties, then he has rights as well; and though she at first seems to wish to disown their connection as she draws her arm from his, by the end of the scene she confesses her love for him, and consequently his later assertion that no one has "so great a claim" on her as he (p. 418) has considerable force. Indeed the strength of her tie to Philip is undermined when, by contrast, she positively cannot bring herself to say that she loves him, and Stephen's description of their previous ties as "mistaken" and "made in blindness" again seems just. The contrast is heightened by her own sense of the likely durability of what binds her to Stephen and her recognition that she will not be able to disengage herself from it as easily as she does her arm, as is indicated when she is tempted to tell Stephen her heart is Philip's, for she knows this can win her release from "outward struggle" only. Finally, if Maggie maintains that she would be "haunted by the suffering" caused Philip and Lucy, and consequently that her love for Stephen "would be poisoned" (p. 394); he makes the more telling point that they could "only pretend to give [themselves] to any one else": "There is wrong in that too—" he says; "there may be misery in it for *them* as well as for us" (p. 394). There would seem to be more to counter the poison in the first instance than in the second.

The positions that Maggie and Stephen take here remain constant, and they stick to them in their final decisive discussion at Mudport. Since neither position is clearly preferable morally, we need perhaps to seek a psychological explanation of her adamant stand in the face of his persuasiveness, even though we do not doubt the sincerity of her feeling. We are given a clue, I think, at a crucial moment during their exchange at aunt Moss's, a moment when Maggie almost gives way:

> Maggie was silent. If it were *not* wrong—if she were once convinced of that, and need no longer beat and struggle against this current, soft and yet strong as the summer stream!
>
> "Say 'yes,' dearest," said Stephen, leaning to look entreatingly in her face. "What could we care about in the whole world beside, if we belonged to each other?"
>
> Her breath was on his face—his lips were very near hers—but there was a great dread dwelling in his love for her.
>
> Her lips and eyelids quivered; she opened her eyes full on his for an instant, like a lovely wild animal timid and struggling under caresses, and then turned sharp round towards home again. (p. 393)

If Stephen has maintained that their previous ties were "made in blindness," this is a moment of open-eyed confrontation. What it reveals is that he has the power to call to life in her the "lovely wild animal" that she has repressed for so long; but their relationship and attraction to each other are entirely on this physical level. When Maggie, therefore, insists that she remains tied to Philip while admitting that she loves Stephen, it would seem that she needs and wants both men, wants Philip too for what Stephen cannot give her. Wanting both, she—like Cathy in relation to Edgar and Heathcliff—is finally incapable of choosing one. This would seem to be the purport of her reference to paradise in the same exchange: "If life were quite easy and simple," she says, "as it might have been in paradise, and we could always see that one being first towards whom . . . . I mean, if life did not make duties for us before love comes, love would be a sign that two people ought to belong to each other" (p. 394). What she seems somewhat confusedly to be saying, if we bear in mind the force of earlier references to Eden, is that when one is whole oneself, one's choices are simple and so life is easy. Torn in two, as she is now, she is incapable of resolving her conflict. The incapacity declares itself in the way she renounces Stephen in the same breath that she confesses she loves him (p. 394).[12]

Maggie's renunciation of the man she loves in the name of principle is strikingly similar to that of Jane Eyre; and it is interesting that water imagery also plays a part in the crucial confrontation between Jane and Rochester: "The crisis was perilous; but not without its charm: such as the Indian, perhaps, feels when he slips over the rapid in his canoe." Jane is indeed in a perilous situation at this point: to repel Rochester, who is poised for violent attack, is to risk death at his hands; to accept him is to risk another kind of destruction, to risk being swept away, in spite of her valid objections, in a rush of passion. What Jane does is, like the Indian, to retain perfect control, riding the rapid and resisting the pull both to and away from Rochester; and what she finally takes her stand on in deciding to leave him—"there I plant my foot"—is "care for [herself]." Jane's renunciation of Rochester, therefore, is essentially self-defensive, a means of self-preservation. Maggie's "care," however, is all for others; and in renouncing Stephen, in refusing to give herself to the current, she is left to "beat and struggle" against it, the frantic nature of the effort seeming to presage self-destruction. One is reminded of Stein's pronouncement in *Lord Jim* about a man who "falls into the sea": "If he tries to climb out into the air as inexperienced people endeavour to do, he drowns—*nicht wahr?*"

In the event what Maggie does is to allow herself to drift. Accepting Stephen's invitation to go on the river, she lets his "stronger presence . . . bear her along" apparently "without any act of her own will" (p. 407). After a while Stephen stops rowing, and says: "See how the tide is carrying us out—away from all those unnatural bonds that we have been trying to make faster round us—and trying in vain"; and Maggie yearns to "glide along with the swift, silent stream, and not struggle any more" (p. 408). In the end they board the Dutch vessel that is heading for Mudport, and this line of imagery culminates in a drowning: "But now nothing was distinct to her: she was being lulled to sleep with that soft stream still flowing over her, with those delicious visions melting and fading like the wondrous aërial land of the west" (p. 412). For Maggie, it appears, there is no way out: to let herself drift into a union with Stephen would seem to lead no less to destruction than to struggle against it—which she again proceeds to do when she rouses herself ("Waking" is the title of the next chapter) and decisively leaves him at Mudport to return to St. Ogg's, ready to brave it alone.

What it means to Maggie to give Stephen up is powerfully suggested by her response to the letter (written some two months after she has left him) in which he begs to be allowed to come to her:

> When Maggie first read this letter she felt as if her real temptation had only just begun. At the entrance of the chill dark cavern, we turn with unworn courage from the warm light; but how, when we have trodden far in

the damp darkness, and have begun to be faint and weary—how, if there is a sudden opening above us, and we are invited back again to the life-nourishing day? The leap of natural longing from under the pressure of pain is so strong, that all less immediate motives are likely to be forgotten—till the pain has been escaped from. (pp. 449–50)

The "chill dark cavern" is the final image of enclosure used in connection with Maggie, and should be related to that which previously evoked her sense of being shut in by a rocky wall in the days of her devotion to Thomas à Kempis. If it was Philip who made an opening in the wall for her then, her feeling of enclosure was in some degree mitigated by the open sky above, even if the prospect it presented was "remote" and "unfathomed." Now the sense of enclosure is intensified, for she has progressed so far in "the damp darkness" of the chill cavern as to feel altogether cut off from "the warm light" and from "the life-nourishing day." What the cavern evokes is a tomb; and indeed Maggie has condemned herself to a kind of living death in choosing to be without both Philip and Stephen, for love, we remember, is her vital principle. If her "life-struggles" have throughout "lain almost entirely within her own soul, one shadowy army fighting another, and the slain shadows for ever rising again" (p. 269); her battles with herself—and with outward circumstance, for by this point St. Ogg's has won and even Dr. Kenn has felt compelled to advise her to leave the town—have so depleted her strength that she seems almost to have lost the will to carry on: "she must begin a new life, in which she would have to rouse herself to receive new impressions—and she was so unspeakably, sickeningly weary!" (p. 449). The "sudden opening" above her which Stephen's call makes in the cavern is thus a call to life itself, a chance to rise from the tomb. The "leap of natural longing" to escape from pain which possesses her is also the leap of the lovely wild animal which Stephen again stirs into being and would make its own bid for life.

But, in a culminating instance of Maggie's self-division, the animal is negated by mind: "her mind [recoils]" and swings her back to her old position (p. 450). Her decision to stand by her renunciation of Stephen may be viewed as a climactic exercise of restraint on her part, the sort of restraint that has been associated with a truly civilized response to life and with an achieved maturity. That would seem to be the view the novelist expects us to take; and it has been said that "Maggie's rejection of Stephen Guest . . . is surely represented as an act of the greatest moral heroism."[13] But what we are also shown is that the decision places her firmly back in the dark cavern:

> She took up the letter, held it to the candle, and let it burn slowly on the hearth. To-morrow she would write to him the last word of parting.

"I will bear it, and bear it till death . . . . . But how long it will be before death comes! I am so young, so healthy. How shall I have patience and strength? Am I to struggle and fall and repent again?—has life other trials as hard for me still?"

With that cry of self-despair, Maggie fell on her knees against the table, and buried her sorrow-stricken face. . . . (p. 451)

Maggie's burning of the letter not only signifies the finality of her renunciation of Stephen but also mutely seems to assert that her passion too can be left to burn itself out. But we have just been told that, if "the old shadowy enemies" that she battles are "for ever slain," they for ever "[rise] again" (p. 447); and her conflict would accordingly appear to be far from resolved. Torn in two as before, left alone in the cavern without either Stephen or Philip, Maggie determines to cleave once again to her old teacher and bear her cross "till death." But she is in fact reduced to the kind of despair that knows and wants only death, to a despair that can issue only in what Philip once called a "long suicide."[14] It is precisely at this point that she feels "a startling sensation of sudden cold about her knees and feet" and realizes that it is "water flowing under her" (p. 451); but the advent of the flood, though carefully prepared for, comes across now as sentimentally contrived. In the flood scenes Maggie is granted an access of strength: with a renewed wholeness of being evocative of her childhood, she rescues Tom and is reunited with him before they drown together. But not even this ending can offset the impression of her irreparable self-division, of the "cry of self-despair" with which she opts for the cavern and which leaves her wanting only to "[bury] her sorrow-stricken face" as her soul goes out to "the Unseen Pity" that will be with her "to the end" (p. 451).

CHAPTER 4

Tess of the d'Urbervilles
Mastery and Abandon

The form of *Tess of the d'Urbervilles* is at first sight deceptively simple: the life of the protagonist is divided into "phases," and her adventures in love seem to be shaped by no more than a traditional triangle. But the antagonists in the triangle, Alec d'Urberville and Angel Clare, are not merely opposed as alternate lovers of Tess Durbeyfield; like Heathcliff and Edgar, and Stephen and Philip, they clearly figure oppugnant principles of being. The nature of this opposition and of the triangle in which it is contained has been suggestively described by D. H. Lawrence:

> Angel Clare has the very opposite qualities to those of Alec d'Urberville. To the latter, the female in himself is the only part of himself he will acknowledge: the body, the senses, that which he shares with the female, which the female shares with him. To Angel Clare, the female in himself is detestable, the body, the senses, that which he will share with a woman, is held degraded. . . .
> Who is he, that he shall be pure male, and deny the existence of the female? This is the question the Creator asks of him. Is then the male the exclusive whole of life?—is he even the higher or supreme part of life? Angel Clare thinks so: as Christ thought. . . .
> The one extreme produces the other. It is inevitable for Angel Clare and for Alec d'Urberville mutually to destroy the woman they both loved. Each does her the extreme of wrong, so she is destroyed.
> The book is handled with very uncertain skill, botched and bungled. But it contains the elements of the greatest tragedy: Alec d'Urberville, who has killed the male in himself . . . ; Angel Clare, who has killed the female in himself . . . : and Tess, the Woman, the Life, destroyed by a mechanical fate, in the communal law.[1]

One need not subscribe to Lawrence's view of the constituents of the male and female principles to grant that he has seized on an opposition that is fundamental to Hardy's vision of life. It is an opposition that runs through Hardy's work, from *The Return of the Native* (1878), with its insistence on "the mutually destructive interdependence of spirit and flesh"—the terms in which Hardy chooses to formulate the conflict—to *Jude the Obscure* (1895), with its searing corroboration of Jude Fawley's intuition that his life is one of "constant internal warfare between flesh and spirit." The conflict, moreover, is so much a question of general principles of being that Hardy duplicates the kind of opposition that is established between the two male rivals in *Tess* in his presentation of the two women whom Jude loves. From the outset, Alec (like Arabella Donn) has the stamp of a creature of the senses: he is first seen emerging "from the dark" of a tent; he has a "bold rolling eye" and full, red, smooth lips; there are "touches of barbarism" in the contours of his face (p. 79).[2] Angel, on the other hand, is "rather bright than hot—less Byronic than Shelleyan," and (like Sue Bridehead) is directly said to be "more spiritual than animal" (p. 257).

The opposition, however, is neither as simple nor as fixed as Lawrence makes it. In the Hardy universe "flux and reflux—the rhythm of change—alternate and persist in everything under the sky" (p. 434), and both Alec and Angel are caught up in that rhythm. If Alec has killed the male in himself, has denied the spirit, that is, he would also appear to hanker after it, for he undergoes a "conversion" and becomes a "ranter," even though his career as an itinerant preacher may be short-lived. And if Angel is pure male and lives by the spirit, he repudiates the Church, which he is expected to enter as a minister, and aspires to a life of the senses, for he seeks a down-to-earth existence as a farmer. Hardy would thus appear to be concerned with a conflict between flesh and spirit that is not only externalized in the opposition between Alec and Angel but also internalized in each of the men. As it is, of course, in Tess herself, for perhaps Hardy's boldest manipulation of his traditional form is the rhythmic duplication of its triangular dynamics: with the swing of a pendulum, Tess moves from Alec to Angel, and then back to Alec before returning to Angel, thus imaging the degree to which she is pulled between one man and the other. What is also suggested is her inability to reconcile within herself the conflicting principles they preeminently embody, as she first negates the spirit in relation to Alec and then the flesh in relation to Angel. And since she moves freely between the two men, choosing her own way though subjected to intolerable pressures, her tragedy would seem to lie not so much in her mutual destruction by Alec and Angel, as has been the critical consensus since Lawrence, as in her own failure to integrate flesh and spirit.[3] It is true that Tess sees herself as a victim—"Once victim, always victim—that's the law!" she bitterly cries out towards the end of her story (p. 411); and that is how the novelist, as he sets the scene for

Tess's arrest at the sacrificial slab at Stonehenge, would seem to wish us finally to see her. But she is as much a victim of herself as others, and should be regarded as ultimately responsible for what happens to her.

Tess of the d'Urbervilles is more fully realized than Lawrence believed, and indeed provides us with a number of its own vivid images as pointers to its comprehension. On one occasion at Talbothays, Angel scrutinizes Tess while she is still heavy with sleep and before she is aware of him:

> . . . her face was flushed with sleep, and her eyelids hung heavy over their pupils. The brim-fulness of her nature breathed from her. It was a moment when a woman's soul is more incarnate than at any other time; when the most spiritual beauty bespeaks itself flesh; and sex takes the outside place in the presentation.
>
> Then those eyes flashed brightly through their filmy heaviness, before the remainder of her face was well awake. With an oddly compounded look of gladness, shyness, and surprise, she exclaimed—
> 'O Mr. Clare! How you frightened me—I—' (p. 231)

At this moment Tess epitomizes a fullness of being that is compounded of a rare harmony of flesh and spirit, when spirit bespeaks itself flesh, and flesh is shot through with the bright flash of spirit. It is a harmony she does not often attain to, but in its plenitude it constitutes an implicit ideal against which partial being is measured—that of both Alec and Angel as well as her quotidian self. This happy balance of flesh and spirit in man has an analogue in nature in the diurnal balance of twilight:

> [Tess] knew how to hit to a hair's-breadth that moment of evening when the light and the darkness are so evenly balanced that the constraint of day and the suspense of night neutralize each other, leaving absolute mental liberty. It is then that the plight of being alive becomes attenuated to its least possible dimensions. (p. 134)

If it is characteristic of Hardy that mere existence should be envisaged as a dire circumstance, it is striking that this should be rendered most tolerable at a moment when opposites are demonstratively balanced. But the "hair's-breadth" of balance that is achieved in nature seems to posit the kind of neutralization that is neither attainable nor desirable in man, as Tess's moment of "brim-fulness" forcefully suggests; and a different view of twilight seems more appropriate to human aspiration:

> The gray half-tones of daybreak are not the gray half-tones of the day's close, though the degree of their shade may be the same. In the twilight of the morning light seems active, darkness passive; in the twilight of evening it is the darkness which is active and crescent, and the light which is the drowsy reverse. (p. 186)

This is a reconciliation in which the opposites retain their separate identity, and which allows for a natural preponderance of one or the other in a rhythm of change. It is notable that when one of the opposites is no more than a "drowsy reverse," as the light is in the evening, it is by no means negated, for its presence modifies the crescent darkness into twilight. The alternation depicted here may serve as a vivid metaphor of what Hardy seems to have had in mind as a principle of characterization while he was at work on *Tess:* "I am more than ever convinced that persons are successively various persons, according as each special strand in their characters is brought uppermost by circumstances."[4]

Like so much in Hardy, this statement points ahead to Lawrence—to Lawrence's theory of character as a series of allotropic states; but it also points more directly, of course, to Hardy's conception of Tess as she moves back and forth between Alec and Angel. Tess's problem, however, is that she does negate one part of herself when another (and opposite) part is uppermost; and it is in terms of the kind of balance that is evoked by a twilight in which neither the light nor the dark is denied that she is found wanting. It is an indication of the imaginative coherence of the novel that Tess's tragic failure to achieve integrated being is played out against the background of the disintegration of the agricultural community of which she is a product.

II

The sort of relationship Alec wishes to impose on Tess is figured when she rides with him in his smart gig on the way to Trantridge. Alec is a "handsome, horsey young buck" (p. 92), and when they reach a long, steep descent and he begins to drive recklessly down it, it seems at first as if this is merely an expression of his natural flamboyance and high spirits: "Why, I always go down at full gallop," he says to the alarmed Tess. "There's nothing like it for raising your spirits" (p. 94). But it soon becomes apparent there is more to his driving than that. For one thing, the horse is a mare; and as the dashing young male urges it into a full gallop, the description of the pell-mell drive downhill, with "the figure of the horse rising and falling in undulations before them" (p. 95), takes on insistent sexual overtones. These are still further emphasized when, before the end of the drive, Tess is reduced to desperation and "her large eyes [stare] at him like those of a wild animal" (p. 96). For another, the mare is no ordinary horse, but "has killed one chap" and has also "nearly killed" Alec himself on another occasion (p. 95). Consequently the drive downhill also becomes a question of Alec's pitting himself against the horse, of his testing his power over it and demonstrating his mastery: "If any living man," he tells Tess, "can manage this horse I can:—I won't say any living man can do it—but if such has the power, I am he" (p. 94). The scene becomes more and more evocative of the episode in *Women in Love* in which Gerald Crich subdues the mare at the railway crossing in the presence of Gudrun Brangwen.

Once Alec has loosened the rein and given the mare its head, what he demonstrates in the ride is the degree to which he can impel it to a wild abandon while he himself coolly—if high-spiritedly—retains control of it (p. 95). The motif of abandon, so sharply concretized in the mare's plunge downhill, is of central importance in Tess's story, and indeed may be said to frame it at its very beginning, if only by way of light adumbration. The opening incident of the novel, in which Parson Tringham informs Jack Durbeyfield of his descent from "the ancient and knightly family of the d'Urbervilles" (p. 43), may be regarded as the first link in the chain of chance that leads Tess—via her father's incapacity and the accident in which the horse Prince is killed—to Alec; but, as always in Hardy, chance is no more than the challenge of character, and the clergyman admits that, though he had resolved not to tell Durbeyfield of his discovery, he unaccountably gave way to an impulse: ". . . our impulses are too strong for our judgment sometimes," he says (pp. 44–45). Similarly, though Tess's fatal involvement with Alec might appear to be quite literally determined by a force beyond her control since she is asleep when Prince is killed, I think she must be seen as abandoning herself to the sleep which overtakes her, despite the fact that she knows she should stay awake. There is, after all, a point at which one *allows* oneself to fall asleep.

As the gig speeds along, alternative possibilities in the development of Tess's relationship with Alec are nicely juxtaposed. At first Tess clings to him, and it is only when they safely reach the bottom of the hill that she disengages herself and realizes how completely she has given way to impulse: "She had not considered what she had been doing; whether he were man or woman, stick or stone, in her involuntary hold on him" (p. 95). Alec then "[loosens] rein" again, they go shooting down a second hill, and the only way Tess can persuade him to stop is by agreeing to let him kiss her. She implores him not to claim his due, but he is "inexorable," and gives her "the kiss of mastery" (p. 96)—a phrase which draws together related significances of the drive. When they come to "yet another descent" and Alec tries to extort another kiss, however, Tess defeats him by allowing her hat to blow off and refusing to get back into the gig after she has retrieved it. Demonstrating that she can take a stand, Tess walks the rest of the way to Trantridge (pp. 97–98).

But she is not always prepared to walk, and the way in which she "abandons herself to her impulse" on another occasion is premonitory of what is to come. She has been drawn into a fierce quarrel with the Queen of Diamonds when suddenly Alec appears on horseback. He urges her to jump up behind him in order to get away from "the screaming cats":

> She felt almost ready to faint, so vivid was her sense of the crisis. At almost any other moment of her life she would have refused such proffered aid and company . . . But coming as the invitation did at the particular juncture when fear and indignation at these adversaries could be transformed by a spring of the foot into a triumph over them, she abandoned herself to her impulse, climbed the gate, put her toe upon his instep, and scrambled into the saddle behind him. The pair were speeding away into the distant gray by the time that the contentious revellers became aware of what had happened. (pp. 112–13)

This episode immediately precedes Tess's seduction; and being a culminating instance of her capacity for abandon in relation to Alec, would strongly seem to suggest that it is a seduction, and not a rape, that follows. This is the general critical view, but Tony Tanner, in one of the very best studies of the novel, repeatedly refers to what happens as a rape.[5] This gives one pause and makes one realize that what happens in the Chase is not, in the formulation of Ian Gregor, "both a seduction *and* a rape,"[6] but so ambiguously presented as to invite the mutually contradictory readings.

Though Hardy is constrained by the conventions of his time to leave us to find our way by indirection, his sudden change of direction is startling. Prior to the scene in the Chase, Alec has certainly not been presented as a rapist. For "near three mortal months" he has pursued Tess, and though riled by her "trifling" with him, has accepted her rebuffs (p. 115). On the night in question he tells her that he loves her and asks whether he may not treat her "as a lover" (p. 115). He also reveals that on that day he has presented her father with "a new cob" to replace Prince and given toys to the children of the family (p. 117). Most revealingly of all, when he leaves Tess to try to find out where they are, he is compassionate to her: " 'Nights grow chilly in September. Let me see.' He pulled off a light overcoat that he had worn, and put it round her tenderly. 'That's it–now you'll feel warmer,' he continued. 'Now, my pretty, rest there; I shall soon be back again' " (p. 118). Neither his concern nor his tenderness suggests the rapist, yet when he returns to "the white muslin figure" which seems to have been swallowed up in the darkness— "everything else was blackness alike"—suggestions of violation become insistent. We are told that philosophy cannot explain "why it was that upon this beautiful feminine tissue, sensitive as gossamer, and practically blank as snow as yet, there should have been traced such a coarse pattern as it was doomed to receive"; and "why so often the coarse appropriates the finer thus." The only explanation proffered is that of retribution, for "doubtless some of Tess d'Urberville's mailed ancestors rollicking home from a fray had dealt the same measure even more ruthlessly towards peasant girls of their time" (pp. 118–19). And for good measure the description of Alec's return to Tess ended, in the first edition of the novel, with the following passage (subsequently omitted from later editions):

> Already at that hour some sons of the forest were stirring, and striking lights in not very distant cottages; good and sincere hearts among them, patterns of honesty and devotion and chivalry. And powerful horses were stamping in their stalls, ready to be let out into the morning air. But no dart or thread of intelligence inspired these men to harness or mount, or gave them by any means the least inkling that their sister was in the hands of the spoiler; and they did not come that way.[7]

This pronouncement is echoed in the edition we now have in the comments of a villager on Tess's baby: "A little more than persuading had to do wi' the coming o't, I reckon. There were they that heard a sobbing one night last year in The Chase; and it mid ha' gone hard wi' a certain party if folks had come along" (p. 140).

If it is difficult to reconcile this view of the matter with what precedes it, with the way in which both Tess and Alec have been presented, it is equally hard to relate it to what follows, to the way in which Tess responds to the experience. It is possible to imagine—or, at any rate, to conceive how a novelist such as Hardy could lead us to imagine—that a woman might fall in love with her rapist; but Tess, both before and after the night in the Chase, repeatedly states that she does not love Alec and has never loved him—and yet, though this episode takes place on "a Saturday in September" (p. 106), it is not until "a Sunday morning in late October" (p. 123) that she leaves him, having freely lived as his mistress, that is to say, for about a month after it. Hardy, apparently, both wishes it to be clear it is not only a rape that is in question (if it is a rape at all) and wants to minimize the extent of Tess's transgression. He is led into inconsistency, it seems to me, not so much because he is intent on presenting Tess as "a pure woman," as has been asserted,[8] as because he wants her to be seen as a victim. Tess is asleep when Alec returns to where he has left her in the Chase, just as she was asleep when the accident with Prince takes place, but it is as a responsible tragic agent—not helpless victim—that we should view her.

Tess emerges as such an agent, and any dispute as to whether she has been raped or seduced becomes supererogatory, in what she reveals about her attitude to Alec during the period she is his mistress. What is most striking about her feeling when she leaves Trantridge is her self-loathing, her self-disgust. When Alec catches up with her, she says to him: ". . . if I had ever sincerely loved you, if I loved you still, I should not so loathe and hate myself for my weakness as I do now! . . . My eyes were dazed by you for a little, and that was all" (p. 125). And when her mother tells her she should have got Alec to marry her, she reflects bitterly how little her mother knows the feeling towards him which has made her "detest herself":

> She had never wholly cared for him, she did not at all care for him now. She had dreaded him, winced before him, succumbed to adroit advantages he took of her helplessness; then, temporarily blinded by his ardent manners, had been stirred to confused surrender awhile: had suddenly despised and disliked him, and had run away. That was all. Hate him she did not quite; but he was dust and ashes to her, and even for name's sake she scarcely wished to marry him. (p. 130)

Tess loathes and hates herself so strongly, it now appears, because she despises and dislikes Alec. Her feeling for him fills her with revulsion from her own body as well as his, and it is not only he who is "dust and ashes" to her. She herself is reduced to dust and ashes because she now realizes that what she gave Alec was a body uninformed by spirit, devoid of the love which could animate it—and which could alone redeem it in her eyes. Though her eyes were "dazed" and "blinded" by him, they see clearly enough now; we cannot help contrasting this view of her with that of her later "brim-fulness" of being when her eyes "flash brightly through their filmy heaviness." It is the spirit that Tess has denied in her relationship with Alec and that now whips back on her. And her "surrender," moreover, was "confused" because there was not even a strong physical passion to move her to it: when Alec begins to pursue her for a second time and says, "Here I am, my love, as in the old times!" she answers: "Not as then—never as then—'tis different! . . . And there was never warmth with me!" (p. 410).

What a cold body is like is indicated in a superb scene, which encapsulates all the elements in their relationship:

> Alec d'Urberville removed his cigar, bent towards her, and said—
> 'You are not going to turn away like that, dear? Come!'
> 'If you wish,' she answered indifferently. 'See how you've mastered me!'
> She thereupon turned round and lifted her face to his, and remained like a marble term while he imprinted a kiss upon her cheek—half perfunctorily, half as if zest had not yet quite died out. Her eyes vaguely rested upon the remotest trees in the lane while the kiss was given, as though she were nearly unconscious of what he did. (p. 126)

Tess may speak ironically here, but in the absence of both love and physical warmth on her part, we must assume she has in fact "succumbed" to Alec because he mastered her—that she was mastered as well as blinded by his "ardent manners." If such mastery implies a subduing of her spirit, that in turn implies (in the end) the marble flesh which she now indifferently yields to him, as if she is "nearly unconscious" of him—and the taste of dust and ashes. Not that she alone is cold. Her marble is matched by the coldness with which Alec pursues her, the coldness that underlies his will to dominance, for coolness, as we have seen in the episode with the mare, is a condition of such mastery. Alec's drive for mastery is more complex than he realizes, however, for it coexists with the genuine tenderness towards Tess that he exhibits on occasion, and with an unacknowledged force of feeling that will later draw him back to her, scattering his evangelical pretensions like so much chaff in the wind; but at this stage of the relationship he is, for the most part, egotistically concerned only with his own needs. The needs of flesh alone are soon sated, though he is slower in reaching satiety than Tess, and Hardy beautifully captures the last flicker of his half-extinguished desire as he kisses Tess "half perfunctorily, half as if zest [has] not yet quite died out." Since, moreover, his desire is fueled not by love but by a will to mastery, it is fired by opposition, not submission; and it is Tess's very yielding which dooms it to extinction—as is suggested by a passage in the manuscript (italicized in the following quotation) which Hardy inserted into his description of Alec's kiss and then deleted (possibly because it was too specific about the length of Tess's stay with him as his mistress): ". . . he imprinted a kiss upon her cheek—half perfunctorily, half as if zest had not yet quite died out *for only a month had elapsed since she had ceased to defend herself against him.*"[9]

III

When Tess, at the beginning of Phase the Third: The Rally, sets out for Talbothays, where Angel is staying, it is not only in a literal sense that her journey is "now in a direction almost opposite to that of her first adventuring" (p. 155). Just what she is journeying towards is mapped out for us, as it were, when she looks down from a hill on the Valley of the Great Dairies, which is her destination:

> It was intrinsically different from the Vale of Little Dairies, Blackmoor Vale, which, save during her disastrous sojourn at Trantridge, she had exclusively known till now. The world was drawn to a larger pattern here. . . .
> The bird's-eye perspective before her was not so luxuriantly beautiful, perhaps, as that other one which she knew so well; yet it was more cheering. It lacked the intensely blue atmosphere of the rival vale, and its heavy soils and scents; the new air was clear, bracing, ethereal. The river itself, which

nourished the grass and cows of these renowned dairies, flowed not like the streams in Blackmoor. Those were slow, silent, often turbid; flowing over beds of mud into which the incautious wader might sink and vanish unawares. The Froom waters were clear as the pure River of Life shown to the Evangelist, rapid as the shadow of a cloud, with pebbly shallows that prattled to the sky all day long. There the water-flower was the lily; the crowfoot here. (pp. 156–57).

As Tess moves into a "world" that is "drawn to a larger pattern" than she has known before, she is given a chance to escape the reduced life of her previous experience, a chance to attain to the sort of fullness of being she indeed momentarily epitomizes on one memorable occasion at Talbothays. As she moves from the turbid, muddy waters of Blackmoor to the pure, clear waters of Froom, that is, from silent streams to those that prattle, and from "heavy soils and scents" to a "new air" that is "clear, bracing, ethereal," she is given the opportunity to move beyond the heavy, inarticulate earthiness of flesh—in which, like "the incautious wader" in the streams of Blackmoor, one may get bogged down—to the free, expressive clarity of spirit. In a word, what is figured by the light rapid Froom waters that coexist with the luxuriance of an earth where "milk and butter [grow] to rankness" (p. 156) is the possibility of a new quickness.

That Hardy is indeed putting the configurations of the Valley of the Great Dairies to symbolic account would seem to be confirmed when Angel, after a visit to his parents at Emminster, is pictured returning to the same valley:

> An up-hill and down-dale ride of twenty-odd miles through a garish mid-day atmosphere brought him in the afternoon to a detached knoll a mile or two west of Talbothays, whence he again looked into that green trough of sappiness and humidity, the valley of the Var or Froom. Immediately he began to descend from the upland to the fat alluvial soil below, the atmosphere grew heavier; the languid perfume of the summer fruits, the mists, the hay, the flowers, formed therein a vast pool of odour which at this hour seemed to make the animals, the very bees and butterflies, drowsy. . . . It was with a sense of luxury that he recognized his power of viewing life here from its inner side, in a way that had been quite foreign to him in his student-days; and, much as he loved his parents, he could not help being aware that to come here, as now, after an experience of home-life, affected him like throwing off splints and bandages . . . (p. 230)

For Angel, the novelist indicates as he now stresses different features of the same valley, the significance of his movement towards Tess (to whom he is hastening on this journey) is the reverse of what her association with him means for her. Coming from his clerical home, he makes a necessary descent to the farm, a descent from the "transcendental aspirations" of

Vicarage life (p. 218) and the rarefied atmosphere of the spirit, to a rich, languid, material sappiness, which the valley now figures. Its materiality is sharply opposed to Angel's inculcated habit of abstraction, which he carries over from theological metaphysics to everyday life, viewing even Tess as "a fresh and virginal daughter of Nature" (p. 176), and being inclined to see her not as a milkmaid but "a visionary essence of woman," whom he calls Artemis and Demeter (p. 187). But as he progressively adapts himself to the earthiness of farm life, and as his relationship with Tess develops, it seems as if he too will be drawn to a larger pattern than he has known. When he feels as if he has thrown off splints and bandages, he registers a sense of having regained a vital freedom and fullness of function after the restrictive dislocations of his upbringing. Having learned at Talbothays to view life "from its inner side," Angel finds he is able to experience an "aesthetic, sensuous, pagan pleasure in natural life and lush womanhood," and to feel "the great passionate pulse of existence, unwarped, uncontorted, untrammelled by . . . creeds" (pp. 218–19). He demonstrates, moreover, that he has developed a capacity for the kind of physical spontaneity that would be quite beyond his brothers, for example: when he overhears a man insulting Tess, he is "stung to the quick," and before he has "considered anything at all," strikes the man "with the full force of his fist, sending him staggering backwards . . ." (p. 274). But vestiges of a creed that has been deeply assimilated remain to slow the pulse of his own existence when it comes to a direct sexual response to Tess, suggesting he has not changed as much as he likes to believe: during his courtship of Tess he is often on the point of kissing her, but repeatedly checks himself, "for tender conscience' sake" (p. 209) or because he is deterred by "his scrupulous heart" (p. 245). Angel, it appears, is as temperamentally averse to abandon as Tess is prone to it.

Tess's passionate nature, however, is not much in evidence at Talbothays—despite the novelist's lavish celebration of the lushness of her surroundings. On one occasion, it is true, she is provoked by Angel to "a distraction of tenderness," and he learns "what an impassioned woman's kisses [are] like" (p. 255); but for the most part it is "his tutelary guidance" that she desires (p. 246). In association with him she is led "to pick up his vocabulary, his accent, and fragments of his knowledge, to a surprising extent" (p. 238); and "his influence over her" is so marked that she catches "his manner and habits, his speech and phrases, his likings and his aversions" (p. 270). The change in her is effectively registered for us by Alec when he meets her again and is surprised by her fluency of speech and her "good English" (p. 389); and her own sense of its extent is so great that she bitterly writes to Angel: "What was the past to me as soon as I met you? It was a dead thing altogether. I became another woman, filled full of new life from you" (p. 417). Tess's own assurance of a fullness of being while she is together with Angel at Talbothays would seem to posit her achievement of a new wholeness, but in fact from the moment she comes to the farm she seems to wish to dispossess herself of her own body.

This tendency first becomes apparent during a conversation with Dairyman Crick at breakfast:

> 'I don't know about ghosts,' [Tess] was saying; 'but I do know that our souls can be made to go outside our bodies when we are alive.'
> The dairyman turned to her with his mouth full, his eyes charged with serious inquiry, and his great knife and fork (breakfasts were breakfasts here) planted erect on the table, like the beginning of a gallows.
> 'What—really now? And is it so, maidy?' he said.
> 'A very easy way to feel 'em go,' continued Tess, 'is to lie on the grass at night and look straight up at some big bright star; and, by fixing your mind upon it, you will soon find that you are hundreds and hundreds o' miles away from your body, which you don't seem to want at all.' (p. 175)

Tess, we remember, may be said to have made her soul go outside her body in her relationship with Alec, but that was by way of leaving her body unimpeded; now what she seems to aspire to is the liberated soul that may burgeon from a discarded body. But that such a severance, in this case as in the other, will no less surely issue in dust and ashes is strikingly suggested by the gallows simile—a comparison which only Hardy could have made. At the very outset of this "phase," what is proleptically implied is that, with her predilection to set aside the body, Tess takes her first step to the gallows, for this will lead her in due course to return to Alec, giving him her body then to do with as he likes, and so to the murder when Angel comes to claim her.

One evening Tess hears Angel playing his harp in the garden, and begins to move towards him, keeping "behind the hedge" so that he may not "guess her presence":

> The outskirt of the garden in which Tess found herself had been left uncultivated for some years, and was now damp and rank with juicy grass which sent up mists of pollen at a touch; and with tall blooming weeds emitting offensive smells—weeds whose red and yellow and purple hues formed a polychrome as dazzling as that of cultivated flowers. She went stealthily as a cat through this profusion of growth, gathering cuckoo-spittle on her skirts, cracking snails that were underfoot, staining her hands with thistle-milk and slug-slime, and rubbing off upon her naked arms sticky blights which, though snow-white on the apple-tree trunks, made madder stains on her skin; thus she drew quite near to Clare, still unobserved of him.
> Tess was conscious of neither time nor space. The exaltation which she had described as being producible at will by gazing at a star, came now without any determination of hers; she undulated upon the thin notes of the

second-hand harp, and their harmonies passed like breezes through her, bringing tears into her eyes. . . . (pp. 178–79)

This passage has been the focus of considerable critical scrutiny with regard to Tess's place "in nature." I think David Lodge is right when he insists that, "even if the reader recoils from the overgrown garden, there is no suggestion that Tess does," and that she seems to be "at home in it." But I doubt whether the point of the passage is to show the "connection between Tess and the natural world" and so to imply "the 'mad', passionate, non-ethical quality of her sensibility."[10] What we are shown, it seems to me, is how unnatural Tess is. She may be at home in the garden as she moves through it like a cat, but whereas the rank grass and mists of pollen and blooming weeds variously epitomize a natural fecundity, and the juices that rub off on to her skin stain her in the flesh, she has abstracted herself from this teeming abundance. "Conscious of neither time nor space," she has abandoned herself to "exaltation," to a condition, that is, as the reference to her stargazing indicates (and the novelist's close juxtaposition of the two passages stresses), in which "you are hundreds and hundreds o' miles away from your body, which you don't seem to want at all." And that is how she approaches Angel.[11]

When Tess knows that Angel loves her and wants to marry her, she cannot decide whether or not to tell him of her relationship with Alec. Her mother, when appealed to, tells her not to be a fool, and Tess concludes that silence would seem to be "best for her adored one's happiness":

> Thus steadied by a command from the only person in the world who had any shadow of right to control her action, Tess grew calmer. The responsibility was shifted, and her heart was lighter than it had been for weeks. The days of declining autumn which followed her assent [to Angel], beginning with the month of October, formed a season through which she lived in spiritual altitudes more nearly approaching ecstasy than any other period of her life.
>
> There was hardly a touch of earth in her love for Clare. To her sublime trustfulness he was all that goodness could be—knew all that a guide, philosopher, and friend should know. She thought every line in the contour of his person the perfection of masculine beauty, his soul the soul of a saint, his intellect that of a seer. . . . He would sometimes catch her large, worshipful eyes, that had no bottom to them, looking at him from their depths, as if she saw something immortal before her.
>
> She dismissed the past—trod upon it and put it out, as one treads on a coal that is smouldering and dangerous. (p. 257)

Tess does not hold to the decision to keep her relationship with Alec secret, but when her attempt to inform Angel of it by letter miscarries, she fails—though "in her conscience" she knows there is "still time" before the marriage (p. 277)—to tell him. For all the mitigating circumstances, Tess must be seen as responsible for this failure, which is at the very heart of her story. It is the kingpin of the plot, for it results in Angel's abandonment of her; it is the essential cause of her tragedy, for it is an irreparable error and leads, in the end, to her murder of Alec and her execution; and it is the crux of her attitude to Angel, for it signifies her shrinking from the facts of flesh in relation to him. It is the sullied flesh that she would countermand: on her wedding night she agrees to keep on the jewels Angel's godmother has bequeathed to his wife because she is struck by the thought that she still has "something to tell" and that there may be "help in these" (p. 288)—as if the stain will be less apparent amid the diamond-radiance of her beauty. It is the nature of her love for Angel, however, that is most strongly expressive of her flight from flesh, for there is "hardly a touch of earth" in it; indeed, when she is with him, the "buoyancy of her tread" is "like the skim of a bird which has not quite alighted" (p. 260). When she does tread firmly, it is to dismiss the past, treading on it as on "a coal that is smouldering and dangerous." It is clearly the fire of passion she wants to stamp out; just as Maggie Tulliver, at seventeen, tries to stifle her passions though, "like a damp fire," they threaten to leap out again when "all seems safe." At Talbothays Tess tries "to lead a repressed life" though she "little [divines] the strength of her vitality" (p. 181). Consequently the coal is liable to flare up suddenly—as when she passionately kisses Angel on the occasion already referred to. In her repression—as in her movement through the unweeded garden—Tess is not in harmony with nature, this being suggested by the implied gap between the "spiritual altitudes" in which she has her being and the lush days of "declining autumn" through which she is actually living. Having lost touch with earth, she also loses touch with reality, transforming Angel into the godlike figure of her idealizations. How far he is from actually possessing the qualities she attributes to him, she speedily and brutally discovers.

When Tess finally confesses to Angel, she is appalled to find that he will not "forgive" her, as she begs him to. "O Tess," he says, "forgiveness does not apply to the case. You were one person; now you are another. My God—how can forgiveness meet such a grotesque—prestidigitation as that!"—and he insists that the woman he has been loving is "another woman in [her] shape" (pp. 298–99). Angel's response suggests that his is a case of love in the head, as Lawrence might have called it; and his recourse to the word "prestidigitation" in such circumstances reveals how he takes refuge in words from the woman in front of him. Angel, that is to say, when shocked back into an old mode of being, is as much given to intellectual altitudes as Tess to spiritual; and in his relationship with her the flesh is as surely and mutually denied as is the spirit in her relationship with Alec.

The mode that Angel slips back to, annulling his hard-won freedom from trammeling creeds, is described when he announces to Tess it is "advisable" they should part:

> Tess stole a glance at her husband. He was pale, even tremulous; but as before, she was appalled by the determination revealed in the depths of this gentle being she had married—the will to subdue the grosser to the subtler emotion, the substance to the conception, the flesh to the spirit. Propensities, tendencies, habits, were as dead leaves upon the tyrannous wind of his imaginative ascendency. (p. 316)

Angel's harshness to Tess is in part occasioned by his sense of having been deceived by her, is in part "the cruelty of fooled honesty . . . after enlightenment" (p. 301); but, more fundamentally than that, it springs from an involuntary revulsion from what he takes to be her defilement, a recoil from tainted flesh that is not unlike her own. He realizes this long afterwards in Brazil and then is "struck" by remorse, perceiving that what he has "inherited with the creed of mysticism" is an "abhorrence of the un-intact state" (p. 422). It is a tyrannous will that now forces him to smother his natural feeling for Tess, all such "propensities" being scattered like so many "dead leaves." The will to subdue the flesh to the spirit meets a capacity to withdraw spirit from flesh in a common sterility, in dead leaves, for on the night of Tess's seduction it was in "a deep mass of dead leaves" that Alec made "a sort of couch or nest" for her (p. 117), and it was to "the white muslin figure he had left upon the dead leaves" that he returned (pp. 118–19). Alec's struggle to master Tess, moreover, is jux-taposed to Angel's to master himself. As he steels himself against her, his air is "calm and cold, his small compressed mouth indexing his powers of self-control; his face wearing still that terribly sterile expression which had spread thereon since her disclosure" (p. 305). Coldness, it appears, is the condition of his kind of mastery as of Alec's, but Angel's coldness is more inhuman, for it is the coldness of metal: though he is generally "gentle and affectionate," deep within him there lies hidden "a hard logical deposit, like a vein of metal in a soft loam, which [turns] the edge of everything that [attempts] to traverse it," and blocks his acceptance of Tess, no less than of the Church (p. 311). With thought subduing substance, battening on it like a cancer and consuming it, for he becomes "ill with thinking; eaten out with thinking, withered by thinking" (p. 313), Angel leaves the woman he loves for an abstraction.

IV

Hardy is as authorially evasive about Alec's conversion as about Tess's seduction. After Alec has backtracked, his conversion is accounted for as being merely "whimsical," no more perhaps than "the mere freak of a careless man in search of a new sensation, and temporarily impressed by his mother's death" (p. 403). But this hardly accords with Alec's readiness to act on his newfound beliefs, or with the steady strenuousness of his life as a preacher, or with the reputation of being "an excellent, fiery, Christian man" (p. 379) that he has acquired by the time Tess meets him. What is suggested rather is his genuine aspiration to a new mode of being, an intense attempt to change his nature:

> It was less a reform than a transfiguration. The former curves of sensuousness were now modulated to lines of devotional passion. The lip-shapes that had meant seductiveness were now made to express supplication; the glow on the cheek that yesterday could be translated as riotousness was evangelized to-day into the splendour of pious rhetoric; animalism had become fanaticism; Paganism Paulinism; the bold rolling eye that had flashed upon [Tess's] form in the old time with such mastery now beamed with the rude energy of a theolatry that was almost ferocious. Those black angularities which his face had used to put on when his wishes were thwarted now did duty in picturing the incorrigible backslider who would insist upon turning again to his wallowing in the mire.
>
> The lineaments, as such, seemed to complain. They had been diverted from their hereditary connotation to signify impressions for which nature did not intend them. Strange that their very elevation was a misapplication, that to raise seemed to falsify. (pp. 383–84)

What this bespeaks is not whimsicality but an effort to yoke opposed qualities by violence together. Alec's "transfiguration" is reminiscent of Heathcliff's "transformation" when he returns to Wuthering Heights after his absence of three years: both men are so strongly cast in an original mold that nothing can change its outlines. When Alec's lineaments seem to complain, they are eloquent of his failure to integrate his new Paulinism with his old Paganism, to bring spirit into a proper and firm relation with flesh; and their "hereditary connotation" proclaims him fundamentally Sensual Man as before.[12]

Alec suddenly sees Tess while he is preaching, and the effect on him is "electric, far stronger than the effect of his presence upon her" (p. 384). What happens to him, that is, is analogous to what happens to Angel when Tess confesses to him: he is shocked back into an earlier mode of being. Within a few days "something of his old passion for her" revives; but, having only now discovered she has borne his child and not knowing she is married, he notably offers "to make the only reparation" he can and asks her to be his wife (p. 394). It is only after he learns she cannot marry him that, in a grotesque parody of his spiritual rebirth, "the corpses of those old fitful passions which had lain inanimate amid the lines of his face ever since his reformation [seem] to wake and come together as in a resurrection" (p. 403). One of the passions that now revive would seem to be his old passion for mastery, for he unguardedly reveals that an important component of his feeling for Tess is that she was not totally subdued by him: "Why I did not despise you was on account of your being un-smirched in spite of all," he tells her; "you withdrew yourself from me so quickly and resolutely when you saw the situation; you did not remain at my pleasure; so there was one petticoat in the world for whom I had no contempt, and you are she" (p. 402). The old compulsion clearly emerges later when, having given up his preaching "entirely" because of his feeling for her, he reappears in "the old jaunty, slap-dash guise" under which Tess first knew him (pp. 408–9); and after Tess has struck him in the face with her heavy leather glove and drawn blood, he takes hold of her "by the shoulders, so that she [shakes] under his grasp," and says, "Remember, my lady, I was your master once! I will be your master again. If you are any man's wife you are mine!" (p. 412).

After Angel deserts her, Tess is brought back to earth with a vengeance; and, reduced to hard physical labour in the swedefields of Flintcomb-Ash, she now lives in a place which is "bosomed with semi-globular tumuli—as if Cybele the Many-breasted were supinely extended there," and where are to be seen "myriads of loose white flints in bulbous, cusped, and phallic shapes" (pp. 355, 360). If Tess succeeds in resisting the temptation of going to Alec when he pursues her at Flintcomb-Ash, she is unable to withstand him after her father dies and she and her family are forced to leave their village home and seek refuge in a nearby town. When even the rooms they hope to rent in Kingsbere are not available to them, and the family is literally in the street, she finally succumbs to Alec's offer to provide for them. This is a new lease of life for her mother and the children, but, though she herself moves with Alec to "a stylish lodging-house" at Sandbourne (p. 464) and has all the material comfort she can want, we are to understand that the spirit goes out of her at this point. "These clothes are what he's put upon me: I didn't care what he did wi' me!" she tells Angel when he returns to England and seeks her out at Sandbourne; and Angel receives an impression then that Tess has "spiri-tually ceased to recognize the body before him as hers—allowing it to drift, like a corpse upon the current, in a direction dissociated from its living will" (pp. 466–67). Tess, of course, is laboring here under the shock of Angel's unexpected return and of the realization that "it is too late" (p. 466), but it is into her whole renewed relationship with Alec that she has, in effect, drifted as mere flesh, like a corpse. In agony she goes back to Alec, who is still in bed, and with "her lips . . . bleeding from the clench of her teeth upon them," says to him: "O, you have torn my life all to pieces . . . made me be what I prayed you in pity not to make me be again!

. . . My own true husband will never, never—O God—I can't bear this!—
I cannot!" (pp. 469–70). Tess's situation is tragic; but, wanting Angel and
having given herself to Alec (like Catherine caught between Heathcliff and
her husband in *Wuthering Heights*), it is she who has torn her life to
pieces—and breakdown is her only recourse. It is in a "moment of mad
grief," Angel later supposes, that "her mind [loses] its balance" and she
kills Alec in final desperate abandon (p. 475).

Tess then runs out after Angel in order to tell him what she has
done:

> By degrees he was inclined to believe that she had faintly attempted,
> at least, what she said she had done; and his horror at her impulse was mixed
> with amazement at the strength of her affection for himself, and at the
> strangeness of its quality, which had apparently extinguished her moral
> sense altogether. Unable to realize the gravity of her conduct she seemed at
> last content . . .
> It was very terrible if true; if a temporary hallucination, sad. But,
> anyhow, here was this deserted wife of his, this passionately-fond woman,
> clinging to him without a suspicion that he would be anything to her but a
> protector. He saw that for him to be otherwise was not, in her mind, within
> the region of the possible. Tenderness was absolutely dominant in Clare at
> last. He kissed her endlessly with his white lips, and held her hand, and
> said—
> 'I will not desert you! I will protect you by every means in my power,
> dearest love, whatever you may have done or not have done!' (p. 475)

It is a moving scene, as Tess, after all her suffering, finds acceptance at
last. But for her there is now nothing left except the week's happiness she
snatches with Angel before her arrest at Stonehenge. For Angel, as he
comes to believe that she has, at the least, attempted murder, the wheel
comes full circle in the rhythm of change, and he is now called on to
respond to a Tess whose "taint" is far worse than when he first rejected
her, a being whose "moral sense" seems to be altogether "extinguished."
What is remarkable is that he is equal to the occasion, his self-mastery
being attained now not through a cold self-control but a readiness to let
go. His instinctive reaction of horror at her deed is at once mediated by a
deeper understanding of what has led her to it. Faced by a supreme test,
Angel does not this time subdue substance to conception: taking "the
gravity of her conduct" into account, he nevertheless fully sets beside it
the woman who is clinging to him, accepting the "passionately-fond
woman" as his "deserted wife"; and it is now that woman in all the anguish
of her frailty and strength who is his first concern. This reconciliation of
hitherto contending forces in Angel is epitomized in the "tenderness" that
is "absolutely dominant" in him at last, in his tender kisses and protec-
tiveness, for it is in such tenderness that spirit bespeaks itself flesh and
flesh is made one with spirit.

Only now, when it is tragically too late, are Tess and Angel ready for full relationship. Within the house in which they take refuge there may be "affection, union, error forgiven," but outside is "the inexorable" (p. 481). The closing pages of the novel imply that for Angel there may still be left the possibility of a new union with Tess's younger sister. But when he joins hands with 'Liza-Lu after Tess's execution and "[goes] on," he leaves ruin behind him. Angel may be said to have found himself in the end, but the lives that have been lost are now irredeemable.

C HAPTER 5

The White Peacock
The Dislocation of Consciousness

Lawrence was disarmingly casual about the way he proposed to set about writing his first novel. He told Jessie Chambers, his girl friend at the time, that "the usual plan is to take two couples and develop their relationships": "Most of George Eliot's are on that plan. Anyhow, I don't want a plot, I should be bored with it. I shall try two couples for a start."[1] Emily Saxton and Cyril Beardsall, the narrator, would seem to have been one of the couples he had in mind for *The White Peacock*, but in the event their relationship is no more than vaguely adumbrated—these characters were to await their more vital reincarnation as Miriam Leivers and Paul Morel in *Sons and Lovers*—and the action is set in motion by the mechanics of a triangle, not of coupling, Lettie Beardsall being attracted to George Saxton when she is already involved with Leslie Tempest. And it is the figure of a triangle that impresses its shape on the three-part structure of the narrative: Part I moves to a seeming resolution of the triangle in the announcement of Lettie's engagement to Leslie; Part II charts her continued fluctuations between the two men prior to the wedding; Part III presents the results for all concerned of Lettie's marriage to Leslie.

In *Wuthering Heights*, *The Mill on the Floss*, and *Tess of the d'Urbervilles*, the novelists were at pains to detail the heroine's relationship with one man before the other appeared on the scene; and our points of departure were the relations between Cathy and Heathcliff, Maggie and Philip, and Tess and Alec. In *The White Peacock* the established relationship is that of Lettie and Leslie, but when she becomes interested in George, we know no more of her relations with Leslie than the one-page account of their meeting at the end of Chapter 1—an account that at first sight is perhaps most notable for being provided, in an early manifestation of the technical

89

insouciance (if not incompetence) that mars the novel, by an absentee narrator. In effect, therefore, Lawrence develops the two relationships *pari passu*, and there is no sharp movement of the heroine from one man to the other; but, as in the other texts, the two men are presented as opposites, and Lettie's indecision between them figures an unresolved opposition within her.

Michael Squires, also linking Lawrence with George Eliot and Thomas Hardy, points to a connection between *The White Peacock* and "the early 'pastoral' novels" of these writers: "All the novels reveal the same structural pattern, the same kind of human conflict: a young woman living in the country is forced to choose between two dissimilar suitors, one rural and one urban. In each novel the motivation for much of the action lies in the conflict that this double attraction ignites in the lives of its characters."[2] The novels of George Eliot and Hardy to which Squires refers are *Adam Bede* and *Silas Marner*, and *Under the Greenwood Tree*, *Far from the Madding Crowd*, and *The Woodlanders;* and the structural pattern he describes makes an interesting parallel to that analyzed in this study, though in its repeated resolution of conflict it is distinct from the figure presented here. But it does not seem to me that the opposition between the rural and the urban throws much light on the central opposition in *The White Peacock* even though George is a farmer and Leslie an industrialist. Certainly Lettie's conflict may more usefully be discussed in other terms.

The terms suggested are those provided by Lawrence himself. In a letter written to Bertrand Russell, Lawrence said:

> I have been reading Frazer's *Golden Bough* and *Totemism and Exogamy.* Now I am convinced of what I believed when I was about twenty—that there is another seat of consciousness than the brain and the nerve system: there is a blood-consciousness which exists in us independently of the ordinary mental consciousness, which depends on the eye as its source or connector. There is the blood-consciousness, with the sexual connection holding the same relation as the eye, in seeing, holds to the mental consciousness. One lives, knows, and has one's being in the blood, without any reference to nerves and brain. This is one half of life, belonging to the darkness. And the tragedy of this our life, and of your life, is that the mental and nerve consciousness exerts a tyranny over the blood-consciousness and that your will has gone completely over to the mental consciousness, and is engaged in the destruction of your blood-being or blood-consciousness, the final liberating of the one, which is only death in result.[3]

Lawrence is also on record as saying that he "began [*The White Peacock*] at twenty";[4] and so what he "believed" when he was "about twenty" and later expressed in discursive terms to Russell may be regarded as relevant to the thematic concerns of the novel—and indeed proves to be at its heart. George and Leslie are men in whom "blood-consciousness" and "mental consciousness," respectively, are predominant; and Lettie veers between giving preponderance to one or the other of these aspects of her nature. Mental consciousness, which most of us are habituated to living in, may be said to speak for itself as a term, and defines itself in the novel in repeated (indeed wearying) passages of talk. Blood-consciousness is both more subtly and more powerfully evoked, perhaps as effectively as anywhere in a simple description of work in the fields. Cyril reports how he one day helps George scatter manure over the "bare red fields":

> Beneath us, the spires of the poplars in the spinney were warm gold, as if the blood shone through. . . . There was nothing in this grey, lonely world but the peewits swinging and crying, and George swinging silently at his work. The movement of active life held all my attention, and when I looked up, it was to see the motion of his limbs and his head, the rise and fall of his rhythmic body, and the rise and fall of the slow waving peewits. (p. 218)[5]

George's movements as he works are not a product of the mental consciousness—if they were directed by the mind, it is not unlikely they would be botched—but of what Lawrence means by blood-consciousness: unconstrained, George rhythmically scatters the manure, "without any reference to nerves and brain." What is concretized here is "blood-being," natural, untrammeled existence in the flesh, as the parallel between the swinging "rise and fall" of George's body and that of the peewits emphasizes; and it is a condition, even outside of "the sexual connection," in which the blood shines through—as with the poplars—directly informing the substance of being.

Lawrence's claim in the letter to Russell that the mental consciousness "exerts a tyranny" over the blood-consciousness is expressive of his sense of how a sustained Pauline insistence on the primacy of the spirit over the flesh had ultimately made for the "tragedy" of modern life—for the dominance of mental consciousness over blood-consciousness. But his assertion that "one lives, knows, and has one's being in the blood" should not be taken, as it still sometimes is, to represent his adherence to a religion of blood—as if he were seeking to counter St. Paul by inverting him. He may seem on occasion to glorify the blood, and certainly the most vivid moments in *The White Peacock* pulse to it, but he is unswerving in his view that blood-consciousness is no more than "one half of life," and his ideal is a wholeness or fullness of being that integrates both kinds of consciousness. "We are creatures of two halves," he said, "spiritual and sensual—and each half is as important as the other. . . . It is halfness, or partness, which causes Judas";[6] but he also believed that "the effort to mate spirit with body, body with spirit, is the crying confusion and pain of our times."[7] It is Lettie's misfortune to be paired with men who have not achieved wholeness; and it is her "tragedy" that she herself cannot bring body and mind together—that in her they are dislocated, as it were, one tending to take the place of the other.

In *The White Peacock* Lawrence set the tale of his lovers in the countryside in which he himself loved to roam as a boy and young man, and the descriptions of nature in this first novel are as sharply meticulous and passionately evocative as comparable passages in the later work. It was this aspect of the novel which most impressed its first readers and reviewers—Jessie Chambers reports how Lawrence proudly told her that "some of the descriptions of nature were considered equal to those in Hardy's *Tess of the d'Urbervilles*"[8]—and which still elicits the greatest praise.[9] But these descriptions, impressive though they may be in their own right, are also functional: the rhythmic movement of the seasons which is so carefully charted is not only the *raison d'être* for the changing rhythms of work in the fields at Strelley Mill; it provides a natural counterpart to the ebb and flow of Lettie's feeling for George and Leslie, validating it in a larger context than that of personal idiosyncrasy. Cyril's rendering of the "spirit of place" in the opening paragraph, moreover, suggests that the novelist's imaginative grasp of his material is unwavering and effectively links the human drama to its setting:

> I stood watching the shadowy fish slide through the gloom of the mill-pond. They were grey, descendants of the silvery things that had darted away from the monks, in the young days when the valley was lusty. The whole place was gathered in the musing of old age. The thick-piled trees on the far shore were too dark and sober to dally with the sun; the weeds stood crowded and motionless. Not even a little wind flickered the willows of the islets. The water lay softly, intensely still. Only the thin stream falling through the mill-race murmured to itself of the tumult of life which had once quickened the valley. (p. 1)

This evocation of a reigning inertia might seem to be designed merely as an appropriate setting for George, who at once makes his appearance, and whose life (Cyril proceeds to inform him) is "nothing else but a doss" (p. 1). The description, however, also emphasizes the pale thinning of life in the valley, the replacement of the once lusty, silvery fish by their shadowy, grey descendants and the substitution of the murmur of a meager stream for the former "tumult of life"; and what this points to is not only the diminished life of George but of Lettie and Leslie as well, the kind of diminished life that in its falling short of wholeness is to be the focus of the tale to follow.[10]

Nor is it in the descriptions of nature alone that the presence of a major writer is revealed. Though *The White Peacock* is in a number of respects immature work, so immature, it once seemed to me, that I did not include it in a book-length study of Lawrence, I have come to realize that

Lawrence's early insights into the disintegrative effects of "partness" nonetheless warrant the closest attention. But then we have to grant that the novel exists in its own right, and refuse to be distracted by portents of what is to come, however tempting it may be, for instance, to discuss the novelist's unconscious homosexuality or the gamekeeper motif. Viewing *The White Peacock*, moreover, in the perspective established by the structural pattern studied here, enables one to see that it is not George who is its major protagonist, as he is generally held to be; and so to do justice— for all the extraneous matter that clings to this first novel—to its firm center in Lettie.

II

The opening description that we are given of Lettie is rather perfunctory, but it contains one striking detail: "She was tall, nearly six feet in height, but slenderly formed. Her hair was yellow, tending towards a dun brown. She had beautiful eyes and brows, but not a nice nose. Her hands were very beautiful" (p. 8). Lettie should possibly qualify as the tallest heroine in the English novel, but if she is statuesque, she abundantly possesses blood-being. Like George in the field with the peewits, she is consequently at one with nature, "[glinting] on like a flower" when she moves "brightly through the green hazels" (p. 9). At the same time, Lettie—like Maggie Tulliver—is a woman with a mind; and though she is proud of her physical appearance, even a little vain, she seems to place the highest value on her mind, saying, in a conversation with George, that she knows how a man will compliment her by the way he looks at her, and suggesting that a discriminating man will respond more to her mind than her body: "Some look at my hair, some watch the rise and fall of my breathing, some look at my neck, and a few—not you among them—look me in the eyes for my thoughts" (p. 26).

In her relations with George, Lettie is both compelled by his physical presence, rousing to it in spite of herself, and made fearful by it. This is forcefully conveyed in a number of fine scenes. On one occasion he comes into the room when she is playing the piano at the farm:

> He asked her why she didn't play something with a tune in it, and this caused her to turn round in her chair to give him a withering answer. His appearance, however, scattered her words like startled birds. He had come straight from washing in the scullery, to the parlour, and he stood behind Lettie's chair, unconcernedly wiping the moisture from his arms. His sleeves were rolled up to the shoulder, and his shirt was opened wide at the breast. Lettie was somewhat taken aback by the sight of him standing with legs apart, dressed in dirty leggings and boots, and breeches torn at the knee, naked at the breast and arms.

"Why don't you play something with a tune in it?" he repeated, rubbing the towel over his shoulders beneath the shirt.

"A tune?" she echoed, watching the swelling of his arms as he moved them, and the rise and fall of his breasts, wonderfully solid and white. Then having curiously examined the sudden meeting of the sunhot skin with the white flesh in his throat, her eyes met his, and she turned again to the piano, while the colour grew in her ears, mercifully sheltered by a profusion of bright curls. (pp. 13–14)

The scene epitomizes the relationship of Lettie and George. When she turns to him, girding her mind to make her "withering answer," she is ready to do what she repeatedly does in fact—to shrivel him up in the hot scorn of her superior intellect. But his appearance, so markedly full and firm of flesh, "scatters her words," seems for a time to annul mental consciousness, consuming it in a different kind of flame, so that the highly articulate, verbal Lettie can do no more than "echo" his words. What *she* "watches" in compliment to him, moreover, is "the swelling of his arms" and "the rise and fall of his breasts"; and when "the colour grows in her ears," the fiery blood speaks in her eyes, not her thoughts: George looks at her "with glowing brown eyes, as if in hesitating challenge," and she "[answers] his challenge with a blue blaze of her eyes" (p. 14). Lettie differentiates George and herself from Cyril, saying to George, "We do not burn our bodies in our heads—or our hearts, do we?" (p. 94); what the scene at the piano dramatizes is the way such a process may be reversed—and Lettie seems both to want and to dread this.

If Lettie's mind is routed in this scene, she shows that it is able to bound back when, on another occasion, she and George look together at a reproduction of Maurice Greiffenhagen's "Idyll" (pp. 28–30). He is roused by the painting, looks at Lettie "with glowing eyes," and "[lights] up curiously," responding particularly to the painter's presentation of the girl, who is "half afraid" in the face of the man's passion. Lettie is at first mockingly disparaging—"She may well be half afraid," she says, "when the barbarian comes out in his glory, skins and all"—but then, when the "unappeased fire in [George's] breast" rises to his eyes, she seems to be overcome by a similar fear herself: "Having become a few degrees calmer, he looked up at her now, his eyes wide and vivid with a declaration that made her shrink back as if flame had leaped towards her face." She evades his eyes in fear, but when they thereafter look "nakedly" at each other and force themselves to undergo the "dazzled, shrinking pain" that this involves, "their veins [are filled] with fluid, fiery electricity" as her blood is finally charged. It is not her thoughts that she now wants George to look for:

At the door she turned. She must steal another keen moment: "Are you admiring my strength?" she asked. Her pose was fine. With her head thrown back, the roundness of her throat ran finely down to the bosom, which swelled above the pile of books held by her straight arms. He looked at her. Their lips smiled curiously. She put back her throat as if she were drinking. They felt the blood beating madly in their necks. (p. 29)

But Lettie is not ready to submit to the madly beating blood—it is "a mad impulse" that "seizes on" Stephen Guest, we recall, when he showers kisses on Maggie Tulliver's arm—and she suddenly leaves the room. When she comes back, she is "talking madly to herself in French," and no matter what George says to her, she answers "in the same mad clatter of French, speaking high and harshly" (pp. 29–30). Lettie thus sets her mad clatter against the mad blood—and succeeds in countermanding it; though when she says goodbye to him, her voice is "full of insurgent tenderness" (p. 30).

If the relationship of Lettie and George is anchored in the blood, that of Lettie and Leslie is founded on the word. Banter is a feature of their relations, this note being sounded clearly on their first appearance together. Leslie pretends he is asleep, and Lettie tickles his nose with a twig:

> "Lettie! I was dreaming of kisses!"
>
> "On the bridge of your nose?" laughed she—"But whose were the kisses?"
>
> "Who produced the sensation?" he smiled.
>
> "Since I only tapped your nose you should dream of—"
>
> "Go on!" said he, expectantly.
>
> "Of Doctor Slop," she replied, smiling to herself as she closed her parasol.
>
> "I do not know the gentleman," he said, afraid that she was laughing at him.
>
> "No—your nose is quite classic," she answered, giving him one of those brief intimate glances with which women flatter men so cleverly. He radiated with pleasure. (pp. 9–10)

Leslie is no match for the quicker and brighter Lettie, who quite undoes him with her witty literary allusion, but he is better able to engage in the game than George, and enters into it "expectantly." Where it is the flame of passion that engenders fear in the encounters between Lettie and George, here it is the thrust of ridicule, which Leslie is "afraid" he is unable to parry. Some time later he calls her "a little tease" (p. 80), and this is evidently a role that she readily adopts: in this instance she not only tickles his nose with her twig but his vanity with her praise, being teasingly willing to appear to promise more than she is in reality disposed to give. This is partly because in relation to him she seems to be most interested in self-gratification, in tickling herself, so to speak, for we note how she "smiles to herself" as she makes her joke about Doctor Slop. And though she lights Leslie up, making him "radiate with pleasure," the "brief intimate glance" she gives him (in contradistinction to the looks she exchanges with George) comes straight from the calculating mind, for she is "cleverly" intent on "flattering" him.

When Lettie and Leslie make love, they characteristically make words, he even being impelled to ask her what she is "making so many words about" (p. 86):

> Twisting a curl round his finger, one of those loose curls that always dance free from the captured hair, Leslie said:
> "Look how fond your hair is of me; look how it twines round my finger. Do you know, your hair—the light in it is like—oh—buttercups in the sun."
> "It is like me—it won't be kept in bounds," she replied.
> "Shame if it were—like this, it brushes my face—so—and sets me tingling like music."
> "Behave! Now be still, and I'll tell you what sort of music you make."
> "Oh—well—tell me."
> "Like the calling of throstles and blackies, in the evening, frightening the pale little wood-anemones, till they run panting and swaying right up to our wall. Like the ringing of bluebells when the bees are at them; like Hippomenes, out-of-breath, laughing because he'd won." (p. 84)

And so on for another page and a half, with references to Atalanta, to Eve, to the "Blessed Damozel," to the Pre-Raphaelites, and to Horace following fast and furious. Though Leslie says he thinks "there's more in the warm touch of a soft body than in a prayer" and that he will "pray with kisses," what more immediately seems to attract him to Lettie is her cleverness: "—you are clever, you are rare," he declares with delight when she embroiders one of his allusions (pp. 84–85). And indeed when he is finally put to it to define her desirability as a wife, it is her social utility that strikes him first: "You'll make a fine wife, Lettie," he says, "able to entertain, and all that." Nor is he outdone by her self-preoccupation in relation to him: "Let me look at myself in your eyes," he says—and she is not slow to mention Narcissus (p. 86).

But Leslie, it should be noted, also has a firm physicality. He has a "fine, lithe physique, suggestive of much animal vigour"; his "person" is "exceedingly attractive"; and one is said to feel pleasure when one watches him "move about" (p. 44). Nor is his blood congealed, for he tells Cyril that it "jumps afire" when he remembers Lettie's kisses, though he feels compelled to add: "You know, I don't think she feels for me as I do for her" (p. 106). And that is the trouble. Able to titillate her mind, he is unable in the irrational and mysterious ways of blood-being to warm her blood, and he is forced to recognize that to him she is "a cold little lover" (p. 83). It is not Leslie but the flattering self-image he can command for her that kindles Lettie, as becomes evident in the look they exchange at the Christmas party at Highclose. She makes "a stir" there, being "decidedly the most distinguished" among the "little belles of the countryside": "Leslie was enraptured, ostentatious in his admiration, proud of being so well infatuated. They looked into each other's eyes when they met, both triumphant, excited, blazing arch looks at one another. Lettie was enjoying her public demonstration immensely; it exhilarated her into quite a vivid love for him" (p. 101). It is with a blaze of self-gratification that they archly shine for each other.

Lettie's relationship with Leslie is thus sharply distinguished from her connection with George, and the differences are accentuated when the three of them are brought together, as in the rabbit chase, for instance. The chase takes place in a chapter entitled "The Scent of Blood," and the scene nicely illustrates the workings of blood-consciousness. One day Leslie, Lettie, and Cyril come upon George and his father mowing corn. Suddenly one of the rabbits that infest the Saxton fields bursts from the standing corn, and the men set off after it "full pelt":

> The bewildered little brute, scared by Leslie's wild running and crying, turned from its course, and dodged across the hill . . . The little wretch was hard pressed; George rushed upon it. It darted into some fallen corn, but he had seen it, and had fallen on it. In an instant he was up again, and the little creature was dangling from his hand.
>
> We returned, panting, sweating, our eyes flashing, to the edge of the standing corn. . . . (p. 49)

If Lawrence remarked in the letter to Russell that the eye is the "source or connector" of the mental consciousness and the "sexual connection" that of the blood-consciousness, the numerous instances referred to above make it clear that the eye as reflector is as revelatory of blood as mind; and the "flashing" eyes of the men here is one overt sign of how their blood is roused when they join in the chase. The scene impels a recognition of the existence within the individual psyche of dark destructive forces as well as the more genial elements to which the mild harvest setting would naturally seem to give rise. And the responses of Leslie and George are at once differentiated. Leslie's blood does not propel him to effective action, for the excess of his "wild running and crying" proves to be self-defeating. George, however, responds with an instinctive sureness and control to the impulsions of the chase.

Cyril becomes the focus of the following episode when he sees another rabbit, and goes after it:

> If I could have let myself fall on it I could have caught it, but this was impossible to me, and I merely prevented its dashing through the hole into safety. . . . As I walked round I caught sight of [another] rabbit skulking

near the bottom corner of the patch. Its ears lay pressed against its back; I could see the palpitation of the heart under the brown fur, and I could see the shining dark eyes looking at me. I felt no pity for it, but still I could not actually hurt it. I beckoned to the father. He ran up, and aimed a blow with the rake. There was a sharp little cry which sent a hot pain through me as if I had been cut. But the rabbit ran out, and instantly I forgot the cry, and gave pursuit, fairly feeling my fingers stiffen to choke it. It was all lame. Leslie was upon it in a moment, and he almost pulled its head off in his excitement to kill it. (pp. 49–50)

Cyril's reactions exemplify that strife between the two modes of consciousness which is the burden of the novel. His initial squeamishness is an inhibitory product of the mind, which prevents his body from doing what it could well do, incapacitating it and so making it "impossible" for him to fall on the rabbit. The father's blow, however, draws blood, for Cyril feels the rabbit's pain as his own, as if he has "been cut." When the rabbit runs out, the scent of blood becomes irresistible, and with blood-consciousness seeming to rise ineluctably and swamp mental consciousness—it is what we have seen happen in some of Lettie's encounters with George—Cyril joins in the chase, "forgets" the rabbit's cry, and aches now with the desire to choke it, directly responding to the blood in his stiffening fingers. It is Leslie, however, who consummates the kill, but once more we note the excess of his response, his blood lust, as he almost pulls the rabbit's head off.

The discussion that follows the scene in the fields is as revealing as the chase itself:

George began, in that deliberate voice that so annoyed Emily:
"It does make you mad, though, to touch the fur, and not be able to grab him"—he laughed quietly.
Emily moved off in disgust. Lettie opened her mouth sharply to speak, but remained silent.
"I don't know," said Leslie. "When it comes to killing it goes against the stomach."
"If you can run," said George, "you should be able to run to death. When your blood's up, you don't hang half way."
"I think a man is horrible," said Lettie, "who can tear the head off a little mite of a thing like a rabbit, after running it in torture over a field." . . .
"Well," said George, "what's the good finicking! If you feel like doing a thing—you'd better do it."
"Unless you haven't courage," said Emily, bitingly.
He looked up at her with dark eyes, suddenly full of anger.
"But," said Lettie—she could not hold herself from asking, "don't you think it's brutal, now—now that you *do* think—isn't it degrading and mean to run the poor little things down?"
"Perhaps it is," he replied, "but it wasn't an hour ago." (pp. 51–52)

Though the issue here is the killing of rabbits, what the protagonists say is expressive of fundamental attitudes and has a direct bearing on the development of their relations. In the light of the gusto with which he pounces on the rabbit, Leslie's assertion that "it goes against the stomach" to kill is a blatant falsification, a disavowal of what has been proved on his own pulses—and this is precisely what his marriage becomes. As it does for Lettie, who seems more particularly to have Leslie in mind when she pronounces that "a man" who can tear the head off a rabbit is "horrible," though she will prove able to discount her revulsion in more important respects than this. Her insistence here on "thinking," moreover, is representative of her tendency to set the mind up over the blood, a tendency that proves to be crucial in her relations with both men. At the same time her condemnation of the chase (which has inevitable sexual overtones) betrays a shrinking from the bare reality which George forces on her, her fear showing through its moral covering. George, in contradistinction to Leslie, stolidly refuses to color the reality he has experienced. His account of what happens when one's "blood is up" is not only substantiated by what has actually taken place in the cornfield, perhaps most strikingly in the case of the usually bloodless Cyril; it also establishes him, on this occasion at least, as the one most directly in harmony with his instinctual life. His quiet insistence, furthermore, that the pursuit of a rabbit makes one "mad" implicitly grants the nonrational drive at work—and we remember, though Lettie may not, the blood that beats madly in her neck when she steals her keen moment with him. He is also the only one to acknowledge the differing perspectives produced by the two kinds of consciousness, being prepared to grant that the chase may be viewed as "degrading and mean" when abstracted from its particular time and place and circumstance, but standing by the truth of the lived moment.

It is a major irony of the novel, however, that though George does not "hang half way" where a rabbit is concerned, he proves to be decidedly "finicky" when the object of the chase is a woman. Certainly in regard to Lettie he does not do what he feels like doing, and his sister's kind remark is intended to remind him of the fact. Not that he is lacking in courage, as she implies. His blood flows smooth and true, but it is channeled by the mind into self-mistrust, a mistrust that becomes habitual, virtually instinctive: his "energy and passion" are "normally . . . bound down by his caution and self-instinct" (p. 140). It is his concern with self that allows the initiative to pass to his rival, for George's failure with Lettie is immediately attributable to a fatal hesitancy on his part, to a dread of being rejected by her which prevents him from acting until it is too late. His self-mistrust, his inability to risk himself, is linked in the narrative with a general fear of being humiliated: the encounter with Annable, for instance, in which he is ignominiously knocked down by the gamekeeper but which he begs Cyril to keep secret, is a clear intimation of this inhibiting anxiety.

Despite Lettie's apparent disgust, the rabbit chase is in fact a means of bringing her and George together. Prior to the chase, George's rhythmic mowing has excited her admiration, Lettie being moved to touch George's arm, drawing her finger-tips along "the smooth brown muscle" and then, revealingly, hiding "her hand into the folds of her skirt, blushing" (p. 48). Lettie's blood, whether or not she admits it, is then further aroused by the killing of the rabbits. Heightened blood-consciousness, however, is not only a sign of increased sexual awareness but itself generates a deep response to the natural world, a general quickening and relatedness. Shortly after the conversation quoted above, the young people go for a stroll and watch the moon rise. ". . . washed off [their] feet in a vague sea of moonlight," their reactions are neatly discriminated: "Lettie was glad, a little bit exalted. . . ; Leslie was frowning, oblivious, and George was thinking, and the terrible, immense moonbeams braided through his feeling" (p. 54). Leslie's obliviousness here is the self-betraying obverse of his excessive excitement during the chase, and it is set against the way Lettie and George stir in common connection with the cosmos. Their need, by this time, for some sort of sexual release is imperative, and when Leslie, oblivious too to Lettie's mood, refuses her invitation to dance a polka on the wet grass, she dances first with Cyril and then with George:

> . . . in a moment they were bounding across the grass. After a few steps she fell in with him, and they spun round the grass. It was true, he leaped, sprang with large strides, carrying her with him. It was a tremendous, irresistible dancing. Emily and I must join, making an inner ring. Now and again there was a sense of something white flying near, and wild rustle of draperies, and a swish of disturbed leaves as they whirled past us. Long after we were tired they danced on.
>
> At the end, he looked big, erect, nerved with triumph, and she was exhilarated like a Bacchante.
>
> "Have you finished?" Leslie asked.
>
> She knew she was safe from his question that day. (p. 55)

The directly sexual nature of the dance is strongly emphasized, and it is also symbolic of what seems to be a natural affinity between Lettie and George: Leslie is left a disconsolate onlooker as the triangle bursts asunder and George carries Lettie with him in the irresistible dancing. But he proves to be unable to carry her with him outside of the dance—and she is not always prepared to trust to her blood, as the subsequent development of her relations with both men shows.

III

Lettie encompasses her fate through a series of willed negations of her own deepest feelings. As she veers between the two men, she becomes "very wilful," and then, crucially, seems to opt for the mind as a *modus operandi:* "she, who had always been so rippling in thoughtless life, sat down in the window-sill to think, and her strong teeth bit at her handkerchief till it was torn in holes. She would say nothing to me; she read all things that dealt with modern women" (pp. 73–74). As her thoughts bite home, it seems clear what sort of choice a modern woman should make. The life of a farmer's wife, for one thing, would seem to rule itself out; and so when George finally summons up courage, some time after her official engagement to Leslie, and tells her that he plans to "take a farm in Canada" and wants her "to set out with," she at first fences with him flippantly, but then says it would be "impossible," given how she is "fixed," and adds: "You know it is—Look at me now, and say if it's not impossible—a farmer's wife—with you in Canada" (p. 166). George, in his self-mistrust, collapses into acquiescence; but farming is not at issue, and in placing the reality of her connection with him in this context, she not only distorts it but defrauds herself. She even seems to be aware of this—"No, I won't come down [to tea]," she says to George, "—let me say farewell—'jamque Vale! Do you remember how Eurydice sank back into Hell?" (p. 213); but she insists on the farewell nonetheless. Both she and Cyril, moreover, place the blame for her parting from George squarely on him, Lettie talking at him when she declares that "you can generally get what you want if you want it badly enough" (p. 188), and Cyril pinpointing his failure as due to his being "afraid to make the struggle, to rouse himself to decide the question for her" (p. 208). Though it is true that George hangs back prior to Lettie's announcement of her engagement to Leslie, he does subsequently make a number of attempts to win her—and if she wants to be compelled by him, what she does is effectively to rebuff him.

It is shortly before her marriage to Leslie that Lettie talks about sinking back into Hell, and on the same occasion she suggests to George that they walk together into the wood. They are met everywhere by signs of natural fecundity: the ridings are "knee deep" in forget-me-nots; hyacinths droop "magnificently with an overweight of purple," or stand "pale and erect, like unripe ears of purple corn"; "heavy" bees are "intoxicated even with the sight of so much blue," and swing in "clinging, clambering riot" (p. 213). Lettie seems urged to riot herself, repeatedly seeking physical contact with George: she ruffles his hair, leaves her hand lying on his knee, gives him her hand to clasp in his, and putting her hand in his, leans softly against him (pp. 213–14). Though she acts freely, she nevertheless insists that she is not free, declaring rather histrionically that, if the "threads of [her] life" were once "untwined," now "another has caught them up": ". . . the chord of my life is being twisted, and I cannot wrench it free and untwine it again—I can't. I am not strong enough" (p. 214). But George is now too roused to be put off by metaphor, and makes his most passionate declaration of love to her:

> "No, Lettie," he pleaded, with terror and humility. "No, Lettie; don't go. What should I do with my life? Nobody would love you like I do—and what should I do with my love for you?—hate it and fear it, because it's too much for me?"
>
> She turned and kissed him gratefully. He then took her in a long, passionate embrace, mouth to mouth. In the end it had so wearied her that she could only wait in his arms till he was too tired to hold her. He was trembling already.
>
> "Poor Meg!" she murmured to herself dully, her sensations having become vague.
>
> He winced, and the pressure of his arms slackened. She loosened his hands and rose half dazed from her seat by him. She left him, while he sat dejected, raising no protest. (p. 215)

This is the climactic moment of Lettie's relationship with George. She is now given a chance to climb out of the Hell into which she feels she is sinking—just as Maggie Tulliver in relation to Stephen Guest has the opportunity to leap out of "the chill dark cavern" in which she finds herself and return to "the life-nourishing day." But Lettie allows the chance to slip through her fingers because she wills herself into being deaf to what her blood-consciousness tells her, just as, analogously, Maggie allows "her mind to recoil" and swing her back into the cavern. Here George both talks and acts strongly, and yet Lettie will not allow this to be enough—even though she is quite overcome by his embrace, and though she is as much overcome by the knowledge the passionate kiss conveys. "Poor Meg," she says, registering the unhappiness that George, loving her as he does with all his being, will doom Meg to by marrying her. And "poor Leslie," she might have murmured as well, for she has not been an unwilling partner in the embrace, has even provoked it, showing unequivocally how much she wants George even while insisting she is bound to Leslie. Though George characteristically "slackens" and accepts her departure, she in turn must be assumed to submerge the truth of that kiss in her sense of the superior attainments, social position, and wealth of Leslie and of her commitment to him, for she proceeds to marry him in spite of it. It is somewhat like Catherine Earnshaw and Heathcliff and Edgar Linton, as a number of critics have remarked.[11]

It is not only *Wuthering Heights* that *The White Peacock* recalls at this point. Alec d'Urberville, we remember, is said to have "touches of barbarism" in the contours of his face; and George makes Lettie "wince" when he holds out "his inflamed, barbaric hands" by way of justifying his refusal to join her prewedding pastoral tea-party. It is the kind of shrinking in Lettie that we have noted before, and it is repeated when George is ultimately persuaded to join the group: she then turns her head away from the sight of "his thick, half-washed fingers fumbling over the fruits," while the "talk [bubbles] and [froths] over . . . the cups" (p. 229). But it is not from his barbaric hands alone that she recoils; she turns away too from a love that could perhaps give meaning to her life.

In her relations with Leslie, Lettie similarly and climactically disavows the revelations of the blood, though what is revealed to her is of negative rather than positive import, as with George. Once during their engagement she proposes that he spend the night at her house, and they look at each other "with wide, smiling eyes—like children on the brink of a stolen pleasure" (p. 172). That evening he seems "to emanate a warmth of physical comfort and pleasure"; and the warmth is suggestive of an overall vitality, for it generates "a certain glow" that "[enhances] his words" as well as his laughter and his movements (p. 173). The next morning she does not join him at breakfast, and when she comes downstairs to say goodbye to him, she keeps her face "half averted" and will "not look at him." Within an hour he returns, and the following conversation takes place:

> "You—are you—are you angry with me?" he faltered.
> Tears suddenly came to her eyes.
> "What did you come back for?" she said, averting her face from him. He looked at her.
> "I knew you were angry—and—" he hesitated.
> "Why didn't you go away?" she said impulsively. He hung his head and was silent.
> "I don't see why—why it should make trouble between us, Lettie," he faltered. She made a swift gesture of repulsion, whereupon, catching sight of her hand, she hid it swiftly against her skirt again.
> "You make my hands—my very hands disclaim me," she struggled to say.
> He looked at her clenched fist pressed against the folds of her dress.
> "But—," he began, much troubled.
> "I tell you, I can't bear the sight of my own hands," she said in low, passionate tones.
> "But surely, Lettie, there's no need—if you love me—"
> She seemed to wince. He waited, puzzled and miserable.
> "And we're going to be married, aren't we?" he resumed, looking pleadingly at her.

She stirred, and exlaimed:
"Oh, why don't you go away? What did you come back for?"
(pp. 175–76)

Leslie's obvious bewilderment at her reception of him, his inability to understand the change in her, would seem to rule out any overt sexual failure on his part, and certainly the description of him the night before would not seem designed to prepare us for that. What his questions convey, as he struggles to make sense of her attitude, is that he believes her to be upset—he thinks unreasonably—by the mere fact of their illicit intercourse. Her refusal to look at him, however, suggests rather that there is something she does not want to face in relation to him. Her "gesture of repulsion" seems to indicate that he repels her physically, but her feeling is more complex than this implies. It is her own hands that she says "disclaim her," her own hands that she "can't bear the sight of," and it is when she sees her own hand that she "hides it swiftly against her skirt" (a gesture that is forcefully contrasted with the way she hides her hand after touching George's arm in the instance previously referred to). Both her words and her actions, that is, suggest that she is filled with self-disgust; and perhaps the best commentary on her feeling is that offered by Tess Durbeyfield's self-hatred in an analogous situation. Tess, we remember, was filled with a sense of loathing after she broke away from Alec and admitted to herself that she had lived with him as his mistress without loving him. And that, we infer, is what Lettie, after all her hesitations in regard to Leslie, has now discovered, what her blood has now made incontrovertibly clear to her—that she does not love him, and cannot respond physically to him. He inadvertently (and perhaps overconfidently) diagnoses what is wrong when he says, "But surely, Lettie, there's no need—if you love me—" and her seeming "to wince" in response (this now being a different kind of shrinking from that evoked by George) tells everything. Yet she is now doubly his.

Lettie does make an effort to break with Leslie, but by then he is recovering from serious injury as a result of a motor accident, and her position is the more difficult in that the accident was caused by his swerving to avoid her. She tells him that she is not sure she "ought to marry" him, and finally asks him to let her go:

"You mean you don't love me?"
"Love—love—I don't know anything about it. But I can't—we can't be—don't you see—oh, what do they say—flesh of one flesh."
"Why?" he whispered, like a child that is told some tale of mystery.
She looked at him, as he lay propped upon his elbow, turning towards hers his white face of fear and perplexity, like a child that cannot understand, and is afraid, and wants to cry. Then slowly tears gathered full in her eyes, and she wept from pity and despair. (pp. 195–96)

Lettie's refusal to refer to the spirit that has failed to animate the flesh constitutes a "mystery" for him because, in his obliviousness (and we remember his responses in the moonlit field), he is not even aware of any incapacity on her part. And it is not only in his inability to understand that he is "like a child"; he betrays an utterly childlike dependence on her, allowing the tears to "[run] down his cheeks" when he asks her if she does not want him "now," in his injured state, though she has previously assured him the problem has to do with herself, not him (pp. 195–96). His unmanning distress, however, is too much for Lettie, and unable to hurt him, responding to him in a way that is not unlike Cyril's initial reaction to the rabbit in the cornfield, she puts her arms round him and finally commits herself to him. But what the price of her support of him—of such an abrogation of the blood—is likely to be is intimated by the end of the scene: "Oh—do you want to go away from me again?" Leslie suddenly asks; and she replies, "No—only my arm is dead," and she draws it "from beneath him, standing up, swinging it, smiling because it [hurts] her" (p. 196).

Lettie marries Leslie, and one measure of her lack of fulfillment is that she can "never quite let [George] be," and that she is subject to "a driving force" that impels her "against her will to interfere in his life" (p. 292). When she returns to Eberwich, it is true she desists from visiting him at his home after he is married because Meg proves to be "too antagonistic," but she keeps up the friendship with him "in spite of all things," and he visits her at Highclose "perhaps once in a fortnight." Some ten years after she first announced her engagement to Leslie, she seems to be no less engaged by George; and while she lets Leslie "forget her birthday" and so be away from home on the occasion, "for some unknown reason, she [lets] the intelligence slip to George," whom she invites to dinner. And ten years after the engagement, they still have much the same effect on each other: "Immediately George saw her his eyes wakened with a dark glow. She stood up as he entered, her hand stretched straight out to him, her body very erect, her eyes bright and rousing, like two blue pennants" (p. 295). But by then the knowledge of what they have made of their lives has bitten into both of them, and when Lettie's children leave the room, "the smile [dies] from their faces" and they look down "sadly," being "very still and heavy with melancholy" (p. 297).

George says that he looks "to marriage" to set him busy on his "house of life, something whole and complete, of which it will supply the design" (p. 235); but the very foundation of his life is undermined when he marries Meg though still in love with Lettie. Years later he tacitly admits his responsibility for the failure of his marriage, unknowingly establishing a parallel between himself and Lettie in relation to her husband: "I can't give [Meg] any of the real part of me," he tells Cyril, "the vital part that she wants—I can't, any more than you could give kisses to a stranger" (p. 298). The result is that Meg, who is "secure in her high maternity," humiliates him and is "hostile to his wishes" (p. 272); and he feels "like a vacuum . . . all loose in the middle of a space of darkness, that's pressing on you" (p. 284). Without marriage as a firm base from which to operate, moreover, George cannot really make a success of anything else, Lawrence's depiction of his failure serving to concretize in his first novel what he enunciated many years later as accepted doctrine:

> Sex holds any *two* people together, but it tends to disintegrate society, unless it is subordinated to the great dominating male passion of collective *purpose.*
>
> But when the sex passion submits to the great purposive passion, then you have fullness. And no great purposive passion can endure long unless it is established upon the fulfilment in the vast majority of individuals of the true sexual passion.[12]

George at first sets out to make money, but, though he becomes quite well-to-do, his money-making—like that of Gerald Crich in *Women in Love* and Clifford Chatterley in *Lady Chatterley's Lover*—is at bottom an escape from an inner nullity, from the vacuum of his being. Becoming disillusioned with mere prosperity, he begins to work for the socialist cause, and that seems to give promise of a true purposive activity, but his political ardor soon peters out. In the end he lets everything go, and subsides into a gradual drunken deterioration. Even the fire of his "evil-drunk" rages soon dies out, and he sinks in the prime of his life into a feeble alcoholic passivity, becoming an alienated outcast. When Cyril sees him for the last time, he is "lamentably decayed," leaning against a gate "like a tree that is falling, going soft and pale and rotten, clammy with small fungi" (pp. 320–21).

Leslie, like George, also goes in for public life after his marriage, becoming a County Councillor and speaking authoritatively as a mine owner on economic questions of the day; but we are to understand that he too does not excel as a public man, one indication of this being that even George, as Lettie reports, is "rather more than a match" for him in "frightful battles" that they have over "the nationalisation of industries" (p. 292). Leslie's deficiency would also seem to be attributable to the nature of his marriage—Lettie encourages him in his political ambitions because "it [relieves] her of him" (p. 295)—though we are not told much about his view of it. Cyril states that after his marriage he seems to "[lose] his assertive self-confidence," and almost at once reports that "Lettie and he [have] separate rooms" when they stay at Woodside (p. 254). As Cyril sees it, the marriage for Leslie, far from being vitalizing, is notable for the ease with which he makes it nonexistent, oblivious once again: "As Lettie was always a very good wife, Leslie adored her when he had the time, and when he had not, forgot her comfortably" (p. 287).

The change in Lettie after her marriage is first apparent when she makes no attempt to conceal a general sense of disillusionment. "The only thing worth doing is producing," she announces at a dinner party. "That is the only thing one finds any pleasure in—that is to say, any satisfaction"; and when George innocently asks her whether she writes poetry, she replies that her ten-month-old son is her "work." And it is at this stage that Cyril offers his summing up of her condition:

> Having reached that point in a woman's career when most, perhaps all, of the things in life seem worthless and insipid, she had determined to put up with it, to ignore her own self, to empty her own potentialities into the vessel of another or others, and to live her life at second hand. This peculiar abnegation of self is the resource of a woman for the escaping of the responsibilities of her own development. Like a nun, she puts over her living face a veil, as a sign that the woman no longer exists for herself: she is the servant of God, of some man, of her children, or maybe of some cause. As a servant, she is no longer responsible for her self, which would make her terrified and lonely. Service is light and easy. . . . [Lettie] had . . . now determined to abandon the charge of herself to serve her children. (pp. 280–81)

Cyril formulates his view of Lettie as a general proposition about the life of women, but we may be allowed to doubt that all women find life worthless at the point when they have been married for a few years and have given birth to a healthy first child. Lettie's disillusionment is clearly personal, and as clearly to be attributed to the vacuity of her marriage. Her condition, pulled as she still is between the man she has married and the man she cannot let be, is analogous to that of Cathy in *Wuthering Heights;* and on occasion it seems to take on the very form and substance of Cathy's situation:

> Like so many women, [Lettie] seemed to live, for the most part contentedly, a small indoor existence with artificial light and padded upholstery. Only occasionally, hearing the winds of life outside, she clamoured to be out in the black, keen storm. She was driven to the door, she looked out and called into the tumult wildly, but feminine caution kept her from stepping over the threshold. (p. 287)

In its wider implications, however, Lettie's condition is similar to that of Maggie in *The Mill on the Floss* and of Tess in *Tess of the d'Urbervilles* as well as to that of Cathy. When in their relations with two men the pressure of the pull between them becomes unbearable, Cathy and Tess suffer a breakdown and Maggie is poised for one though it is not actualized; shortly thereafter they all die. Lettie does not overtly break down, nor does she die, but she falls apart at the innermost core of her being—and in effect ceases to be, certainly as Lawrence understands meaningful being. This is emphasized over and over in Cyril's account, but perhaps the central indication of it is her determination "to empty her own potentialities into the vessel of another or others": Lettie allows herself to lapse into the life of her child, permitting the core of the self to dissolve, as it were, and pouring herself into her son. The result, of course, is her own vital inanition, and a negation of self that is almost suicidal in its self-destructiveness: she decides "to ignore her own self" and "to live her life at second hand"; she engages in a "peculiar abnegation of self," and makes it clear that she "no longer exists for herself"; and she "abandons the charge of herself to serve her children." Such a sacrifice of self is an evasion of "the responsibilities of her own development," as she has previously evaded the truths of the blood, and it is seen as no less pernicious.[13] And what is behind her collapse, as we know, is her retreat from the flesh, a retreat which she now carries about with her, "like a nun" who veils her "living face." It is the kind of retreat, as we shall see, that Mrs. Dalloway will also assay.

An oblique comment on Lettie's situation is provided by the symbol of the white peacock, which gives the book its title. The symbol is overtly connected with Annable and with the story of his first marriage. Annable tells Cyril that Lady Crystabel was infatuated with him but chose to view him in an aesthetic light—"I was Greek statues for her"—and refused to have children. To his great humiliation, she became "really glutted" with him after three years, and then began "to get souly," treating him as "her animal," until after a further year he revolted and left her (pp. 149–50). Just before Annable tells his story to Cyril, he points to a peacock which has settled on one of the tombstones in the graveyard where they have met:

> "The proud fool! —look at it! Perched on an angel, too, as if it were a pedestal for vanity. That's the soul of a woman—or it's the devil."
> He was silent for a time, and we watched the great bird moving uneasily before us in the twilight. . . .
> "Just look!" he said, "the miserable brute has dirtied that angel. A woman to the end, I tell you, all vanity and screech and defilement." (pp. 147–48)

When, at the end of his story, Annable admits that "it wasn't all [Lady Crystabel's] fault," Cyril replies: "A white peacock, we will say" (p. 150), using the word "white," it seems, in much the same extenuating sense as in the phrase "a white lie." And to be white, we also note, is to be bloodless.

In so far as the white peacock relates to Annable and Lady Crystabel, therefore, the symbol is self-explanatory, even crudely so. The trouble arises when it is also related later to Lettie. One night, flirting with George in the presence of her husband, she is described in the following terms:

> As she turned laughing to the two men, she let her cloak slide over her white shoulder and fall with silk splendour of a peacock's gorgeous blue over the arm of the large settee. There she stood, with her white hand upon the peacock of her cloak, where it tumbled against her dull orange dress. She knew her own splendour, and she drew up her throat laughing and brilliant with triumph. (p. 251)

With her white shoulder and her white hand on her peacock cloak, Lettie too is clearly intended to be seen as a white peacock; and in her case too the adjective may be taken extenuatingly to indicate that it is not "all her fault," the two men having failed her as much as she them.[14] But it is difficult to reconcile Annable's description of the peacock with her, for it is clearly colored by his own resentments and by his aggressive attribution of blame for the sexual disharmony he has experienced. Lettie may be vain, but she has certainly not defiled either George or Leslie; and if she may be said to have messed up anyone's life, it is her own.[15] We need perhaps to avoid Annable's explicit symbolizing, and place the peacock scene in a wider context. The context provided is one of an overall death-liness. When Cyril makes his way to the abandoned church, he has to push through a path "clogged with decayed leaves"; inside the church the pews lean "in ghostly disorder," prayerbooks are scattered in "the dust and rubble," and there is "a rustle of many birds like spirits." He is relieved to go outside and "drink" fresh air again, but he wanders among the graves in the churchyard. It is then that the peacock flaps beyond him, "on to the neck of an old bowed angel, rough and dark, an angel which [has] long ceased sorrowing for the lost Lucy, and [has] died also" (pp. 146–47). To the extent that Lettie is to be seen as a peacock, she too has taken her stand on death, the death of her married self, despite all the showy luxuriance of its outward manifestation. That, at all events, is the final view we are offered of her. She tells Cyril that she has "nothing at all in her life," and declares it is "a barren futility": "I hope I shall have another child next spring," she writes; "there is only that to take away the misery of this torpor. I seem full of passion and energy, and it all fizzles out in day-to-day domestics—" (p. 287). When, after ten years of continued flirtation, George forces the issue, declaring "it must be one way or another," she "coldly" opts for a final parting (pp. 300–301)—but then she is not left with very much, and her own blood is now virtually stilled: "Lettie's heart would quicken in answer to only one pulse, the easy, light ticking of the baby's blood" (p. 311).

C̲HAPTER̲6

Mrs. Dalloway
The Splitting of Experience

In "Modern Fiction" (1919) Virginia Woolf announced the need to liberate the novelist from a number of constraints, most particularly from the traditional requirement of having to provide a plot; and in *Mrs. Dalloway* (1925), after the unsuccessful experiment of *Jacob's Room* (1922), she discovered an effective substitute for plot as an organizing principle. Instead of relating her characters by means of a series of causally connected events, she simply juxtaposed them in time and space, such a juxtaposition being the form of relationship natural to the flux of experience, to the onward flow of time from minute to minute. It is the need to provide fixed points of reference in the flux, to ground the juxtapositions, that accounts for all the references in the novel to the striking of clocks and the precise location of scenes—as in the following representative passage:

> "I will tell you the time," said Septimus, very slowly, very drowsily, smiling mysteriously at the dead man in the grey suit. As he sat smiling, the quarter struck—the quarter to twelve.
> And that is being young, Peter Walsh thought as he passed them. To be having an awful scene—the poor girl looked absolutely desperate—in the middle of the morning. But what was it about, he wondered; what had the young man in the overcoat been saying to her to make her look like that; what awful fix had they got themselves into, both to look so desperate as that on a fine summer morning? The amusing thing about coming back to England, after five years, was the way it made, anyhow the first days, things stand out as if one had never seen them before; lovers squabbling under a tree; the domestic family life of the parks. Never had he seen London look so enchanting—the softness of the distances; the richness; the greenness; the civilisation, after India, he thought, strolling across the grass. (p. 108)[1]

Septimus Warren Smith and Peter Walsh are major characters in the

111

novel, yet this is the only occasion on which their paths cross (while Septimus is alive, at any rate). The relationship the novelist is prepared to allow them seems to be merely that of their juxtaposition in Regent's Park at a quarter to twelve on the one particular day in June with which the novel is immediately concerned. What is striking in this typical scene is the lack of communication among the people in it, a lack which is not only attributable to their being strangers, for as Peter impinges on the Smiths in time and space and passes on, he completely misapprehends what he witnesses, assuming a lovers' quarrel where Rezia in her desperation is trying to cope with her husband's insanity.

Where people are not strangers and there is some contact between them, it is regarded as fragile, so tenuous that it may disintegrate at a touch—as the image of the spider's thread suggests in the following instance: when Richard Dalloway and Hugh Whitbread leave Lady Bruton, they are said to be "attached to her by a thin thread (since they had lunched with her) which would stretch and stretch, get thinner and thinner as they walked across London; as if one's friends were attached to one's body, after lunching with them, by a thin thread, which (as she dozed there) became hazy with the sound of bells, striking the hour or ringing to service, as a single spider's thread is blotted with raindrops, and, burdened, sags down" (p. 170). Even the relationship of marriage is presented in similar terms, for, when Richard Dalloway leaves Lady Bruton, his mind sets on his wife, "as a single spider's thread after wavering here and there attaches itself to the point of a leaf"; and, deciding to "go straight to her," he is eager "to travel that spider's thread of attachment between himself and Clarissa" (pp. 172, 173).

Virginia Woolf's method, we realize, is not idiosyncratic but calculated, in an effective union of form and substance, to support the exploration of her theme: the isolation of the individual; and in its pattern of juxtapositions it is as deliberate and artificial as any melodramatic connection in a Victorian novel. Her "discovery," moreover, of a new method of presenting individual character, her digging out "beautiful caves" behind her characters which "connect" and "[come] to daylight at the present moment"—what she called her "tunnelling process"[2]—is also related to thematic preoccupations. Her use of the method in order to evoke the past (in its dark cave) and her consequent emphasis on an inner rather than an external reality are directly expressive of her sense that people lead their real lives not in contact with their fellows but in self-communion. For Peter Walsh, as he strolls across the grass in the park, the Smiths become objects of inner reflection, on a par in the end with "the softness of the distances" or "the greenness" that, among other things, attract his attention and are taken into himself. Certainly Virginia Woolf wished to portray states of self-enclosure in the novel, as another diary entry reveals: "I want to bring in the despicableness of people like Ott. [i.e., Lady Ottoline Morrell] . . . The truth is people scarcely care for each other. They have this insane instinct for life. But they never become attached to anything outside themselves."[3]

In scene after scene, however, the novelist shows how people long for such attachments, for a sense of contact and of communication with others, even if they cannot attain them. Sally Seton's comment towards the end of the novel might serve as an epigraph to all the scenes of this kind that precede it: "Are we not all prisoners?" she asks. "She had read a wonderful play about a man who scratched on the wall of his cell, and she had felt that was true of life—one scratched on the wall" (p. 290). Peter, for instance, not only exemplifies during much of the day the sort of solitary confinement behind the bars of his own consciousness that Sally's remark suggests; he is also shown, in one notable scene, making an ineffectual attempt to scratch on the wall. Walking "across Trafalgar Square in the direction of the Haymarket," he sees a young woman whom he finds "extraordinarily attractive" and begins to follow her, believing that she sheds on him "a light which [connects] them," and that her cloak blows out "with an enveloping kindness, a mournful tenderness, as of arms that would open and take the tired." But nothing comes of the pursuit. It is a fantasy, and anyway "other people [get] between them in the street, obstructing him, blotting her out"; then, after he catches up with her, she eventually stops, opens a door, and is "gone" (pp. 80–83). Other people are always getting between, we realize, as (to consider only some of Clarissa Dalloway's main relationships) Richard Dalloway comes between her and Peter, or Lady Bruton between her and Richard, or Miss Kilman between her and her daughter Elizabeth. Not that other people alone are to blame, as we might expect, given the cell. The desire to scratch through the wall is frustrated not only by its thickness on the other side but by the prisoner's own shrinkings and hesitations. In another significant though apparently trivial scene, Peter comes into dinner that night at his hotel to be met by such hesitations in the people who are already in the dining-room:

> . . . [with] their desire, pulsing in them, tugging at them subterraneously, somehow to establish connections if it were only a birthplace (Liverpool, for example), in common or friends of the same name; with their furtive glances, odd silences, and sudden withdrawals into family jocularity and isolation; there they sat eating dinner when Mr. Walsh came in and took his seat at a little table by the curtain. (p. 240)

The diners, with "their desire . . . to establish connections" set against their "sudden withdrawals into . . . isolation," directly figure the "truth about our soul" which Peter later analogously and metaphorically formulates (p. 242). They also figure the central opposition on which the novel is based; and in restrained miniature, enact the conflict that threatens to pull Clarissa Dalloway in two.

II

Clarissa would like to believe that her capacity for detachment, for remaining on the outside of experience, happily coexists with a proclivity for cutting through to its core: "She sliced like a knife through everything; at the same time was outside, looking on" (p. 15). This combination of qualities is certainly apparent in her responses to the London scene with which the book opens. On the one hand she "plunges" into the fine June morning, which is "fresh as if issued to children on a beach" (p. 7), seeming to throw herself joyously into the midst of city life in all its flux; on the other, she has "a perpetual sense, as she [watches] the taxi cabs, of being out, out, far out to sea and alone"; and she "always" has the feeling that it is "very, very dangerous to live even one day" (p. 15). In the busy London street, we see, surrounded by crowds of people and thronging vehicles, she feels completely isolated. Her feeling is remarkably like that of one of the characters in modern literature whose sense of isolation is most piercing, Conrad's Razumov, who in *Under Western Eyes* is said to be "as lonely in the world as a man swimming in the deep sea." Clarissa's feeling of isolation appears to be almost overwhelming, for it is this that seems to account for her dread of life, for her feeling that just to be alive is very dangerous. Her experience of isolation is so strong, indeed, that it not only makes her feel withdrawn from all around her, from people and taxi cabs, but even from herself, her own body: her body seems "nothing—nothing at all," and she has "the oddest sense of being herself invisible; unseen; unknown; there being no more marrying, no more having of children now, but only this astonishing and rather solemn progress with the rest of them, up Bond Street, this being Mrs. Dalloway; not even Clarissa any more; this being Mrs. Richard Dalloway" (p. 18).

Clarissa's ability to abstract herself, to be her essential self when withdrawn into invisibility, is opposed to a sense of self that is social and public, to a self that finds the meaning of "this thing she [calls] life" in the giving of her parties (for which she is well known), a self whose distinctive "gift" it is to be able to bring people together and establish connections:

> Oh, it was very queer. Here was So-and-so in South Kensington; some one up in Bayswater; and somebody else, say, in Mayfair. And she felt quite continuously a sense of their existence; and she felt what a waste; and she felt what a pity; and she felt if only they could be brought together; so she did it. And it was an offering; to combine, to create; but to whom? (p. 184)

Unable to answer her own question, Clarissa concludes that her parties are "an offering for the sake of offering, perhaps" (p. 184). They would seem to be less an offering to a public god of combinations, to the creativity of social conscience, than the propitiation of a private demon of despair in a flight from an engulfing sense of isolation. Nor would it seem that this urge easily conjoins with a desire to withdraw, for her sense of the existence of others which she feels "quite continuously" is opposed but not balanced by the "perpetual sense" she has of being "far out to sea and alone." Subject to such conflicting pulls at the same time and all the time, Clarissa would seem to be ripe for breakdown.

During a moment of intense self-scrutiny, Clarissa seems implicitly to realize that it is not as easy to cut through things and "at the same time" remain on the outside as she had thought. What she contemplates then is the self-division with which she has to contend:

> She pursed her lips when she looked in the glass. It was to give her face point. That was her self—pointed; dart-like; definite. That was her self when some effort, some call on her to be her self, drew the parts together, she alone knew how different, how incompatible and composed so for the world only into one centre, one diamond, one woman who sat in her drawing-room and made a meeting-point, a radiancy no doubt in some dull lives, a refuge for the lonely to come to, perhaps . . . (pp. 57–58)

Clarissa acknowledges here that the different parts of her self are so "incompatible" as to be in a state of disjunction. It is only by a sheer effort of will, and in response to "some call on her to be her self," that—having to face "the world"—she is able to "[draw] the parts together" and "compose" them into a self. The "pointed, dart-like, definite" shape she presents to the world, therefore, and would like to believe is really her, the hard, concentrated, diamond-like self functioning from a firm center, is a fiction, made up as required, assembled—as on this occasion she "[assembles] that diamond shape, that single person" (p. 58)—the moment she leaves the privacy of her room. The question Clarissa does not confront as she studies herself in the glass is how long she can continue to compel such disarray.

The process of fragmentation, it emerges, can be traced back some thirty years, to the time when Clarissa chose to reject Peter Walsh and marry Richard Dalloway instead. Her relations with the two men externalize her inner conflict, for they figure the opposed aspects of self between which she is torn, Peter demanding of her unreserved connection, and Richard being ready to grant her the right to withdrawal into the privacy of the self. Not that the men are thinly one-sided; they too are torn between the opposed desires, and thus reflect Clarissa's conflict. Peter, for instance, though he is planning to marry, feels that he "[wants] nothing so much as to be alone" (p. 121); and he clings to "the privilege of loneliness," believing that in its "secrecy, complete and inviolable," life is "like an unknown garden" (pp. 228–29). Richard, on the other hand, after lunching with Lady Bruton, is suddenly impelled to assert his connection with Clarissa, to go to her and tell her he loves her (though when it comes to it he is not able to say the words), reflecting that to want to go to her and be with her is what "happiness" is (p. 177), and deciding it is "a miracle, that he should have married [her]" (p. 175).

Thirty years after her decisive choice Clarissa is still married to Richard, but she is no less drawn to Peter, and her situation (though much more protracted than theirs) is analogous to that of both Cathy in *Wuthering Heights* and Lettie in *The White Peacock*. The extent to which Clarissa is still torn, still balancing one man against the other, one possible life against another, is indicated by the steady modification (as the day progresses) of her conviction that, if she had married Peter, "they would have been destroyed, both of them ruined" (p. 14). When Peter visits her, she finds him "enchanting! perfectly enchanting!" and wonders why she decided not to marry him (p. 64); she cannot "down the brandishing of silver-flashing plumes like pampas grass in a tropic gale in her breast" when she kisses him, and thinks, "If I had married him, this gaiety would have been mine all day!" (pp. 71–72); and, finally, she makes the damaging admission (since she has spent her whole adult life with Richard) that it is with Peter and Sally, "with the two of them (more even than with Richard)" that she "[shares] her past" (p. 274).

The central opposition between Richard and Peter has further, if subsidiary, dimensions. Richard comes from a family in which there is a "tradition of public service" (p. 208); he habitually puts the public before the personal, deciding, for instance, when Clarissa tells him how it "came over" her earlier in the day that she might have married Peter, and Richard wonders whether she wishes she had, not to pursue the matter because he "must go" to his parliamentary committee on Armenians (pp. 179–81); he is disparagingly classified by Sally Seton as a "perfect gentleman" (along with the Hugh Whitbreads of the world) (p. 115); and he is dismissed by Peter as possessing "the public-spirited, British Empire, tariff-reform, governing-class spirit" (p. 117). Richard's strength is a capacity for action, based on what Clarissa thinks of as an "adorable, divine simplicity" which enables him to "go and do the thing" while people like Peter or herself "[fritter] their time away bickering" (p. 181). Richard, however, is intellectually timid and narrow, content to limit his views to those of the *Morning Post* (p. 117) and, in the name of propriety, ready to proscribe the reading of Shakespeare's sonnets (pp. 114–15). If, moreover, he is "preserved in his simplicity," he has "at the same time grown rather speechless, rather stiff" (p. 175), this indication of an inner lack of vitality being attributed to him not by a jealous Peter but by the novelist in a rare authorial pronouncement.

Peter, by contrast, is unconventional and holds to a direct, personal response to life, Clarissa reflecting how "she [owes] him words: 'sentimental', 'civilized'; they [start] up every day of her life as if he [guards] her" (p. 56). He is an intellectual, having "ideas about everything," and able (Clarissa recalls) to talk "about Pope, say, or Addison, or just . . . nonsense, what people [are] like" (pp. 191–92); and he is not only "bookish" but dreams of writing books himself when he retires, wanting to "get at the truth about one or two little matters that [interest] him" (pp. 235, 237–38). Peter, however, as he himself reflects, is "a failure . . . in the Dalloways' sense," all he can oppose to their material success and prosperity being a life of "journeys; rides; quarrels; adventures; bridge parties; love affairs; work; work, work!" (p. 67); and in fact he has not accomplished much, falling into fantasy more readily than moving into effective action, thinking of himself when he pursues the girl in the scene earlier referred to, for instance, as "an adventurer, reckless . . . swift, daring, indeed (landed as he was last night from India) a romantic buccaneer, careless of all [the] damned proprieties" (p. 82).[4]

The two sides of Clarissa that correspond to the two men and are respectively activated in relation to them are clearly revealed in the "sketch" of her Peter makes after he first sees her on his return to England (pp. 116–20). Like Peter, she has a capacity for "[enjoying] life immensely," finding enjoyment in "practically everything," and responding directly and personally to everything around her, so that, Peter thinks, remembering the "lovers" whom he assumed to be squabbling in Regent's Park, "very likely she would have talked to those lovers, if she had thought them unhappy." And like Peter, she has a keen intellect—Lady Bruton even thinks of it as sharp, for she believes Clarissa is given to "cutting people up" (p. 157)—and Peter remembers how interested she was in ideas, so that "all the time they argued, discussed poetry, discussed people, discussed politics" (p. 232). She has, too, an "indomitable vitality" (p. 234). At the same time—and like Richard—she is also "worldly," admitting that she cares "too much for rank and society and getting on in the world"; believes in behaving "like a lady"; and "from a natural instinct" lends herself to keeping up an "interminable traffic" in the social decencies. Even as a girl she—like Richard—was conventional, as her response to Sally's story about the man who married his housemaid reveals (p. 90); and in middle age she has developed into "the perfect hostess" (p. 13). If she is "straight as a dart," like Richard she is also "a little rigid"; is even more "unyielding," indeed, being, Peter thinks, "like iron, like flint, rigid up the backbone" (p. 98).

Temperamentally, Clarissa would seem to be poised so evenly between the two men that it is not a greater propensity for the sort of life Richard has to offer that can explain her choice of him. Her choice would appear to be dictated, rather, by a fear of Peter, though it is not at first evident why this should be so strong or what lies behind it. What she finds immediately "intolerable" about Peter, as we have seen, is that with him "everything [has] to be shared," and it is this need which she believes would have destroyed them both; whereas what Richard gives her, as she him, is the "little licence," the "little independence" which she feels "there must be between people living together day in day out in the same house" (p. 14). Clarissa's choice of Richard, it becomes clear, reflects an obsessive fear of being absorbed—of giving herself to anything.

This note is struck on the opening page of the novel when she "plunges" into the morning, the act of plunging seeming for her to epitomize a giving of self. Her going outside into the London street on this occasion becomes simultaneously a plunge into the past, for her exhilaration at once evokes the memory of how, as a girl of eighteen, she "plunged at Bourton into the open air"; but this memory speedily gives way to another, to the recall of her feeling, as she stood at the window before going out, that "something awful was about to happen." Plunging, that is, is associated with dread; nor is it evocative merely of a movement that is like throwing herself into the sea, for the air at Bourton is not only "like the flap of a wave" but "the kiss of a wave" (p. 7). Plunging is also associated, and the dread further particularized, with a fear of death, with Clarissa's distinctive "horror of death" (p. 230): she is said to fear "time itself," the "dwindling of life," and this is related to the "exquisite suspense" she now often feels in middle age, the suspense, as she stands "hesitating one moment on the threshold of her drawing-room," which might "stay a diver before plunging while the sea darkens and brightens beneath him . . ." (p. 47). A little later this complex of associations is again repeated:

> Laying her brooch on the table, she had a sudden spasm, as if, while she mused, the icy claws had had the chance to fix in her. She was not old yet. She had just broken into her fifty-second year. Months and months of it were still untouched. June, July, August! Each still remained almost whole, and, as if to catch the falling drop, Clarissa (crossing to the dressing-table) plunged into the very heart of the moment, transfixed it, there—the moment of this June morning on which was the pressure of all the other mornings, seeing the glass, the dressing-table, and all the bottles afresh, collecting the whole of her at one point (as she looked into the glass), seeing the delicate pink face of the woman who was that very night to give a party; of Clarissa Dalloway; of herself. (pp. 56–57)

Clarissa's frightful existential dilemma is powerfully evoked in this passage. Seized by the icy spasm as her sense of the irrevocable onward flow of time and so of death (her death) takes possession of her, for she has just been wondering whether Peter will think she has grown older, all she can do is attempt to arrest the flow. With the claws still "fixed" in her, she tries to "transfix" the moment, "to catch the falling drop." In order to do that she has first to compose a self—to "[collect] the whole of her at one point"—and then to transfix the moment, to hold it there, by piercing through to and making it yield its essence. But to do this she must be prepared, paradoxically, to yield the pointed self she has assembled to the flux of experience, to "[plunge] into the very heart of the moment"—and such a plunge is itself an icy harbinger.

The fear related to plunging is given further, if indirect, definition. Immediately after the passage just referred to, Clarissa sits mending her green dress for the party, and her motions suggest another water image: "So on a summer's day waves collect, overbalance, and fall; collect and fall; and the whole world seems to be saying 'that is all' more and more ponderously, until even the heart in the body which lies in the sun on the beach says too, That is all" (p. 61). To plunge, to commit oneself to the sea, is to give oneself to its rhythms, to "collect, overbalance, and fall"—to be flung down, in the end, and disintegrate. It is not unlike "being laid out like a mist between the people [one knows] best" (p. 16), which is the way Clarissa, in an interesting image, envisages life after death, for what the image also vividly suggests is once again the disintegration of the hard, pointed self. Both wave and mist seem to me to be furthermore related to the refrain that recurs throughout the novel. As the clocks strike, marking the onward movement of time, "the leaden circles" are repeatedly said to "dissolve in the air": what is imaged, as the circles dissolve, is the change from a solid to a liquid state, such a change effectively suggesting the way the fixed moment of time that is recorded in the striking of the clocks is caught up in its onward flow; but the refrain, like the one from *Cymbeline* which Clarissa thinks of at intervals during the day, also directly evokes the fact of dissolution in time.

The act of plunging, therefore, is associated in various ways with death, disintegration, and dissolution—in short, with a loss of self;[5] and it would seem to be a fear of this that lies behind Clarissa's refusal to give herself in marriage to Peter:

> Love and religion! thought Clarissa, going back into the drawing-room, tingling all over. How detestable, how detestable they are! For now that the body of Miss Kilman was not before her, it overwhelmed her—the idea. The cruellest things in the world, she thought, seeing them clumsy,

hot, domineering, hypocritical, eavesdropping, jealous, infinitely cruel and unscrupulous, dressed in a mackintosh coat, on the landing; love and religion. Had she ever tried to convert any one herself? Did she not wish everybody merely to be themselves? And she watched out of the window the old lady opposite climbing upstairs. Let her climb upstairs if she wanted to; let her stop; then let her, as Clarissa had often seen her, gain her bedroom, part her curtains, and disappear again into the background. Somehow one respected that—that old woman looking out of the window, quite unconscious that she was being watched. There was something solemn in it—but love and religion would destroy that, whatever it was, the privacy of the soul. The odious Kilman would destroy it. Yet it was a sight that made her want to cry. (p. 191)

If it is of Miss Kilman that Clarissa thinks here, the fervent Christian who would love her daughter, she immediately afterwards reflects that "love [destroys] too": "Everything that was fine, everything that was true went. Take Peter Walsh now" (p. 191); and so makes clear that her view of Miss Kilman has its bearing on Peter too. Miss Kilman may long to "grasp" Elizabeth, to "clasp her," to "make her hers absolutely and for ever and then die" (p. 199), but this is not notably different from what Clarissa feels is implied by Peter's wish to share everything, a desire which would make her his as absolutely. What love and religion have in common—and Clarissa would say they share this too with medicine as practiced by doctors such as Sir William Bradshaw—is a need "to convert" the person on whom feeling is concentrated. The need is seen to express itself as a demand that the targets of conversion should, precisely, cease "to be themselves," unyielding and inviolable, holding as their greatest good "the privacy of the soul"; it is a demand that they freely give themselves to love or religion, fully expose themselves, and, all privacy gone, welcome a change of condition. But to give oneself is to be possessed, and that may arouse an obsessive fear of a loss of self. This is the sort of fear, it slowly becomes evident, that accounts for Clarissa's feeling that she would have been "destroyed" if she had married Peter. Having opted to preserve the self, and having turned to the less intense Richard who leaves her room to be herself, Clarissa herself now converts "the old lady opposite," who, behind panes of glass, is securely isolated, into an epitome of the privacy she respects and values above all. There may indeed be "something solemn" in her observation of the lady, who is "quite unconscious that she [is] being watched," but there is a touch of the voyeur too. That the "sight" of the lady should make her "want to cry" seems to be expressive not so much of a reverential joy as of a sense of desolation.

Clarissa's memory of "the most exquisite moment of her whole life" suggests that it is not exactly love (or religion) she despises. The memory is of her relationship with Sally Seton at Bourton, and particularly of the night when, walking with others on the terrace, Sally and she "fell a little behind":

> Then came the most exquisite moment of her whole life passing a stone urn with flowers in it. Sally stopped; picked a flower; kissed her on the lips. The whole world might have turned upside down! The others disappeared; there she was alone with Sally. And she felt that she had been given a present, wrapped up, and told just to keep it, not to look at it—a diamond, something infinitely precious, wrapped up, which, as they walked (up and down, up and down), she uncovered, or the radiance burnt through, the revelation, the religious feeling!—when old Joseph and Peter faced them:
> "Star-gazing?" said Peter. (p. 55)

If this is love, for, looking back on the relationship, Clarissa asks herself "what was [it] except being in love?" (p. 54)—and religion, for it is a "revelation" and she is suffused with "religious feeling"—it is love and religion which do not seek to convert her, or ask her in any way to give of herself. Instead it is she who is given something, the "present," which she is told "just to keep." It seems to be not insignificant that she thinks of the present she may keep, the "something infinitely precious," as "a diamond," since it is as a diamond that the self in its concentrated wholeness is repeatedly imaged; and though the present is "wrapped up," this is "the radiance"—and "the revelation"—that "[burns] through."

This revelation should be related to another which Clarissa suddenly has when—in an astonishing passage—she imagines, having herself "[yielded] to the charm of a woman," what a man might feel:

> . . . she did undoubtedly then feel what men felt. Only for a moment; but it was enough. It was a sudden revelation, a tinge like a blush which one tried to check and then, as it spread, one yielded to its expansion, and rushed to the farthest verge and there quivered and felt the world come closer, swollen with some astonishing significance, some pressure of rapture, which split its thin skin and gushed and poured with an extraordinary alleviation over the cracks and sores! Then, for that moment, she had seen an illumination; a match burning in a crocus; an inner meaning almost expressed. But the close withdrew; the hard softened. It was over—the moment. (pp. 49–50)

If the joy Clarissa feels when Sally kisses her is associated with the revelation that the self may be kept intact in a passionate relationship with a woman, in this passage she plays with the idea of "yielding" herself in such a relationship—but only at two removes, in imagination and in the role of the man. Though it is her capacity for such an imaginative transposition that makes the vicarious experience possible, it touches greater mysteries than she seems to be aware of. Whereas, in her relations with men, as in her relationship with her husband (as we shall see), she is always cold and contracted, here she imagines being warm and expansive. And if the imagined yielding begins innocuously, being like that to a blush

which cannot be checked, it rapidly becomes—in another transposition—
a yielding to the rush of orgasm, as she imagines this is experienced by a
man. Clarissa's imagination is so vivid that it provides her with all the
terms necessary for an understanding of the "inner meaning" of the experience, a meaning that is "almost expressed" but in the end eludes her. If
sexual consummation is a kind of disintegration or spilling over of self, a
"gushing" and "pouring" when the skin splits, this is nonetheless restora-
tive, for it brings "an extraordinary alleviation," sores being assuaged and
cracks filled in and smoothed over in an access of wholeness. But though
Clarissa thinks she has "seen an illumination," she fails to let the vivid
images she conjures up throw their full light, for she is unable to perceive
what lies behind her denial of the flesh—or accept that one must be ready
to lose the self to find it. In the end the illumination is reduced to that of "a
match burning in a crocus," like the momentary light of the flame in a
Marabar cave that is swallowed up in darkness in *A Passage to India*. Even
in middle age she does not really grasp why she turned away from Peter—
and married Richard.

When Richard cannot bring himself to tell Clarissa he loves her and
goes off to his Armenians, she thinks there is "a dignity in people" and "a
solitude," and that "even between husband and wife" there is "a gulf"
which "one must respect": "for one would not part with it oneself, or take
it, against his will, from one's husband, without losing one's independence, one's self-respect—something, after all, priceless" (p. 181). In this
account of the nature of people and of marriage it is "independence"—or
being and remaining oneself—that is presented as a prime virtue, a
"priceless" attribute, but the cost of the licence Richard and Clarissa grant
each other so willingly is the creation of "a gulf" between them. It is on
this same day in her fifty-second year that Clarissa really begins to take its
measure:

> Like a nun withdrawing, or a child exploring a tower, she went up-
> stairs, paused at the window, c..me to the bathroom. . . . There was an
> emptiness about the heart of life; an attic room. . . . She pierced the pincush-
> ion and laid her feathered yellow hat on the bed. The sheets were clean,
> tight stretched in a broad white band from side to side. Narrower and
> narrower would her bed be. The candle was half burnt down and she had
> read deep in Baron Marbot's *Memoirs*. She had read late at night of the
> retreat from Moscow. For the House sat so long that Richard insisted, after
> her illness, that she must sleep undisturbed. And really she preferred to
> read of the retreat from Moscow. He knew it. So the room was an attic; the
> bed narrow; and lying there reading, for she slept badly, she could not
> dispel a virginity preserved through childbirth which clung to her like a
> sheet. Lovely in girlhood, suddenly there came a moment—for example on

the river beneath the woods at Clieveden—when, through some contraction of this cold spirit, she had failed him. And then at Constantinople, and again and again. She could see what she lacked. It was not beauty; it was not mind. It was something central which permeated; something warm which broke up surfaces and rippled the cold contact of man and woman, or of women together. . . . (pp. 48–49)

Clarissa's analysis of how she has "failed" Richard is in line with what we know about her, though it proceeds somewhat circuitously round the same idea. What she thinks of as "some contraction of [her] cold spirit" is a pulling back into self which results in sexual frigidity; her "lack" of "something warm which [breaks] up surfaces and [ripples] the cold contact of man and woman" is the absence of a passionate readiness to plunge through that surface; and her inability to "dispel a virginity preserved through childbirth" is an emotional incapacity to give herself in the flesh. But what she devastatingly registers here are the consequences of that failure. The "solitude" that she deems worthy of such respect is concretized in her having a separate bedroom from her husband and "[sleeping] undisturbed" in the narrow bed over which the sheets are "tight stretched." This suggests another view of the "gulf" that exists between Richard and her, and the narrow tightness of her bed is expressive of the shrinking of her world. Her room is no longer lived in, as it were—it is "an attic room"; and the "emptiness about the heart of life" is, more specifically, her own sexual emptiness. Faced with such a diminution of her world, what Clarissa begins to do—ominously—is withdraw from it, as she does from her own sexuality. When she goes upstairs, she is "like a nun withdrawing," withdrawing into the safety of an accustomed self as into the known security of a convent—as previously, when she enters her home after her walk in the city streets, "she felt like a nun who has left the world and feels fold round her the familiar veils and the response to old devotions" (p. 45). We remember Lettie in *The White Peacock* who in her marriage is said to be "like a nun" who veils her "living face." The amendment of the nun simile here, moreover—going upstairs, Clarissa is also like "a child exploring a tower"—further emphasizes the idea of withdrawal, as a subsequent passage indicates:

It was all over for her. The sheet was stretched and the bed narrow. She had gone up into the tower alone and left them blackberrying in the sun. The door had shut, and there among the dust of fallen plaster and the litter of birds' nests how distant the view had looked, and the sounds came thin and chill (once on Leith Hill, she remembered), and Richard, Richard! she cried, as a sleeper in the night starts and stretches a hand in the dark for help. Lunching with Lady Bruton, it came back to her. He has left me; I am alone for ever, she thought, folding her hands upon her knee. (p. 72)

The consequence of that withdrawal into the tower is a distancing and thinning of the life that goes on outside it; and, inside the tower, what presents itself to contemplation is the detritus of time.

Having failed to establish the kind of connection that leaves no "gulf" between a man and a woman because it encompasses a ready bridging of individual separateness, Clarissa—like the people who watch Peter's entry into the hotel dining-room—withdraws into isolation. We realize now what underlies her feeling of isolation in the midst of a busy street scene; and fully understand why her parties are so important to her. Her sense of isolation is excruciating, for it gives rise to the waking nightmare depicted in the passage quoted above, when, like a sleeper, she "stretches a hand in the dark for help," having been left "alone for ever." This nightmare is the more extraordinary in that she has it in the presence of Peter, having indeed just kissed him and thought how gaiety could have been hers all day if she had married him. But that, of course, is the point. Alone in her tower, Clarissa is her own victim.

III

Virginia Woolf's use of the method of juxtaposition is most audacious in her handling of Clarissa and Septimus Warren Smith, for, though they are the two major protagonists in the novel, they do not even meet. Yet the method ensures their juxtaposition, forces the reader, indeed, to juxtapose and seek to relate them, as they go about their business in London on that June day, doing different things at the same time throughout the day. The readiest relation such a juxtaposition yields is clearly that of contrast; and Virginia Woolf's first rough intention, as she began to work at the novel, is certainly realized and easily recognized in the finished work: "I adumbrate here," she wrote in her diary, "a study of insanity and suicide; the world seen by the sane and the insane side by side—something like that."[6] But the more complex relation between Clarissa and Septimus that the novel challenges us to discover is that of analogy, alerting us to similarity first by a recurrent physical detail in the opening pages—Clarissa has "a ridiculous little face, beaked like a bird's" (p. 18), and Septimus is "pale-faced [and] beak-nosed" (p. 24)—and then slowly revealing further and more significant points of correspondence. In this respect a hint from the novelist, casually given some years after the completion of the novel, is of the greatest interest. In an Introduction which she wrote in 1928 for the Modern Library edition of *Mrs. Dalloway*, Virginia Woolf said:

> Of *Mrs. Dalloway* then one can only bring to light at the moment a few scraps, of little importance or none perhaps; as that in the first version

Septimus, who later is intended to be her double, had no existence; and that Mrs. Dalloway was originally to kill herself, or perhaps merely to die at the end of the party. Such scraps are offered humbly to the reader in the hope that like other odds and ends they may come in useful. (p. vi)

Never was an important indication of method more disarmingly conveyed.

The method of characterization used in most of the novel—the tunneling process—breaks down when it comes to Septimus. He is already insane when we first meet him, and the insane mind cannot be used to communicate a sane past. In Septimus's "case," therefore, the novelist resorts to more or less straightforward omniscient narration to relate his past; but, not wishing perhaps to draw attention to the change of method, makes the presentation of the crucial event in his life too cursory. That event is the death of Evans, his officer, to whom he is greatly attached. We simply have to take the novelist's account of Septimus's response to the death of Evans on trust, accepting it as her *donnée*, and elaborating its significance:

> [Septimus and Evans] had to be together, share with each other, fight with each other, quarrel with each other. But when Evans . . . was killed, just before the Armistice, in Italy, Septimus, far from showing any emotion or recognizing that here was the end of a friendship, congratulated himself upon feeling very little and very reasonably. The War had taught him. It was sublime. He had gone through the whole show, friendship, European War, death, had won promotion, was still under thirty and was bound to survive. He was right there. The last shells missed him. He watched them explode with indifference. When peace came he was in Milan, billeted in the house of an innkeeper with a courtyard, flowers in tubs, little tables in the open, daughters making hats, and to Lucrezia, the younger daughter, he became engaged one evening when the panic was on him—that he could not feel. (pp. 131–32)

Septimus and Clarissa are alike, we see, in the way they are drawn to close relationships, his having to be together with Evans, share with him, fight with him, and quarrel with him suggesting the kind of intensity that characterizes her relationship with Peter. They are alike, furthermore, in the way they draw back at crucial moments from such intimacies. Septimus may not "show any emotion" when Evans is killed, may even "congratulate himself upon feeling very little," but must be assumed to feel so deeply as to be shocked into numbness since he is a highly emotional man—as his attachment to Miss Isabel Pole has previously indicated. The numbness is instinctive, a means of preserving himself, for to give himself to his grief would mean to be overwhelmed by it. Like Clarissa, Septimus instinctively seeks to keep a threatened self intact; and, contracting into a cold numbness, is "bound to survive," the last shells that miss him not being all he has to contend with. But to contract and withdraw into the self, as we have seen in the case of Clarissa, is to distance the world outside it; and Septimus is able to watch the last shells explode "with indifference." It is also, as Clarissa shows, to be subject to an intense isolation; and Septimus's precipitate marriage is a panic-stricken flight not so much from a lack of feeling as from his sense of isolation: "That was it," he later reflects: "to be alone for ever. That was the doom pronounced in Milan when he came into the room and saw them cutting out buckram shapes with their scissors; to be alone for ever" (pp. 218–19).

From its outset, therefore, Septimus's story presents a number of apparent analogies to that of Clarissa; and the novelist's method of relating her two protagonists is straightforward enough—like setting up parallel bars on opposite sides of a room. But in her further development of Septimus—in what she does with her *donnée*—she is more subtle, using him as Clarissa's "double" in order to amplify the significance of *her* story. We can perhaps best get at this dimension of the novel through a passage which presents Septimus in his insanity:

> Look, the unseen bade him, the voice which now communicated with him who was the greatest of mankind, Septimus, lately taken from life to death, the Lord who had come to renew society, who lay like a coverlet, a snow blanket smitten only by the sun, for ever unwasted, suffering for ever, the scapegoat, the eternal sufferer, but he did not want it, he moaned, putting from him with a wave of his hand that eternal suffering, that eternal loneliness. (p. 40)

It is a complex passage. Presenting Septimus in his madness, as a man who hears the voice of "the unseen" when his wife tells him to look at some boys playing cricket, and who in his delusion thinks of himself as "the Lord" whose task it is "to renew society," as "the scapegoat" and "eternal sufferer," it also adverts us to the scapegoat motif in the novel. Jean M. Wyatt, in a fine essay, has pointed out that Septimus really is a scapegoat, that "this is the role he plays in the novel" since, as Virginia Woolf herself indicated, "he dies in [Clarissa's] place."[7] It is a rewarding suggestion, and one that we might well take further: Septimus not only dies in Clarissa's place but lives in her stead as well. He is her double, and in his "eternal loneliness" he not only reveals to us tendencies that are inherent in Clarissa's condition but magnifies them, and—with his greater intensity—pursues them to their bitter end.[8]

Though he survives, more or less intact, for some five years in the postwar world, being what Sir William Bradshaw refers to as a case of "the deferred effects of shell shock" (p. 276), Septimus begins more and more to withdraw into himself, marveling that for him, when Rezia nudges him to look at a beautiful woman, beauty is "behind a pane of glass," and beginning more and more to worry about what he takes to be an inability to feel (pp. 133–34). The withdrawal into self is also the reflex of a withdrawal from a world that he steadily finds more loathsome. He begins to believe that "the world itself is without meaning"; reading Shakespeare, he finds everywhere "loathing, hatred, despair"; he refuses to consider bringing children into "a world like this"; and he concludes that "human beings have neither kindness, nor faith, nor charity beyond what serves to increase the pleasure of the moment" (pp. 134–36). When Rezia cries in her unhappiness (as he becomes more and more remote), he hears her sobs but they seem "far away" and he feels nothing. Finally he "[drops] his head on his hands" and gives in, but Dr. Holmes, when called, finds nothing wrong with him, insisting on this in repeated visits (pp. 137–40). In desperation Septimus tells Rezia their "only chance [is] to escape" from Dr. Holmes, but she "[cannot] understand him":

> So he was deserted. The whole world was clamouring: Kill yourself, kill yourself, for our sakes. But why should he kill himself for their sakes? Food was pleasant; the sun hot; and this killing oneself, how does one set about it, with a table knife, uglily, with floods of blood, —by sucking a gaspipe? He was too weak; he could scarcely raise his hand. Besides, now that he was quite alone, condemned, deserted, as those who are about to die are alone, there was a luxury in it, an isolation full of sublimity; a freedom which the attached can never know. Holmes had won of course; the brute with the red nostrils had won. But even Holmes himself could not touch this last relic straying on the edge of the world, this outcast, who gazed back at the inhabited regions, who lay, like a drowned sailor, on the shore of the world.
>
> It was at that moment (Rezia had gone shopping) that the great revelation took place. A voice spoke from behind the screen. Evans was speaking. The dead were with him.
>
> "Evans, Evans!" he cried.
>
> Mr. Smith was talking aloud to himself, Agnes the servant girl cried to Mrs. Filmer in the kitchen. "Evans, Evans!" he had said as she brought in the tray. She jumped, she did. She scuttled downstairs. (pp. 140–41)

Septimus's assumption, with the last vestiges of his sanity, of the role of scapegoat that is to dominate his madness is not only an objectification of the guilt that grips him but also, as he considers the various ways he might kill himself, an indication of that deep desire for death—here legitimized, so to speak—which ultimately drives him to suicide. What diverts him from thoughts of death is his realization of what he takes to be the totality of his isolation, which he savours at first, trying to adjust to it, as a "luxury" and a "sublimity." Now that Rezia too may be assumed to have "deserted" him, he feels "quite alone," having broken through that final attachment into "freedom." But "no human being could bear a steady

view of moral solitude," Joseph Conrad has said, "without going mad"[9]—
and this is what is strikingly presented as happening in Septimus's case
too. It is precisely at the moment when his sense of isolation becomes
intolerable that he withdraws completely into himself, "[gazing back]" at a
world with which he has now severed all connection, being in effect dead
to it ("like a drowned sailor")—it is at this moment that his reason snaps,
and he is able to alleviate his anguish by resurrecting Evans.

Septimus therefore demonstrates to us what Clarissa's compulsion
to withdraw into herself may lead to if taken far enough. Clarissa is saved
from insanity by a spider's thread. Her continuing relationship with
Richard (for all their separateness and her feeling for Peter) and the giving
of her parties ensure that she never actually snaps her thin connection
with the world. But just how precarious her condition is becomes evident
when we now juxtapose two passages that appear at the very beginning of
the novel. The first passage has already been quoted (on p. 114 above), the
passage in which Clarissa, walking up Bond Street, reflects that her body
seems "nothing at all," and that she is "not even Clarissa any more"
(p. 18). A few pages later there follows this description of Septimus:

> "Now we will cross," [Rezia] said.
> She had a right to his arm, though it was without feeling. He would
> give her, who was so simple, so impulsive, only twenty-four, without
> friends in England, who had left Italy for his sake, a piece of bone. (p. 26)

Like Clarissa, Septimus too—only he is insane—has withdrawn so deeply
into himself as to be withdrawn even from his own body. He gives Rezia a
piece of bone because he is not there anymore—is, indeed, not all there.

Before he goes mad, Septimus witnesses a curious scene in a city
street:

> In the street, vans roared past him; brutality blared out on placards; men
> were trapped in mines; women burnt alive; and once a maimed file of
> lunatics being exercised or displayed for the diversion of the populace (who
> laughed aloud), ambled and nodded and grinned past him, in the Tot-
> tenham Court Road, each half apologetically, yet triumphantly inflicting his
> hopeless woe. And would *he* go mad? (pp. 136–37)

The maimed, ambling, grinning lunatics seem to be more than a nightmarish prefiguration of what awaits Septimus, the means by which he
first senses the extent of his own predicament. The "hopeless woe" which
the lunatics inflict on all who see them is associated with the woes of the
brutal and violent world through which they move. So violent is this
world that, on another occasion, an ordinary, everyday street scene is
transformed into a battlefield, as "the last relics" of a clock striking are
"beaten up, broken up by the assault of carriages, the brutality of vans,

the eager advance of myriads of angular men, of flaunting women" (p. 193). The lunatics, therefore, not only prefigure Septimus's coming madness but seem also to image a likely breakdown in the world around them, the sort of breakdown from which it—like Septimus, and all those, like him, who had "survived"—had just emerged. Published in 1925, the little, apparently irrelevant description seems today to be prophetic—and adds another dimension to Septimus's collapse.

His madness, however, does not turn out to be an ultimate stage of withdrawal, nor—though the birds speak to him in Greek and Evans is at his side—a secure refuge from isolation. Sir William Bradshaw pronounces his to be "a case of complete breakdown—complete physical and nervous breakdown" (p. 145); and prescribes as cure his isolation in one of his homes, ordering "rest in bed; rest in solitude; silence and rest; rest without friends, without books, without messages; six months' rest" (p. 150). Rather than face this final turn of the screw, Septimus withdraws altogether: "Holmes was at the door. 'I'll give it you!' he cried, and flung himself vigorously, violently down on to Mrs. Filmer's area railings" (p. 225). Though he sees himself once again as the scapegoat, giving his life to those who are clamouring for it, rather than taking it himself, his death should not be romanticized:[10] it is a last despairing flight, the culmination of a disaster that began on the battlefield.

IV

At her party that night Clarissa experiences a number of revelations. Though she feels an "intoxication of the moment" when she escorts the Prime Minister down the room and bids him farewell, she suddenly sees her parties and herself in a new light:

> for, though she loved it and felt it tingle and sting, still these semblances, these triumphs (dear old Peter, for example, thinking her so brilliant), had a hollowness; at arm's length they were, not in the heart; and it might be that she was growing old, but they satisfied her no longer as they used; and suddenly, as she saw the Prime Minister go down the stairs, the gilt rim of the Sir Joshua picture of the little girl with a muff brought back Kilman with a rush; Kilman her enemy. That was satisfying; that was real. Ah, how she hated her—hot, hypocritical, corrupt; with all that power; Elizabeth's seducer; the woman who had crept in to steal and defile (Richard would say, What nonsense!). She hated her: she loved her. It was enemies one wanted, not friends . . . (pp. 262–63)

What Clarissa realizes is that, if she has hitherto plunged joyfully into the "tingle and sting" of her parties, such contact is no longer satisfying, offering only a "semblance" of the real thing. Suddenly seeing through the outer brilliance of her parties to their inner "hollowness," she registers too that it is not a party that can fill the emptiness at the heart of life, since it is what is "in the heart" that matters, whereas even her triumphs no longer touch her, being "at arm's length." The "real" thing that she surprisingly sets against the glittering semblance is hatred, the hatred of Miss Kilman which "rasped" her so painfully earlier in the day:

> It rasped her, though, to have stirring about in her this brutal monster! to hear twigs cracking and feel hooves planted down in the depths of that leaf-encumbered forest, the soul; never to be content quite, or quite secure, for at any moment the brute would be stirring, this hatred, which, especially since her illness, had power to make her feel scraped, hurt in her spine; gave her physical pain, and made all pleasure in beauty, in friendship, in being well, in being loved and making her home delightful, rock, quiver, and bend as if indeed there were a monster grubbing at the roots, as if the whole panoply of content were nothing but self love! this hatred! (pp. 21–22).

The "brutal monster," which for Clarissa is the image of her hatred, suggests not only a brute force that tramples and devastates the "leaf-encumbered forest" but also a rough animality that vitalizes it. It also suggests, that is, the thrust of sex, and indeed Clarissa later thinks of "love" as a "monster" too (p. 69). The monster, at all events, whether of love or of hatred, is firmly repressed, being allowed to grub and to stir only "at the roots" down "in the depths" of the forest. It is, we realize, Clarissa's repressed sexuality which has festered and turned to hatred. Hence the significance of the "rush" of hatred for Miss Kilman which she feels—and welcomes—at the party. It is a real passion which she at last gives herself to, allowing the monster to rise to the surface; and if it is released as hatred, that is but the dark side of love—so that she both hates Miss Kilman and loves her. It has taken an enemy, not a friend, to liberate her passion.

Clarissa has her second revelation a little later when she withdraws from the party and goes alone into the little room in which the Prime Minister had sat with Lady Bruton. Once again it is as if she first has to shake herself free of the party—its "splendour [falls] to the floor" like a discarded dress—before she can concentrate on something which, like her passion of hatred, is real. The new reality she confronts is death, specifically the death of the "young man" who the Bradshaws have reported has just killed himself. First, she experiences his death herself, registering it on her own body: "He had thrown himself from a window. Up had flashed the ground; through him, blundering, bruising, went the rusty spikes. There he lay with a thud, thud, thud in his brain, and then a suffocation of blackness." Then she wonders why he has killed himself, and, with an intuition that leaps from her own despair, reflects how, when human relationships fail, there is a refuge from isolation in death: "closeness drew apart; rapture faded; one was alone. There was an embrace in death" (pp. 276–78). This touches her own position so closely that she is soon compelled to confront it:

> Then (she had felt it only this morning) there was the terror; the overwhelming incapacity, one's parents giving it into one's hands, this life, to be lived to the end, to be walked with serenely; there was in the depths of her heart an awful fear. Even now, quite often if Richard had not been there reading the *Times*, so that she could crouch like a bird and gradually revive, send roaring up that immeasurable delight, rubbing stick to stick, one thing with another, she must have perished. She had escaped. But that young man had killed himself.
>
> Somehow it was her disaster—her disgrace. It was her punishment to see sink and disappear here a man, there a woman, in this profound darkness, and she forced to stand here in her evening dress. . . .
>
> Odd, incredible; she had never been so happy. Nothing could be slow enough; nothing last too long. No pleasure could equal, she thought, straightening the chairs, pushing in one book on the shelf, this having done with the triumphs of youth, lost herself in the process of living, to find it, with a shock of delight, as the sun rose, as the day sank. . . . (pp. 278–79)

What Clarissa looks straight at here is her own compulsion to suicide. That morning, as we have seen, she had reflected how dangerous it was to live (being "far out to sea and alone"), but only now does she confront her "overwhelming incapacity" in the face of life, the life she has been given to live to its natural end but which, in "the terror" and "awful fear" of her isolation, she must have been driven time and again to end herself if not for the sustaining presence of Richard. And every time she hears of a suicide, of a man or a woman who, like the Bradshaws' young man, has "plunged" (p. 278) into the "profound darkness" to "sink and disappear" in it, it is "her disaster—her disgrace" and "her punishment" too because she lives the suicide herself, giving herself to it. Then, as she thinks oddly and incredibly, comes the revelation that she has "never been so happy." But it is not odd at all: her happiness is that of a survivor, so glad merely to be alive that "nothing [can] be slow enough; nothing last too long." Finally, she trembles on the edge of another revelation, though she is not quite able to formulate it. She realizes that she has survived because, for all her failures and promptings to death, she nevertheless has given herself to life, "lost herself in the process of living," as she did earlier that day when she plunged into the fine June morning; and that to lose oneself in this way is after all to find oneself—though it is a highly ambiguous "it" which she sees herself as finding. But this too is associated with the idea of renewal, with the sun rising as well as sinking. It is too late for Clarissa to begin to live her life all over again, and as she goes to look for Peter she is still subject to the old conflicting pulls; but (the breakdown and suicide which are implicit in her condition having been worked through at second hand, as it were, in the presentation of Septimus) she alone of all the heroines studied in this book is able in the end to contend effectively with her conflict. The series of revelations she has had at her party now enable her to assume her diamond shape with more assurance: "But she must go back. She must assemble. She must find Sally and Peter. And she came in from the little room" (p. 281).

CHAPTER 7

The End of the Affair
The Eternal Triangle

An immediately notable feature of Graham Greene's *The End of the Affair* is its time scheme. The narrative darts back and forth in time, making for a complex movement, though the chronology itself does not prove to be especially complicated when we disentangle it: Maurice Bendrix, the narrator and main male protagonist, tells his story in early 1949, some three years (p. 17) after the point at which he chooses to begin it—his chance meeting in January 1946 with Henry Miles (p. 1);[1] this encounter takes place some eighteen months after the termination of his affair with Henry's wife Sarah in June 1944 (p. 28), and the affair begins in "the early summer of 1939" (p. 24); Sarah dies at the end of February or in early March 1946 (pp. 150, 159, 161). Bendrix, who is himself a novelist, asserts that his point of departure is arbitrary—"A story has no beginning or end: arbitrarily one chooses that moment of experience from which to look back or from which to look ahead" (p. 1)—but the novelist who lurks behind his narrator-novelist has in fact chosen the point with care. If a narrative may normally be supposed either "to look back" from its beginning or "to look ahead," the point chosen here ensures that this narrative must do both. It must look back, that is, to the beginning of the affair, to its development, and to its end; and at the same time it must look ahead to the new affair which Sarah seemingly has started and to the discovery of the identity of the lover, for Bendrix turns to Parkis, a private detective, to elicit this information. The narrative thus seems at first to encompass two separate stories (though they prove to be inextricably linked); and for about half of the novel—throughout the first two of the five books into which it is divided—the two stories are presented to us in parallel narrative blocks, the account of the launching of the investigation and its prog-

133

ress to a successful conclusion alternating, stage by stage, with that of the beginning of the first affair and its movement to an apparent culmination in the separation of the lovers. What the method subtly achieves, in other words, is the establishment of a parallel between the two affairs and consequently between the two main triangles in which Sarah figures: with her husband and Bendrix, and with Bendrix and the mysterious new lover. (Less significantly, because she does not return his love, she also figures in a third triangle with Smythe, the strawberry-marked rationalist to whom Parkis's sleuthing leads, and Bendrix.) By the time it turns out that Sarah's new involvement is with God, not Smythe, the narrative parallelism has quietly prepared us to view God not only as a lover but as the third (together with Sarah and Bendrix) in a Greenean version of an Eternal triangle.[2]

The novelist provides for the transformation of the expected lover by building the notion of transformation into the narrative structure. This he does through the device of Sarah's journal, which Parkis obtains and presents to Bendrix, and excerpts from which constitute Book Three. Books One and Two bring both stories to apparent points of completion, leading up to the episode which results in the separation of Bendrix and Sarah, and also to the identification of Smythe and the termination of the investigation. The material in this section of the narrative is presented exclusively from Bendrix's point of view; and then in Book Three the same material is reviewed, as it were, by Sarah, and major episodes are presented through her eyes. The result, for us, is a transformation of the narrative, nothing now being what it previously seemed. From first to last, indeed, this is the narrative mode: on the opening page, for instance, Bendrix wonders why he stopped to speak to Henry on that evening in January 1946, for he affirms he hates both him and his wife; and when he asks him how Sarah is, he reports that "nothing would have delighted [him] more than to have heard that she was sick, unhappy, dying" (p. 3), thus marking a starting point for the kind of transformation of feeling—and of being—which the book treats.

Triangular entanglements, however, of the sort explored in this study, have their own inexorable dynamic; and though Sarah is overtly transformed into a saint who embraces God, this is not the only view we are given of her. Sarah, I shall argue, is more aptly seen as a woman who, caught between two lovers, is driven to destroy herself.

II

Greene's sense of individual duality is strikingly like that of Hardy. Hardy, it will be recalled, stated that "persons are successively various persons" in accordance with the predominance of different "strands" in their characters; and his description of the twilight in *Tess of the d'Urbervilles* provided a natural analogue of this belief, the "twilight of the morning" being characterized by the predominance of light, and the "twilight of evening" by that of darkness. The analogous image in *The End of the Affair* is the pendulum, which first appears in an extract from Sarah's journal: "It's strange how the human mind swings back and forth, from one extreme to another. Does truth lie at some point of the pendulum's swing, at a point where it never rests, not in the dull perpendicular mean where it dangles in the end like a windless flag, but at an angle, nearer one extreme than another?" (pp. 130–31). Bendrix later uses the same image: after Sarah's death he cannot fall asleep, and "the pendulum of [his] desire [swings] tiringly to and fro, the desire to forget and to remember, to be dead and to keep alive a while longer" (p. 169). In their behavior and in their attitudes all the main characters swing, pendulum-like, between opposed poles.

The major opposition figured by the two male opponents in the first main triangle, Henry the husband and Bendrix the lover, is that between trust and mistrust. Henry's trust in both Sarah and Bendrix is apparent in the complete absence of any suspicion on his part as to the true nature of their relationship throughout the time of their affair. Bendrix, when he stops him on "that black wet January night on the Common, in 1946" (p. 1), is even struck by his foolishness in not having registered the end of the affair, the eighteen-month cessation of contact during which he has "fallen out of their sight as completely as a stone in a pond" (p. 4). To Bendrix, Henry's trustfulness appears entirely negative and limiting: he is a man who goes about with "blinkers . . . firmly tied" (p. 4); if he has hitherto enjoyed "the serenity of innocence" (p. 11), it is at the cost of being "easy . . . to deceive" (p. 12), so easy that he may even be regarded as Sarah's pimp, as having "pimped with [his] ignorance" (p. 77). Yet, with the swing of the pendulum, Henry is roused to suspicion of Sarah by her recent behavior; and he confesses to Bendrix he has gone so far as to seek the name of a suitable private detective from a friend: "It seems so silly, doesn't it," he says, "that I can trust her absolutely not to read [the friend's letter] though she comes in here a dozen times a day. I don't even put it away in a drawer. And yet I can't trust . . . she's out for a walk now [i.e., in the rain]. A *walk*, Bendrix" (p. 11).

The concomitants of Henry's trustfulness are, first, a natural openness, even naïveté, in personal relationships, of which the devious Bendrix is one beneficiary: when, in view of Henry's embarrassment, Bendrix offers to see the detective for him, his response is: "'Would you really do that for me, Bendrix?' and there were tears in his eyes, as though he had never expected or deserved this supreme mark of friendship" (p. 14). Second, in the very teeth of his suspicion, he possesses an instinctive capacity for loyalty: the upshot of his opening conversation with Bendrix, he declares, is that talking about the matter "[has cleared] his head," and in front of Bendrix he burns the letter that contains the name and address of the detective agency (p. 14); similarly, when Bendrix later reveals to Henry that he has himself employed the detective and baits him with his findings, Henry asks for the report only to "put it straight into the fire" (p. 74). Finally, though the trust and the openness and the loyalty seem to go with the lack of passion that characterizes Henry's relationship with Sarah, they support the "gentleness and affection" that he invariably shows her—and which Bendrix refuses to regard as "love" (p. 15).

If Henry's trust in Sarah makes for his contentment in the marriage, it is Bendrix's mistrust of her that undermines their relationship. His mistrust, as he himself clearly understands, springs fundamentally from a disbelief in himself, from a personal insecurity in relation to her—his self-mistrust recalling that of George Saxton in its intensity. Bendrix loves Sarah "obsessively," and yet he can "feel no trust": "in the act of love I could be arrogant, but alone I had only to look in the mirror to see doubt, in the shape of a lined face and a lame leg—why me?" (p. 53). Like that other unbeliever, the rationalist Smythe with his strawberry disfigurement, Bendrix, with his physical disability, is a marked man. And since "insecurity twists meanings and poisons trust" (p. 62), he is from the outset of the affair certain that he is "only one of many men—the favourite lover for the moment" (p. 53). The result is that he and Sarah quarrel often, for he "[picks] on her with nervous irritation," and he becomes aware that their love is "doomed": "I was pushing, pushing the only thing I loved out of my life" (p. 37). Haunted by fear, it is for Bendrix "as though all [Sarah's] men in the past and all the men in the future cast their shade over the present" (p. 50); and in her journal she strikingly pinpoints the way his love is predicated on a lack of trust when she asserts that it is "like a medieval chastity belt" (p. 107). At the same time he too is capable of swinging to the other extreme, as on the afternoon when she says to him, "I've never loved anybody or anything as I do you," and he feels "complete trust" (p. 57). After he knows from her purloined journal why she has given him up (and though it was he, in "hate and suspicion" and a "passion to destroy," who earlier set the detectives on to her [p. 18]), there is also the occasion just before her death when he feels that he has "never loved her so much": "The more we know the more we love, I thought. I was back in the territory of trust" (p. 153).

The concomitants of Bendrix's mistrust are ranged in opposition to those of Henry's trust. As opposed to Henry's openness, Bendrix's native

ground is deceit, and it is as if he is exiled into truth when he grasps that
there is no need to lie on the renewal of his relationship with Sarah and
Henry after the eighteen-month break: "Then I realised that there was
nothing wrong any more with the truth. Lies had deserted me, and I felt
as lonely as though they had been my only friends" (p. 28). Henry's
capacity for loyalty is matched by Bendrix's for betrayal, and not only in
his affair with Sarah but also in the way he initiates the private investigation despite Henry's wish to drop the matter. And Henry's affection for
Sarah, an affection which for many years has not been sustained by any
sexual contact with her, is set against Bendrix's passion, his fiercely sexual
desire for her.

Since the opposition between trust and mistrust and their concomitants would appear to be the novelist's immediate concern in this work, it
will be apparent how effectively he concretizes the opposed qualities in
the story of an affair. But the twist that he gives this story also enables him
to achieve what Bendrix (his narrator-novelist) asserts is the novelist's
major aim—"the release of the real subject" (p. 24); for, when Bendrix is
posed against a new rival in the second triangle, the initial opposition
smoothly modulates, as we shall see, into one between belief and skepticism. The story, moreover, which so prominently details Parkis's efforts
to track down Sarah's mysterious lover, is primed for a revelation.

III

Sarah is strongly drawn to Bendrix sexually and falls passionately in love
with him. When he makes an advance to her while they are having dinner
together at a restaurant, she unhesitatingly responds, and so their affair
begins without either "pursuit [or] seduction": "We left half the good steak
on our plates," says Bendrix, "and a third of the bottle of claret and came
out into Maiden Lane with the same intention in both our minds"; and
they at once declare their love for each other (pp. 48–49). The affair is
marked by a full reciprocity of desire; and Sarah, who (we are to understand) has had many lovers, finds herself saying to him: "I have never,
never loved a man as I love you, and I never shall again" (pp. 31–32). She
seems to believe the affair can continue indefinitely—in fact it begins in
the summer before the war and goes on until June 1944—but we become
aware of the contradictions of being it enforces on her, and wonder how
long she will be able to tolerate the opposed pulls to which she is subject.

Though the affair by definition involves her in repeated acts of
betrayal, a feature of her relationship with Henry is her loyalty to him.
When Bendrix tells her that he has "only taken Henry up for the purpose
of copy," copy for a character who is "the ridiculous, the comic element"

in the novel he is writing, her response makes him realize she has "an enormous loyalty" to her husband, a loyalty, he grudgingly and parenthetically admits, that he "could never deny" (pp. 5–6). And when Bendrix believes that his vindictive account of the detective's investigation will provoke Henry into hitting him, it is as though he prepares to strike back not only at his rival but at Sarah's outrageous loyalty to him: "If he had [hit me], I would have struck back with such pleasure, struck back at this oaf to whom Sarah had remained in her way so stupidly loyal for so many years, but at that moment the secretary of the club came in" (p. 73).

Likewise, Sarah has a free and open disposition. When Bendrix suddenly falls in love with her in the restaurant, it is her "frankness" (together with his "sudden sense" of her as "an individual woman") that particularly attracts him (p. 48); and throughout the affair he is impressed by her insistence on telling the truth, so that whenever he tries "to get her to say more than the truth," such as that they will marry one day, she always refuses to play "that game of make-believe" (p. 31). Yet she is also "a consummate liar," as Bendrix says after her death (p. 222); and where it is a matter of deceiving her husband, she is like a fish in water in the niceties of deception: when Henry disturbs her in an early embrace with her lover, Bendrix is sad to note "the calmness of her face," fearing the significance of her practiced response; and he notes too "how well she knows how to conduct an affair like this," as she is the one to introduce a proper caution into their arrangements (pp. 50–51). But she is also reckless, seeming wantonly to revel in deception, so that when Henry one day stays in bed with a cold, she is the one to devise a pretext for a visit by Bendrix and to plan their love-making: "Henry had his tray, sitting up against two pillows in his green woollen dressing-gown, and in the room below, on the hardwood floor, with a single cushion for support and the door ajar, we made love. When the moment came, I had to put my hand gently over her mouth to deaden that strange sad angry cry of abandonment, for fear Henry should hear it overhead" (p. 55).

Sarah's contemptuously wanton conduct appears the more puzzling on such occasions not only because of her loyalty to Henry but also because of her genuine love for him. In her journal she affirms her love a number of times. One entry is dated long after she has told Bendrix she has never loved anyone as much as him, is written, indeed, on the day after she has decided to give up Bendrix—though never loving him more. Noting that she often forgets her own telephone number, she wonders why: "I suppose Freud would say that I want to forget it because it's Henry's number too. But I love Henry: I want him to be happy"— though, with a characteristic swing of feeling, she adds: "I only hate him to-day because he *is* happy, and I am not and Maurice is not, and he won't know a thing" (p. 110). Sarah is not prepared to deny her love for Henry even when she contemplates leaving him and has gone so far as to write him a farewell note. She ends the note with "God bless you," but then changes her mind: "I crossed out 'God bless you' very deeply so that it couldn't be read. It sounded smug, and anyway Henry doesn't believe in God. Then I wanted to put Love, but the word sounded unsuitable although I knew it was true. I do love Henry in my shabby way" (p. 140). Sarah, in other words, like Catherine Earnshaw and Clarissa Dalloway before her, truly loves both the men in her life. But it is not merely a question of her loving two men. She wants Bendrix in addition to her husband because she urgently needs him, needs him for what Henry cannot give her.

Sarah's relationship with Henry comes in the end to eschew sex. She reflects that she "must have wanted him, in a way, once," but that she has "forgotten why," and that she was "too young to know what [she] was choosing" (pp. 122–23). Certainly he has been quite unable to satisfy her sexually: on the occasion previously referred to when she and Bendrix make love with Henry in the room above them, he unexpectedly comes downstairs and Bendrix wonders whether he heard her cry "as he passed"; but she says, "He wouldn't have known what it was," and adds: "Poor Henry. It's never happened—not in the whole ten years" (p. 55). By the time of her affair with Bendrix, Sarah is sure that Henry has "long ceased to feel any physical desire for her," and Bendrix doubts whether at that point there is "much else" between them beyond a "kiss on the cheek" (p. 46). She later tells Bendrix she has not slept with Henry "since the first year" of the affair (p. 177). Denuded of sex, the marriage becomes a matter of "fondness," as far as Henry is concerned (p. 78)—or "friendship," as Sarah terms it (p. 139).

Sarah assures Bendrix that her previous affairs have "meant nothing at all," but he cynically thinks she has possibly been driven to them by "the unconscious desire to find that final spasm Henry [has] so woefully failed to evoke" (p. 61). He is altogether too reductive. Sarah has no doubt been driven to her affairs, but for more profound reasons, which she reveals in a diary entry some three weeks after she has broken with Bendrix:

> I looked at Henry's chief. He was a man called Dunstan. He had a broken nose and his battered face looked like a potter's error—a rejected-for-export face. All he would do, I thought, was smile: he wouldn't be cross or indifferent—he would accept it as something that human beings did. I had a sense that I had only to make a move and he would reply to it. I wondered, why shouldn't I? Why shouldn't I escape from this desert if only for half an hour? I haven't promised anything about strangers, only about Maurice. I

> can't be alone for the rest of my life with Henry, nobody admiring me, nobody excited by me, listening to Henry talking to other people, fossilising under the drip of conversation like that bowler hat in the Cheddar Caves. (p. 116)

It might appear that Sarah is simply a promiscuous woman, ready to settle at the drop of a hat (even a bowler hat) for any man who presents himself, even though she registers him as a second-best article of the "rejected-for-export" variety; and she seems to be eager to justify herself in advance for any move she may make by classifying her promiscuity as natural, as "something that human beings do." But her thoughts are revelatory of an imperative need on her part to snatch at vital sustenance. It is a need to flee from an overwhelming sense of inanition which is not unlike that of Lettie in her marriage in *The White Peacock*, to "escape" from the "desert" in which she now finds herself; and the desert image is one that recurs in her journal. Deprived of sexual contact with Bendrix and left to Henry's talk and fondness, it is as if she feels her very life dripping away, "fossilising," turning into a mere effigy of what it has been. Indeed, in an entry written a few weeks later, she records how she has gone on a tour with Henry of civil defense installations in southern England, and how she has had to concern herself with problems of blast and shelters when she is preoccupied with "the problem of pretending to be alive": "Henry and I sleeping side by side night after night like figures on tombs" (pp. 116–17).

In the diary entry about Dunstan, Sarah also artlessly reveals what has furthermore impelled her into her affairs. She feels she is essentially "alone" in her life with Henry not only because there is no physical contact between them but also because there is an absence of what goes with such contact, the kindled warmth of regard and attention, for she now is left with "nobody admiring [her], nobody excited by [her]." The lack of such admiration is so important to her because what she has sought in her affairs is reassurance, a countermanding of her own consuming mistrust of herself, even though in her heart of hearts she knows the disbelief remains:

> That's asking me to believe too much, that there's anything lovely in me. I want men to admire me, but that's a trick you learn at school—a movement of the eyes, a tone of voice, a touch of the hand on the shoulder or the head. If they think you admire them, they will admire you because of your good taste, and when they admire you, you have an illusion for a moment that there's something to admire. All my life I've tried to live in that illusion—a soothing drug that allows me to forget that I'm a bitch and a fake. (p. 119)

An illusion, even if one lives one's life in it, can be maintained only if it is constantly renewed, and a craving for drugs cannot be satiated. It is Sarah's disbelief in herself—after her death Bendrix thinks that "it's just as

well that one of us should believe in her: she never did in herself"
(p. 158)—that drives her to her affairs. It is thus her own mistrust that
makes her violate the trust Henry reposes in her; but (at least for as long as
she is taking the "soothing drug") she contrives to preserve a trusting
confidence in relation to him, even though the nature of the trust and the
confidence is diminishing of him: "Last night I looked at Henry when he
was asleep. So long as I was what the law considers the guilty party, I
could watch him with affection, as though he were a child who needed my
protection" (p. 122). But *she* needs the admiring Bendrix—whose own
disbelief soon becomes focused on her.

Until the very end of her affair with Bendrix, Sarah—unlike the
other heroines studied in this book—is not torn between the two men with
whom she is caught up in a lovers' triangle. As the affair goes on for years
and years, she seems successfully to have found a *modus vivendi*, though we
may suspect it is not actually possible to have one's cake and eat it, and
that the strain of her self-division (as she moves like a pendulum between
her husband and her lover) must be considerable. It is only when she gives
up Bendrix, however, that she experiences a wrenching conflict. At first,
as she records a few months after the break with Bendrix, she feels,
strangely, that she now loves neither man: "It's so unfair. While I loved
Maurice, I loved Henry, and now I'm what they call good, I don't love
anyone at all" (p. 123). But when Bendrix suddenly comes back into her
life after his meeting with Henry and she has lunch with him, the old
longing for him revives. It is so strong, indeed, that she is now ready to
leave Henry for him. In the farewell note that she writes to Henry she
tells him that she has not seen Bendrix for nearly two years, but that she
now knows she cannot "live happily without him," and that she loves him
even more than "[she] did in 1939": "I've been childish, I suppose," she
writes, "but now I realise that sooner or later one has to choose or one
makes a mess in all directions" (pp. 139–40).

In the event, however, Sarah proves incapable of acting on the
choice she has determined to make. Henry comes home before she has
left, and she does not give him the letter. He has that day lunched with
Bendrix and discovered the true nature of his relationship with Sarah; in
pain he goes straight to his room, where she finds him crying. When he
says he has a headache, her response is one of spontaneous love for him: "I
came behind him and put my hand on his forehead." At this point,
Henry, who is still crying, tells her that he loves her, and that he cannot
do without her; seeming to divine her intention, he also begs her not to
leave him. Like Lettie when she asks Leslie to release her from their
engagement in *The White Peacock*, Sarah cannot withstand the misery she is
forced to confront. But we are to understand it is not through pity alone

that she agrees to stay: "I said, 'I won't leave you, I promise.'" Though she says she cannot bear to be with him once she has made her promise, it is with one half of her being that she has responded to his appeal, and in love and loyalty as well as compassion that she stands by him (pp. 140–43). But this is not the only vow she makes.

IV

Sarah makes her earlier commitment on the night in June 1944 when the Germans begin their V1 robot attacks on London; and the second triangle is created, paradoxically, when she vows to give up Bendrix. A robot explodes on the Common nearby, but, embarrassed at the prospect of having to face Bendrix's landlady, Sarah refuses to take shelter in the basement as he suggests. He goes downstairs to see whether the landlady may not be away. Another robot lands very close to the house, and he wakes "after five seconds or five minutes in a changed world." When he comes to, he finds himself lying on his back with the front door of the house suspended by debris a few inches above him. He manages to free himself, and on going up to his room finds Sarah "crouched on the floor—from fear," he supposes. When she sees him, she says: "Oh God, you're alive"; and she later tells him she had gone downstairs, seen him under the door, and thought he was dead: "I knew for certain you were dead," she declares. He questions her as to what she was doing on the floor, and she says she was praying, praying "to anything that might exist," for when "you are hopeless enough, you can pray for miracles" (pp. 81–84). She goes home, and thereafter breaks off all contact with Bendrix. It is nearly two years later that he first discovers the explanation of her behavior when he reads her account of what happened in her journal:

> I knelt and put my head on the bed and wished I could believe. Dear God, I said—why dear, why dear?—make me believe. I can't believe. Make me. I said, I'm a bitch and a fake and I hate myself. I can't do anything of myself. *Make* me believe. I shut my eyes tight, and I pressed my nails into the palms of my hands until I could feel nothing but the pain, and I said, I will believe. Let him be alive, and I *will* believe. Give him a chance. Let him have his happiness. Do this and I'll believe. But that wasn't enough. It doesn't hurt to believe. So I said, I love him and I'll do anything if you'll make him alive. I said very slowly, I'll give him up for ever, only let him be alive with a chance, and I pressed and pressed and I could feel the skin break, and I said, People can love without seeing each other, can't they, they love You all their lives without seeing You, and then he came in at the door, and he was alive, and I thought now the agony of being without him starts, and I wished he was safely back dead again under the door. (pp. 112–13)

I have suggested previously that the story of an affair provides a perfect mechanism to release the oppositions the novelist is concerned with; the episode of the robot similarly serves most aptly to precipitate the religious theme, which is the concealed end of the affair. The way the central issue in this episode is left open illustrates the delicacy with which Sarah's conversion is handled. One critic, it is true, states that Sarah promised to leave Bendrix if God "restored [him] to life after his actual death from the buzz bomb he thought only stunned him";³ but I doubt whether we are expected to flatten the ambiguity quite so roughly. It is enough that Sarah at the time believes Bendrix is dead and that only a miracle can save him. She herself, preserving ambiguity, swings between two utterly opposed views of what has happened: when she looks back on her behavior the next day, she regards it as hysterical: "I knew that if I took his hand and pulled it towards me, it would come away, all by itself, from under the door. Now, of course, I know that this was hysteria. I was cheated. He wasn't dead. Is one responsible for what one promises in hysteria?" (p. 112); but some three weeks later when she first stops on the Common to listen to Smythe, she thinks: "if only he could convince me that you don't have to keep a promise to someone you don't believe in, that miracles don't happen . . ." (p. 114). In passing, we may deplore that Greene is more insistent and less artistic, for he then forces improbabilities on us, when he later seems to ascribe something like miracle-working powers (not to mention sainthood) to Sarah herself: after her death Parkis's son recovers from a serious illness when he is given one of her children's books, and he tells the doctor "it was Mrs. Miles who came and took away the pain" (p. 220); and Smythe's strawberry mark disappears after he has slept with his cheek on "a scrap of hair" he has cut from her corpse (pp. 174, 233).⁴

The real issue, then, in the episode of the robot is not Bendrix's "miraculous" restoration but Sarah's response in the face of his apparent death. Her immediate reaction, when she finds him under the door, is to try to get the door off him, but she cannot lift it (p. 84). It is when she is convinced both that he is dead and that there is nothing she can do, that she goes back to the room and—in despair and in helplessness—begins to pray. Perhaps the best commentary on her response is that provided by an analogous episode in *Anna Karenina*, when Levin's wife gives birth and he hears her moaning in pain:

> "Yes, that is she," he said to himself, and clutching at his head he ran down-stairs.
>
> "Lord have mercy on us! pardon us! aid us!" he repeated the words that for some reason came suddenly to his lips. And he, an unbeliever, repeated these words not with his lips only. At that instant he knew that all his doubts, even the impossibility of believing with his reason, of which he was aware in himself, did not in the least hinder his turning to God. All of that now floated out of his soul like dust. To whom was he to turn if not to Him in whose hands he felt himself, his soul, and his love?

In moments of extremity it may be a sense of powerlessness that impels an unbeliever to turn for help to some force outside himself, but that he should find himself unwittingly praying to God becomes for him a revelation of what he truly feels—and believes in. In the case of Sarah, a wish to believe even precedes her prayer, but it is likewise to God that she turns to *make* her believe. "Man has places in his heart which do not yet exist," the epigraph to the novel from Léon Bloy declares, "and into them enters suffering in order that they may have existence."

It is not only that Sarah's helplessness is extreme—she feels she "can't do anything of [herself]"; it is compounded by an utter disbelief in herself—"I'm a bitch and a fake and I hate myself," she says. It is with a sense that her world, both inner and outer, has collapsed, and that she must hold on to something, that she turns to God. But it is also with a recognition that a great bounty is not to be had for the asking, that it must be paid for, that she makes her vow, seeking to ensure that her prayer should be selfless, untainted by hope of personal gain. Her prayer recalls that of Lizzie Hexam in *Our Mutual Friend*, when she prays to God to help her save the life of Eugene Wrayburn while at the same time she renounces him: "And grant, O Blessed Lord God, that through poor me he may be raised from death, and preserved to some one else to whom he may be dear one day, though never dearer than to me!" It is a fine touch in *The End of the Affair* that makes us see that selflessness is not easily attained—or maintained, for when Bendrix walks into the room and Sarah thinks of "the agony" that now awaits her, she wishes he were "safely back dead again under the door."[5]

Even after Sarah's death and after he has read her journal, Bendrix is not disposed to accept that it is to God he has lost her: "Sarah had really believed that the end began when she saw my body. She would never have admitted that the end had started long before: the fewer telephone calls for this or that inadequate reason, the quarrels I began with her because I had realised the danger of love ending" (p. 176). The chronology of the journal makes it clear, however, that not only "the end" but also her concern with God starts before the explosion of the robot bomb on that momentous night. Four days before the bombing she records that both she and Bendrix fear the "desert" which would be around them "if [their] love were to end," and she asks rhetorically: "If one could believe in God, would he fill the desert?" She goes on to say, with her own "terrible insecurity" rising to the surface, that people who believe in God "don't need admiration, they don't need to sleep with a man, they feel safe"; and she confesses her own need for such belief, her need to be loved by God (pp. 107–108). When, therefore, she greets Bendrix after her prayer and vow with "Oh God, you're alive," this is more than a conventional exclamation; it is an involuntary expression of first belief.

Immediately after she makes her vow, Sarah seems to believe she will be able to go on loving both God and Bendrix (as she has previously loved both her husband and him): almost "the last words" Bendrix hears from her before she breaks with him are, "You needn't be so scared. Love doesn't end. Just because we don't see each other. . . ."; and she adds: "My dear, my dear. People go on loving God, don't they, all their lives without seeing Him?" (p. 79). But within six weeks, torn between her wish to keep her vow and desire for Bendrix, she phones her lover, determining to "go back tomorrow" if he answers—though in the event he proves to be away. And while she waits for the call to come through, Sarah registers the beginning of her own inner disintegration: "I said to God, I've kept my promise for six weeks. I can't believe in you, I can't love you, but I've kept my promise. If I don't come alive again, I'm going to be a slut, just a slut. I'm going to destroy myself quite deliberately. . . . I'm falling in pieces already" (p. 117).

As Sarah veers between wanting to love God and wanting to overcome her love for Bendrix—and being unable to do either—it is clear how the second main triangle is superimposed on the first, taking the impress of its configurations though in a new form. Sarah's vow becomes for her not only a question of "keeping her promise," of keeping faith, but also of another kind of faith; and the previous opposition between trust and mistrust shifts easily into one between belief and skepticism. "A vow's not all that important," she tries to assure herself, "—a vow to somebody I've never known, to somebody I don't really believe in. Nobody will know that I've broken a vow, except me and Him—and He doesn't exist, does he?" (p. 110); and more than eighteen months later she is still arguing the case with herself: "Suddenly I felt free and happy. I'm not going to worry about you any more, I said to God as I walked across the Common, whether you exist or whether you don't exist, whether you gave Maurice a second chance or whether I imagined everything" (p. 139).

For Sarah the struggle between belief and skepticism is also a contest between spirit and flesh. Six weeks after she binds herself to belief, the sense of deadness attendant on her continence so appalls her that she can determine to be "a slut" in order to "come alive again." More than a year later she records how (like Tess Durbeyfield after her initial experience with Alec d'Urberville) she is "trying to escape from the human body and all it [needs]"—and how in pursuit of the spirit she wants "the body . . . destroyed for ever"; but at the same time she thinks of a scar on Bendrix's shoulder and knows that she wants "that scar to exist through all eternity": "Then I began to want my body that I hated, but only because it could love that scar" (pp. 130, 131). And Sarah continues to be torn between flesh and spirit until her death. With *The End of the Affair*, therefore, this study seems to come full circle. I have suggested that, though the self-division of the heroines who precede Sarah takes various forms, it is an opposition between flesh and spirit that underlies their conflicts; and that though the novelists concerned transpose and even transvalue the terms of the fundamental opposition, its recurrent implication in their work is a measure, despite the fact that most of them were avowedly non-Christian, of the continued power of the Pauline dichotomy. With Graham Greene, a professing Catholic, the opposition between flesh and spirit is clearly in the foreground from the time of Sarah's vow, and is prepared for before that when Sarah's passionate affair with Bendrix is set against her asexual relationship with her husband. Greene, however, goes beyond the Pauline injunction that man must die to the flesh in order to live in the spirit, for, in the case of Sarah, at any rate, he asserts that the way to the spirit lies *through* the flesh.

Sarah, we are invited to register, moves to *agape* through *eros*. "Did I ever love Maurice as much before I loved You?" she asks in her journal. "Or was it really You I loved all the time? Did I touch You when I touched him? Could I have touched You if I hadn't touched him first, touched him as I never touched Henry, anybody?" (p. 147). It is almost as if the lover's bed is a spiritual gymnasium. If Sarah's sexuality is characterized by her abandon, by her ability to give herself—the quality crucially lacking in Clarissa Dalloway—her desire to live for the moment only is crossed with intimations of the timeless, as Bendrix perceives: "The moment only mattered. Eternity is said not to be an extension of time but an absence of time, and sometimes it seemed to me that her abandonment touched that strange mathematical point of endlessness, a point with no width, occupying no space" (p. 57). Sarah's readiness to give herself to a lover, moreover, prefigures her willingness to give herself to God, for her capacity for abandon may be seen as proleptic of that for renunciation: "I know I am only beginning to love," she writes, "but already I want to abandon everything, everybody but you [i.e., You]: only fear and habit prevent me" (p. 59). And she comes to apprehend sexual love as virtually an expense of flesh in a conservation of spirit:

> For [Bendrix] gave me so much love, and I gave him so much love that soon there wasn't anything left, when we'd finished, but You. For either of us. I might have taken a lifetime spending a little love at a time, eking it out here and there, on this man and that. But even the first time, in the hotel near Paddington, we spent all we had. You were there, teaching us to squander, like you taught the rich man, so that one day we might have nothing left except this love of You. (p. 148)

When Sarah gives up Bendrix and registers on her own flesh what it is like to "have nothing left," she desolately feels as if she has been abandoned in a "desert" (p. 110). But it is a desolation which leads to the Promised Land.

Sarah believes that Bendrix's experience must necessarily follow the same course as her own, that in the end there is nothing left but God "for either of [them]." But when he has read her journal and understands her position, he determines to fight for her, pitting himself against God, the flesh against the spirit. He follows her into a church, and even looks "with charity towards the altar and the figure dangling there": "She loves us both, I thought, but if there is to be a conflict between an image and a man, I know who will win. I could put my hand on her thigh or my mouth on her breast: he was imprisoned behind the altar and couldn't move to plead *his* cause" (p. 154). The very terms of Bendrix's physical challenge, we see, make the contest intellectual as well, for he is led to oppose his skepticism to any belief in the power of the dangling figure. In the end, furthermore, the opposition that is figured by the second triangle is given a metaphysical dimension too: in opposing himself to God, it is very much as a latter-day devil that Bendrix tries to get Sarah to turn to the world and the flesh.[6]

The first sign of the crumbling of Bendrix's skepticism is his unwitting Manichaeism, his acceptance of the devil in himself. "I have never understood," he says, "why people who can swallow the enormous improbability of a personal God boggle at a personal Devil. I have known so intimately the way the demon works in my imagination" (p. 67); and *his* personal devil becomes a demon of mistrust and suspicion and disbelief. When he meets Henry at the beginning of the narrative and is told that Sarah is "out for the evening somewhere," the "devil in [his] mind" is set to work, and he remembers "other days when Henry must have replied just like that to other inquirers, while [he] alone knew where Sarah was" (p. 3); when Henry confesses his fears about Sarah to Bendrix and then says he must think him a fool, it is "the demon [who speaks]": "Oh no, I don't think you a fool, Henry" (p. 12); and after he has humiliated Henry with talk of the detective's report, he registers that "the demon [has] done its work," and he feels "drained of venom" (p. 74). Bendrix's most notable essay in the demonic is his attempt, in the closing pages of the narrative, to transform God into the devil:

> I sat on my bed and said to God: You've taken her, but You haven't got me yet. I know Your cunning. It's You who take us up to a high place and offer us the whole universe. You're a devil, God, tempting us to leap. But I don't want Your peace and I don't want Your love. I wanted something very simple and very easy: I wanted Sarah for a lifetime and You took her away. With Your great schemes You ruin our happiness like a harvester ruins a mouse's nest: I hate You, God, I hate You as though You existed. (p. 236)[7]

Bendrix may revile God, but he addresses him. By the end of the narrative it is apparent that the epigraph about places in the heart coming into existence applies as much to Bendrix as to Sarah, for despite the qualification expressed in the above passage, he certainly seems to believe in the existence of God since he adds almost at once: "I said to Sarah, all right, have it *your* way. I believe you live and that He exists, but it will take more than your prayers to turn this hatred of Him into love" (p. 236). Sarah, however, has previously adverted us to the significance of hatred: "I thought, sometimes I've hated Maurice, but would I have hated him if I hadn't loved him too? Oh God, if I could really hate you, what would that mean?" (p. 133); and Bendrix himself, though in respect of sublunary affairs, has earlier remarked that "hatred seems to operate the same glands as love" (pp. 26–27), and that "hatred is very like physical love" (p. 70). By the end of the narrative, indeed, Bendrix even seems to have accepted the miraculous view of his own survival on the night of the V1 explosion: ". . . on the other side of the grass was the house with the ruined steps where He gave me back this hopeless crippled life" (p. 236). Perhaps the greatest—and most dubious—of the miracles which mar the closing section of the narrative is that by its end the devil himself seems well on the way to conversion.

But by then Sarah is dead. Bound to her vow (and so to God), Sarah—some three months after she has broken with Bendrix—begins her association with Smythe, seeking a way back to her lover: "I thought, I have been pulled about long enough. Now I'll take a different medicine. If [Smythe] can persuade me that nothing happened, that my promise doesn't count, I'll write to Maurice and ask him if he wants to go on again. Perhaps I'll even leave Henry" (p. 125). It is incipient faith she wants to be cured of, to find an effective "medicine" for, though it is later suggested her search is futile, for she has been vaccinated against disbelief: after her death her mother reveals to Bendrix that at the age of two she had Sarah "baptized . . . a Catholic," and she adds, "I always had a wish that it would 'take'. Like vaccination" (p. 201). Bendrix skeptically thinks that "you can't mark a two-year-old child for life with a bit of water and a prayer": "If I began to believe that, I could believe in the body and the blood" (p. 202); but Henry seems ready to give larger credence to the possibly insidious effect of holy water: "It's an extraordinary coincidence, isn't it," he says. "Baptized at two years old, and then beginning to go back to what you can't even remember . . . It's like an infection" (p. 231).

Towards the end of her life, Sarah may therefore be regarded as having to contend with a double infection, that of the flesh as well as the spirit, for by the time she sees Bendrix again after their long separation, she is physically ill. After their lunch he moves to kiss her, but she turns away:

> She turned her head sharply away, as though she were looking to see if anyone were coming, to see if there was time . . . but when she turned again

the cough took her. She doubled up in the doorway and coughed and coughed. Her eyes were red with it. In her fur coat she looked like a small animal cornered. (p. 35)

Sarah's racking cough, which doubles her up and makes her look like a cornered animal, is an overt indication of how at this stage she is trapped by the flesh—and in more than one way. The image of a trapped animal is repeatedly used to suggest both the appetite and the confinement of flesh: catching "a glimpse" of a prostitute one night, Bendrix sees "something young, dark and happy and not yet spoiled: an animal that didn't yet recognise her captivity" (p. 65); and thinking of how he begins more and more to quarrel with Sarah, driven to a dead end by his mistrust despite their consummate passion, he sees their love in not dissimilar terms: "It was as though our love were a small creature caught in a trap and bleeding to death: I had to shut my eyes and wring its neck" (p. 37). Sarah, too, as Bendrix moves to kiss her on the occasion referred to, is trapped by her desire—despite her vow, as she admits in her account in the journal: "I thought he was going to kiss me again, and I longed for it, and then a fit of coughing took me and the moment passed" (p. 137). Indeed, the last entry that she makes in her journal shows how impossible it is for her to break away from the pull of the flesh: "I'm not at peace any more. I just want him like I used to in the old days. . . . I want Maurice. I want ordinary corrupt human love" (pp. 148–49). But she is also trapped, of course, as that cough forcefully reveals, by her own mortality.

At the same time Sarah is trapped by her vow, and, held by it though straining repeatedly towards Bendrix, she also moves closer and closer towards an acceptance of the Catholic faith. Some fifteen months after the break with Bendrix, she finds herself leaving a church "in a flaming rage," and "in defiance of Henry and all the reasonable and the detached," she does what she has seen "people do in Spanish churches": "I dipped my finger in the so-called holy water and made a kind of cross on my forehead" (p. 134). Her act may be motivated more by defiance of the skeptical Henry than by a wish to demonstrate belief, but—like her vow—it has meaning and is not easily discounted. And even "so-called" holy water, we are to understand, may take. On the very day that she makes up her mind to leave Henry and go to Bendrix (though in the end she promises her husband not to abandon him), she records in her journal that she has bought a crucifix the day before, and adds: "Dear God, I've tried to love and I've made such a hash of it. If I could love you, I'd know how to love them [i.e., the men in her life]. I believe the legend. I believe you were born. I believe you died for us. I believe you are God. Teach me to love. . . . (pp. 143–44). In the letter which she writes to Bendrix shortly before her death and which he receives after she has died, she informs him that she has recently been to a priest and told him she wants "to be a

Catholic" (p. 177); the nurse reports that on her deathbed she "kept on asking for a priest," and "kept on saying, Father, Father," (pp. 165–66). And in the letter to Bendrix her statement of faith (which draws together some of the main motifs in the narrative) is unqualified: "I believe there's a God—I believe the whole bag of tricks, there's nothing I don't believe . . . I've caught belief like a disease. I've fallen into belief like I fell in love. I've never loved before as I love you, and I've never believed in anything before as I believe now. I'm sure. . . ." (p. 178).

Loving Bendrix as never before and believing in God as never before, but bound by her vow to give her lover up, Sarah is subject to an intolerable disjunction between flesh and spirit. In the same letter to Bendrix, she tells him she is not willing to go away with him as he has urged, and adds: "I love you but I can't see you again. I don't know how I'm going to live in this pain and longing and I'm praying to God all the time that he won't be hard on me, that he won't keep me alive" (p. 177). Having lost the will to live, Sarah does not in this respect rely only on God. On the night in January 1946 when she is out in the rain—it is the night on which Bendrix comes back into her life after the long separation—she catches a bad cold, but she does nothing about it. Though her cold gets worse and her cough seems to be tearing her apart, she refuses—suicidally—to call a doctor. When her husband finally makes her see the doctor, it is too late: Henry tells Bendrix the doctor said "if she'd had penicillin a week earlier, he'd have saved her" (p. 164).[8] It is apparent, that is to say, that the wheel has not come full circle after all, that Sarah has not moved through the flesh to the spirit but has in fact been torn in two by the conflict between them. Like the other heroines considered in this study—though Clarissa Dalloway, given her double, may be regarded as a partial exception—Sarah too in the end is the victim of her own self-division. She too is caught, like them, between opposing forces, and, like them, is drawn apart—as though by Plato's horses pulling at the same time in opposite directions.

CHAPTER 1

1. *Phaedrus, The Dialogues of Plato*, tr. B. Jowett (New York, 1937), I, 242–43.

2. *Love and Death in the American Novel* (New York, 1960), p. xx.

3. *The Divided Self: A Perspective on the Literature of the Victorians* (New York, 1969), p. 211. I have omitted Miyoshi's page references to *Jane Eyre*.

4. *Raw Material* (London, 1978, revised edition; first published 1972), p. 171.

5. The love triangle to be studied here, it should also be noted, has nothing in common with the figure of "triangular desire" which the French critic René Girard describes in *Deceit, Desire, and the Novel: Self and Other in Literary Structure*, tr. Yvonne Freccero (Baltimore, Maryland, 1965). The kind of desire Girard analyzes is not direct but imitative and therefore mediated; and he posits the "universal structure" (p. 94) of a triangle which comprises the subject, the mediator, and the object. It could be argued that the desire of the heroine, in the pattern I wish to study, is mediated in the way Girard proposes—to take some simple examples, Cathy's desire for Edgar Linton in *Wuthering Heights* may be said to be mediated by generally accepted notions of what constitutes a good marriage; or Tess Durbeyfield's love for Angel Clare may be viewed as being mediated by that of the other dairymaids for him—but mediation *per se* has no place in the love triangles I discuss. The focus of interest is the heroine's desire for two men, and in the triangle thus established there is no mediator.

Similarly, the pattern I trace should be distinguished from what Jean E. Kennard calls the "convention of the two suitors" in *Victims of Convention* (Hamden, Connecticut, 1978). One of the two suitors, in her study, is regarded as the "wrong" one, and embodies qualities the heroine must learn to reject; whereas, in the novels I discuss, I argue that both suitors embody tendencies that she should not only accept but seek to integrate in a unified self. Furthermore, in most of the novels Kennard analyzes, the heroine resolves her conflict by choosing the "right" suitor in the end; whereas the fundamental feature of the love triangles I consider is the heroine's need for both men and her ultimate inability to give up either.

6. *Dissent and Dogma*, ed. R. H. Super, *The Complete Prose Works of Matthew Arnold*, vol. 6, (Ann Arbor, 1968), p. 40.

7. Noel Gilroy Annan, *Leslie Stephen* (London, 1951), p. 110.

8. George H. Ford, Introduction to "The Victorian Age," *The Norton Anthology of English Literature*, 4th ed. (New York, 1979), vol. 2, p. 939.

9. *Works* (New York, 1826), vol. 5, pp. 120–21.

10. Emily's sister Charlotte directly reveals an awareness of such an opposition in her own life: "If I could always live with you, if your lips and mine could at the same time drink the same draught at the same pure fountain of mercy, I hope, I trust, I might one day become better, far better than my evil wandering thoughts, my corrupt heart, cold to the spirit and warm to the flesh, will now permit me to be." Letter to Ellen Nussey, 6 December 1836, *The Letters of the Brontës, A Selection*, ed. Muriel Spark (London, 1954), p. 60.

11. Letter to Sara Sophia Hennell, 7 October 1859, *The George Eliot Letters*, ed. Gordon S. Haight (New Haven, 1954–55), vol. 3, p. 174.

12. Walter E. Houghton, *The Victorian Frame of Mind 1830–1870* (New Haven, 1957), p. 362.

13. Letter to Frederic Harrison, 15 August 1866, *Letters*, vol. 4, p. 300.

14. Notebook entries for 29 January 1890 and 17 October 1896, Florence Emily Hardy, *The Life of Thomas Hardy* (London, 1962), pp. 224, 285.

15. *Three Guineas* (London, 1938), p. 300.

16. *Madonnas and Magdalens: The Origins and Development of Victorian Sexual Attitudes* (New York, 1976), p. 157.

17. *The City of Dickens* (London, 1971), p. 160.

18. *The Victorian Frame of Mind*, p. 346.

19. See H. M. Daleski, *Dickens and the Art of Analogy* (London, 1970), pp. 49–50.

20. *Oliver Twist*, ed. Kathleen Tillotson (Oxford, 1966), pp. 187–88. This passage is also cited by Alexander Welsh in his fascinating discussion of "The Hearth" in Dickens, in which Rose Maylie is adduced as representative of the kind of "cheerful female eidolon" who "presides" over the Dickensian hearth (*The City of Dickens*, p. 150).

21. *The Angel in the House*, book 1, canto 10, *The Poems of Coventry Patmore*, ed. Frederick Page (Oxford, 1949), p. 121.

22. See "Contributions to the Psychology of Love: A Special Type of Choice of Object Made by Men," tr. Joan Riviere, *The Complete Psychological Works*, ed. James Strachey, vol. 11 (London, 1957), pp. 163–75. The quoted reference is to p. 170.

23. "Professions for Women," *The Death of the Moth* (London, 1942), p. 151.

Cf. Sandra M. Gilbert and Susan Gubar, who talk of the split in terms of "angel" and "monster": "Specifically . . . a woman writer must examine, assimilate, and transcend the extreme images of 'angel' and 'monster' which male authors have generated for her. Before we women can write, declared Virginia Woolf, we must 'kill' the 'angel in the house.' In other words, women must kill the aesthetic ideal through which they themselves have been 'killed' into art. And similarly, all women writers must kill the angel's necessary opposite and double, the 'monster' in the house, whose Medusa-face also kills female creativity"; and: "If we define a woman . . . as indomitably earthly yet somehow supernatural, we are defining her as a witch or monster, a magical creature of the lower world who is a kind of antithetical mirror image of an angel. . . . But now, as a representative of otherness, she incarnates the damning otherness of the flesh rather than the inspiring otherness of the spirit . . ." (*The Madwoman in the Attic: The Woman Writer and the Nineteenth-Century Literary Imagination* [New Haven & London, 1979], pp. 17, 27–28).

In a still more recent study, Nina Auerbach sets out "to resurrect the central female paradigms that presided over the Victorian imagination," and states that woman appears in Victorian "art and literature as four central types: the angel, the demon, the old maid, and the fallen woman" (*Woman and the Demon: The Life of a Victorian Myth* [Cambridge, Massachusetts & London, 1982], pp. 9, 63). Auerbach's study thus provides further support for the view advanced here of the importance of the opposed images of angel and fallen woman (though she inclines to regard the angel as an epitome of selflessness rather than sexlessness); and she too stresses that such images leave the woman out: "According to [the Victorians'] governing imaginative convention, women exist only as spiritual extremes: there is no human norm of womanhood, for she has no home on earth, but only among divine and demonic essences. This imaginative scheme does not believe in a human woman" (p. 64). Auerbach also strikingly ascribes the force of one of her images to the impact of Dickens and Thackeray on the Victorian consciousness: "Angels proliferate most freely in novels of the 1840s and 1850s. They collaborate in the shaping visions of Dickens and Thackeray, whose spectacular popularity at mid-century formulated and helped to create the mythologies of their culture" (p. 82)—though the "angels" of Dickens that she refers to are Little Nell in *The Old Curiosity Shop* and Agnes Wickfield in *David Copperfield*, and Thackeray's Becky Sharp is regarded (among others) as a "demon" (pp. 82, 90).

24. *The Disappearance of God* (Cambridge, Mass., 1963), p. 9.

25. Introduction to the Grove Press edition of *The Monk* (New York, 1959), p. 11. This edition, prepared by Louis F. Peck, follows Lewis's unexpurgated text. Further references are to this edition.

26. *The Literature of the Second Self* (Tucson, Arizona, 1972), pp. 189–90, 100.

27. The views of Keppler and the writers he cites may all doubtless be traced back to a pronouncement of Freud's in 1908:

> It has struck me that in many of what are known as "psychological" novels only one person—once again the hero—is described from within. The author sits inside his mind, as it were, and looks at the other characters from outside. The psychological novel in general no doubt owes its special nature to the inclination of the modern writer to split up his ego, by self-observation, into many part-egos, and, in consequence, to personify the conflicting currents of his own mental life in several heroes.

"Creative Writers and Day-Dreaming," tr. I. F. Grant Duff, *The Complete Psychological Works*, vol. 9 (London, 1959), p. 150.

28. *A Psychoanalytic Study of the Double in Literature* (Detroit, 1970), pp. 4, 13.

29. *The Works of Robert Louis Stevenson*, Vailima Edition (London, 1922), vol. 3, p. 429.

30. *The Literature of the Second Self*, p. 8.

31. For the same reason, the self-division of the protagonists should be distinguished from the condition known as "multiple personality." The heroines studied never cease to be unitary personalities even though they are not well integrated; whereas in the case of multiple personality there is a disintegration into wholly separate and distinct personalities, with the "original personality" being quite unconscious of the existence of the personality or personalities that supplant it.

32. *Great Expectations*, The New Oxford Illustrated Dickens (London, 1953), pp. 161, 162, 188.

CHAPTER 2

1. All page references are to the Clarendon Edition of the novel, ed. Hilda Marsden and Ian Jack (Oxford, 1976).

2. David Cecil, "Emily Brontë and *Wuthering Heights*," *Early Victorian Novelists* (London, 1934), p. 164.

3. Dorothy Van Ghent says that "essentially, *Wuthering Heights* exists for the mind as a tension between two kinds of reality: the raw, inhuman reality of anonymous natural energies, and the restrictive reality of civilized habits, man-

ners, and codes ("On *Wuthering Heights*," *The English Novel: Form and Function* [New York, 1953], p. 157); and U. C. Knoepflmacher refers to an opposition, among other things, between "civilization and Eros" (*Laughter and Despair: Readings in Ten Novels of the Victorian Era* [Berkeley, 1971], p. 107). The central opposition in the novel between wildness and cultivation may also be regarded as a variation of Claude Lévi-Strauss's basic binary opposition between the raw and the cooked or nature and culture. See *The Raw and the Cooked* (New York, 1970); and Sandra M. Gilbert and Susan Gubar, who also refer to the opposition in these terms, in *The Madwoman in the Attic*, pp. 273–74.

4. Dorothy Van Ghent, to whom I am indebted for this idea, suggestively connects it with a symbolic incest motif in the novel: "The foster kinship provides an imaginative implicit reason for the unnaturalness and impossibility of their mating. Impassioned by their brother-and-sisterlike identity of kind, they can only destroy each other, for it is impossible for two persons to *be* each other . . . without destruction of the physical limitations that individualize and separate. . . ." (*The English Novel*, p. 169).

5. "Lockwood's Dreams and the Exegesis of *Wuthering Heights*," *Nineteenth-Century Fiction*, 14 (September 1959), 101.

6. Cf. Q. D. Leavis, who says that on his return Heathcliff "releases the now repressed part of [Cathy's] nature (the 'half savage'), which has no relation to the fact that she is happy with Edgar as a lover . . ." ("A Fresh Approach to 'Wuthering Heights,'" *Lectures in America*, with F. R. Leavis [London, 1969], p. 125). Cf. too David Sonstroem, who says "characteristically, in spite of her best intentions, [Catherine] disregards one or the other [i.e., Heathcliff or Edgar]. . . . Divided against herself, Catherine characteristically denies or disregards one aspect of herself" ("*Wuthering Heights* and the Limits of Vision," *PMLA*, 86 [Jan. 1971], 53).

7. Cf. Masao Miyoshi: "[Cathy's] existence . . . created out of fusion with . . . Heathcliff, is torn in two, one part enmeshed in the legitimate order of family and institutions, the other in the Heathcliff that is herself. She cannot choose either to abandon Edgar or deny herself. In this self-destruction she herself has invited, her life ebbs" (*The Divided Self*, p. 215).

8. Cf. Albert J. Guerard, who says Cathy "*cannot* live unless she possesses both men, the two reconciled as it were within her" ("Preface to *Wuthering Heights*," in *Twentieth Century Interpretations of Wuthering Heights*, ed. Thomas A. Vogler [Englewood Cliffs, N.J, 1968], p. 66).

9. "The Brontës, or, Myth Domesticated," *Forms of Modern Fiction*, ed. William Van O'Connor (Bloomington, Indiana, 1959), p. 118. The essay was originally published as "The Brontës: A Centennial Observance," in *The Kenyon Review*, 9 (Autumn 1947).

CHAPTER 3

1. All page references are to the Riverside paperback edition of the novel, ed. Gordon S. Haight (Boston, 1961), which follows the text of the third edition (December 1861).

2. "Anality in *The Mill on the Floss*," *Novel*, 5 (Fall 1971), 50.

3. "A Reinterpretation of *The Mill on the Floss*," *PMLA*, 87 (Jan. 1972), 57–58.

4. Such a view of Eden has a long tradition behind it. See M. H. Abrams,

who says "the Neoplatonic tradition, persisting from the Church Fathers to the German Idealists, . . . equates the fall from paradise with a splintering of primal unity . . ." (*Natural Supernaturalism: Tradition and Revolution in Romantic Literature* [New York, 1971], p. 222). Thomas L. Jeffers regards the significance of the myth of Eden in *The Mill on the Floss* in similar terms, specifying wholeness (among other things) as a paradisal feature: "*The Mill on the Floss's* vision of childhood as an Edenic pre-history, the no-time before the time of 'the thorny wilderness,' is squarely in the romantic tradition. [George Eliot] creates a credible childhood world that forwards the tradition's central idea . . . that children . . . are closer to the world 'as God made it,' exhibiting a humanity still uncorrupted by experience."

". . . *The Mill on the Floss* suggests a myth that human nature once was whole but now is divided into 'parts.'"

"Why do these divisions between mind and body and within mind itself, these deep causes of the loss of Eden, occur?" ("Myths and Morals in *The Mill on the Floss*," *The Midwest Quarterly*, 20 [Summer 1979], 332, 336, 339).

5. *The Novels of George Eliot* (New York, 1959), p. 46. Sara M. Putzell claims that since both Tom and Maggie are "a complex mixture of Dodson and Tulliver," this "renders absolutely untenable the customary explanation of their unhappy relationship as yet another Dodson-Tulliver conflict with Tom representing the Dodsons and Maggie the Tullivers"; but she nevertheless keeps to the same terms: "all her life [Maggie] is torn between the claims of filial and social duty, upheld by the Dodsons, and a Tulliverish impulsiveness which responds to the vagrant desires of the self" ("'An Antagonism of Valid Claims': The Dynamics of *The Mill on the Floss*," *Studies in the Novel*, 7 [Summer 1975], 230, 228).

6. Letter to François D'Albert-Durade, 29 January 1861, *The George Eliot Letters*, vol. 3, p. 374.

7. *George Eliot* (Cambridge, 1962), p. 119.

8. The metaphor of the opening in the wall is strikingly similar to one that is used in *The Rainbow* to describe the coming together of Anna and Will Brangwen: for her he is "the hole in the wall, beyond which the sunshine [blazes] on an outside world."

9. C. B. Cox, who refers both to the wood and plain image and to the opening in the rocky wall, says that "this kind of image, describing a movement towards a free, full life, is often used to describe Maggie's desires" (*The Free Spirit* [London, 1963], p. 13).

10. *George Eliot* (London, 1902), pp. 100, 103, Cf. F. R. Leavis, who says Stephen is "universally recognized to be a sad lapse on George Eliot's part "(*The Great Tradition* [London, 1948], p. 40); and W. J. Harvey, who calls him "a worthless popinjay," and maintains "he isn't really there as a force in the novel at all" (*The Art of George Eliot* [London, 1961], pp. 123–24).

11. George Eliot's presentation of the relationship of Maggie and Stephen is so sure—and convincing—that one can sympathize with her resentment of Edward Bulwer-Lytton's criticism of it: "The other chief point of criticism—Maggie's position towards Stephen—is too vital a part of my whole conception and purpose for me to be converted to the condemnation of it. If I am wrong there—if I did not really know what my heroine would feel and do under the circumstances in which I deliberately placed her, I ought not to have written this book at all, but quite a different book, if any." Letter to John Blackwood, 9 July 1860, *The George Eliot Letters*, vol 3, pp. 317–18.

12. Cf. F. R. Leavis, who claims that Maggie has "no sense that Stephen Guest . . . is not worthy of her spiritual and idealistic nature. There is no hint that, if Fate had allowed them to come together innocently, she wouldn't have found him a pretty satisfactory soul-mate" (*The Great Tradition*, pp. 43–44).

13. John Hagan, p . 53.

14. Joan Bennett takes a similar view: "After [Maggie] has burnt [Stephen's] letter she has nothing left to hope for except an early death and the author provides the timely, wish-fulfilling death by drowning" (*George Eliot*, p. 130); and Bernard J. Paris says that at this point "there is in Maggie a profound wish for death, for only in death is there the peace of a sure refuge" (*A Psychological Approach to Fiction* [Bloomington & London, 1974], pp. 185–86). Joseph Wiesenfarth, however, seemingly ignoring the despair to which Maggie is reduced before the flood begins, maintains that Maggie succeeds in resolving her conflict: "Critics who say that Eliot never satisfactorily resolves Maggie's conflicts are quite wrong. Maggie learns how to imitate Christ. . . . The life of the semipagan Dodsons . . . cannot comprehend the soul of a Maggie Tulliver, working out for herself the meaning of the *Imitation of Christ*" ("Legend in *The Mill on the Floss*," *Texas Studies in Literature and Language*, 18 [Spring 1976], 33).

CHAPTER 4

1. "Study of Thomas Hardy," *Phoenix*, I, ed. Edward D. McDonald (London, 1936), pp. 484, 485, 488.

2. All page references are to the Penguin edition of *Tess of the d'Urbervilles*, ed. David Skilton (1978). This edition reproduces the text of the definitive 1912 Macmillan *Wessex Novels* edition.

3. A notable exception to this consensus is Robert B. Heilman, who sees Tess as "caught between incomplete options" in her relations with Alec and Angel; and maintains Hardy makes her "more of a person and less of a helpless victim, more of an agent and less a passive recipient of the actions of others" than is generally thought ("*Gulliver* and Hardy's *Tess*: Houyhnhnms, Yahoos, and Ambiguities," *The Southern Review*, 6 [New Series] [April 1970], 286, 288).

4. Notebook entry of 4 December 1890, Florence Emily Hardy, *The Life of Thomas Hardy* (London, 1962), p. 230.

5. See "Colour and Movement in Hardy's *Tess of the d'Urbervilles*," *Critical Quarterly*, 10 (Autumn 1968), 221, 222, 223, 226.

6. *The Great Web: The Form of Hardy's Major Fiction* (London, 1974), p. 182.

7. See the New Wessex (paperback) edition of *Tess of the d'Urbervilles*, ed. P. N. Furbank (London, 1974), p. 470.

8. Cf. Mary Jacobus, who wittily says that, "like Milton, Hardy has produced two versions of the fall—one, comprehensible in human terms, the other retrospectively imposed for the sake of his argument" ("Tess's Purity," *Essays in Criticism*, 26 [October 1976], 328).

9. J. T. Laird, *The Shaping of Tess of the d'Urbervilles* (Oxford, 1975), p. 72.

10. *Language of Fiction* (London, 1966), pp. 182, 185.

11. Bruce Johnson argues that she approaches him sensually, that it is "clearly a sensual preoccupation on Tess's part [which] turns the notes of Angel's distant harp into his body itself: 'They [the sounds] had never appealed to her as

now, when they wandered in the still air with a stark quality like that of nudity.' " But he grants that "her mind transforms the scene" since she is not conscious of either space or time, and says: "The garden is fecund and sensuous, in keeping with her perception of Angel's harp notes as nudity itself, but it is also deceptive, as is her transcendent state of mind" (" 'The Perfection of Species' and Hardy's Tess," *Nature and the Victorian Imagination*, ed. U. C. Knoepflmacher and G. B. Tennyson [Berkeley, 1977], pp. 266–67). It seems to me, however, that Tess's "state of mind" functions to dissipate that nudity, to deprive it of substance: by the end of the scene she is said to undulate "upon the thin notes of the second-hand harp, and their harmonies [pass] like breezes through her, bringing tears into her eyes."

12. Robert Heilman calls Alec "Sensual Man" and Angel "Ascetic Man." See "*Gulliver* and Hardy's *Tess*," p. 286.

CHAPTER 5

1. E. T. (Jessie Chambers), *D. H. Lawrence: A Personal Record*, 2nd ed., ed. J. D. Chambers (London, 1965; first published 1935), p. 103.

2. "Lawrence's *The White Peacock*: A Mutation of Pastoral," *Texas Studies in Literature and Language*, 12 (Summer 1970), 264. The essay is reprinted in Squires's book, *The Pastoral Novel: Studies in George Eliot, Thomas Hardy, and D. H. Lawrence* (Charlottesville, 1974).

3. Letter of 8 December 1915, *The Collected Letters of D. H. Lawrence*, ed. Harry T. Moore (London, 1962), vol. 1, p. 393.

4. Letter to William Hopkin, 20 February 1911, *The Letters of D. H. Lawrence*, ed. James T. Boulton, vol. 1 (Cambridge, 1979), p. 233.

5. All page references are to the Phoenix Edition of the novel (London, 1955). *The White Peacock* was first published in 1911.

6. Letter to Dorothy Brett, conjectured date 26 January 1925, *Collected Letters*, vol. 2, p. 828.

7. "Study of Thomas Hardy," *Phoenix*, vol. 1, p. 474.

8. *A Personal Record*, p. 179.

9. See, for instance, Keith Alldritt, *The Visual Imagination of D. H. Lawrence* (London, 1971), p. 12; and John Alcorn, *The Nature Novel from Hardy to Lawrence* (London, 1977), p. 80.

10. Keith Alldritt also points to a connection in the opening description between "the human . . .[and] the natural life of the valley," if in somewhat different terms, but then he goes on to say that "the major theme" of Lettie's relations with George and Leslie is "not clearly related to the opening assumption" (*The Visual Imagination of D. H. Lawrence*, pp. 5–6).

11. See George H. Ford, *Double Measure: A Study of the Novels and Stories of D. H. Lawrence* (New York, 1965), p. 50; Keith Sagar, *The Art of D. H. Lawrence* (Cambridge, 1966), p. 10; F. B. Pinion, *A D. H. Lawrence Companion* (London, 1978), p. 128; and Alastair Niven, *D. H. Lawrence: The Novels* (London, 1978), p. 19.

12. *Fantasia of the Unconscious* (London, 1931; first published 1923), p. 99.

13. Lawrence was unequivocal about this when faced with an analogous situation at a crisis in his own life: "If Frieda and the children could live happily

together, I should say 'Go' . . . But if she would only be sacrificing her life, I would not let her go if I could keep her. Because if she brings to the children a sacrifice, that is a curse to them. If I had a prayer, I think it would be 'Lord, let no one ever sacrifice living stuff to me—because I'm burdened enough!' " Letter to Else Jaffe, 14 December 1912, *Letters*, vol. 1, p. 486.

14. Cf. George Ford, who says: "Whiteness evokes not merely Lettie's favorite color of dress but indicates how her character itself is to be estimated. It is her nature to dazzle by beauty, but she is distinctly not evil. Whiteness here is an evaluative test of character more than a color" (*Double Measure*, p. 55); Stephen J. Miko, who refers to Ford's reading: "Certainly Lettie is not evil, yet she is vain. Her whiteness is not an indication of moral purity but a reference to a form of sterility, or, if that word seems too strong, at least to a lack of commitment" (*Toward "Women in Love": The Emergence of a Lawrentian Aesthetic* [New Haven, 1971], p. 25); and Keith Alldritt, who says the word "white" implies "a lack of consciously malicious purpose" (*The Visual Imagination of D. H. Lawrence*, p. 6).

15. Cf. Gavriel Ben-Ephraim: " . . . Annable verbalizes what the increasingly negative portrait of woman in *The White Peacock* suggests: that females direct de-energizing forces at the vitality in men. . . . [But] Annable's view [is] inharmonious with the text of the novel, especially the characterization of Lettie, [and] the symbol which incarnates his conceptions is unsuccessful" ("The Pastoral Fallacy: Tale and Teller in D. H. Lawrence's *The White Peacock*," *The Literary Review*, 19 [Summer 1976], 426). The essay is reprinted in Ben-Ephraim's book, *The Moon's Dominion: Narrative Dichotomy and Female Dominance in Lawrence's Earlier Novels* (Rutherford, N. J., 1981).

CHAPTER 6

1. All page references are to the first edition of the novel (London, 1925).

2. *A Writer's Diary*, ed. Leonard Woolf (London, 1953), entries of 30 August 1923 and 15 October 1923, pp. 59, 60.

3. Entry of 4 June 1923, p. 55. Leon Edel was one of the first to note Virginia Woolf's general indebtedness, in respect of the method she developed, to James Joyce. See *The Modern Psychological Novel* (New York, revised edition 1964; first published 1955), p. 133.

4. Alex Zwerdling remarks that "we come to know Peter better than he knows himself," and that "his whole personality in middle age is a flimsy construct designed to reassure himself that the passion and radicalism of his youth are not dead" ("*Mrs. Dalloway* and the Social System," *PMLA*, 92 [Jan. 1977], 77).

5. J. Hillis Miller thinks it is much more ambiguous: "If *Mrs. Dalloway* is organized around the contrary poles of rising and falling, these motions are not only opposites, but are also ambiguously similar. They change places bewilderingly, so that down and up, falling and rising, death and life, isolation and communication, are mirror images of one another rather than simply a confrontation of negative and positive penchants of the spirit" ("Virginia Woolf's All Souls' Day: The Ominiscient Narrator in *Mrs. Dalloway*," in *The Shaken Realist: Essays in Modern Literature in Honor of Frederick J. Hoffman*, ed. Melvin J. Friedman and John B. Vickery [Baton Rouge, 1970], p. 110). The essay is reprinted (with some modifications) in Miller's *Fiction and Repetition: Seven English Novels* (Cambridge, Massachusetts, 1982).

6. *A Writer's Diary*, entry of 14 October 1922, p. 51.

7. "*Mrs. Dalloway*: Literary Allusion as Structural Metaphor," *PMLA*, 88 (May 1973), 440.

8. Alex Page has also remarked that "Septimus' character is in all essentials Clarissa's, but taken to a deadly extreme"—though he has a different view of what these essentials are ("A Dangerous Day: Mrs. Dalloway Discovers Her Double," *Modern Fiction Studies*, 7 [Summer 1961], 123).

9. *Under Western Eyes*, Dent Collected Edition, p. 39.

10. Cf. Avrom Fleishman, for instance: "Septimus as the outcast whose death reinvigorates his society is matched by Clarissa as social organizer who raises her activity from mindless social climbing to principled life affirmation" (*Virginia Woolf: A Critical Reading* [Baltimore, 1975], p. 89). A more meaningful "match" is suggested by Blanche H. Gelfant: "Septimus Smith's sense of inviolability [i.e., as expressed in his suicide], though symptomatic of his paranoia, makes him Mrs. Dalloway's dark complement. He represents her possible destiny were she to lose her tenuously free contact with other people which gives her a hold on sanity" ("Love and Conversion in *Mrs. Dalloway*" *Criticism*, 8 [Summer 1966], 241).

CHAPTER 7

1. All references are to the first edition of the novel (London, 1951).

2. David Lodge plays with the same phrase. He says *The End of the Affair* is "the story of an 'eternal triangle' in a highly significant sense: Bendrix's rival for Sarah's love is not another man, not Henry, but God" (*Graham Greene* [New York & London, 1966], pp. 33–34). Cf., too, Laurence Lerner, who says the novel is "a story of several love-triangles. There is Henry-Sarah-Bendrix: husband-wife-lover. Then there is Bendrix-Sarah-Smythe: Sarah really belongs to Bendrix, Smythe wants her. Slowly we realize that behind these two triangles is another, Bendrix-Sarah-God. God is a lover, having an affair with Sarah, using the dirtiest tricks he can to win her from Bendrix" ("Graham Greene," *Critical Quarterly*, 5 [Autumn 1963], 230). See too a similar account of *The End of the Affair* in Lerner's *Love and Marriage: Literature and its Social Context* (London, 1979), pp. 50–52.

3. Harvey Curtis Webster, "The World of Graham Greene," *Graham Greene: Some Critical Considerations*, ed. Robert O. Evans (Kentucky, 1963), p. 21.

4. John Atkins maintains that since Greene, as a Catholic, "believes in miracles," it would be "impertinent" on our part to tell him they are not permissible. See *Graham Greene* (London, 1957), pp. 193–203 for his account of *The End of the Affair*. Greene himself, however, invites the application of different standards: "There are leaders of the Church," he wrote in a letter to Elizabeth Bowen, "who regard literature as a means to an end, edification. That end may be of the highest value, of far higher value than literature, but it belongs to a different world. Literature has nothing to do with edification" (Elizabeth Bowen, Graham Greene, and V. S. Pritchett, *Why Do I Write* [London, 1948], pp. 31–32). Indeed Greene is directly critical of this aspect of *The End of the Affair*: "The incident of the strawberry mark had no place in this book; every so-called miracle should have had a natural explanation, and the coincidences ought to have continued over the years, battering at the mind of Bendrix, forcing on him a reluctant doubt" (*Introductions to Three Novels* [Stockholm, 1962], p. 47).

5. Cf. Ian Gregor, who maintains Sarah is inhuman: "At the heart of

Sarah's warmth there is something which Greene seeks to persuade us is divinity, but its features uncomfortably resemble inhumanity"; and "The upshot of [the] presentation of Sarah . . . is to tend to make [her], in her relations with Bendrix, 'selfless' to the point of inhumanity" (Ian Gregor & Brian Nicholas, *The Moral and the Story* [London, 1962], pp. 196, 199).

6. Cf. G. L. Arnold, who says Bendrix is "meant to sit for a portrait, if not of the Prince of Darkness in person, at least of one of his minions" ("Adam's Tree," *The Twentieth Century*, 150 [October 1951], 340).

7. R. W. B. Lewis would perhaps not altogether disagree with Bendrix's view of God. He says that in *The End of the Affair*, as in *The Heart of the Matter* and *The Potting Shed*, "God moves in a singularly Mephistophelean manner, His wonders to perform—a deity with whom one bargains away one's peace or love or beliefs, for the life of someone else" ("The 'Trilogy' of Graham Greene," *Modern Fiction Studies*, 3 [Autumn 1957], 214).

8. Cf. Laurence Lerner, who says it is God who "[carries] Sarah off when she's in danger of relapsing" (*Love and Marriage*, p. 51); and David H. Hesla, who states it is Bendrix who "destroys Sarah," though he also says her death is "suicidal," if "ambiguously so" ("Theological Ambiguity in the 'Catholic Novels,'" *Graham Greene*, ed. Evans, pp. 106, 97).

INDEX

Characters are indexed under the names by which they are commonly referred to.